APPLIED PSYCHOLOGY

APPLIED PSYCHOLOGY: INDIAN PERSPECTIVE

Edited by
QAMAR HASAN

GYAN PUBLISHING HOUSE
NEW DELHI-110002

APPLIED PSYCHOLOGY: INDIAN PERSPECTIVE
[*Psychology, Health, Sports, Women's Studies*]

ISBN: 9788121206112

Published in 1998 in India by
Gyan Publishing House
5, Ansari Road
New Delhi 110 002

Laser Typeset at Alphabet, Delhi
Printed at Mehra Offset Press, New Delhi.

To

My Late Colleague

Prof. Afzal Kureshi

Contents

List of Tables

Preface

The present volume is an attempt to showcase the contribution of Indian psychologists to applied psychology. To make it possible for readers to appreciate the range of the contribution, let us refer to different fields of applied psychology in the USA. J.P. Guilford in his book *General Psychology* has given a chart showing fields of life that depends upon psychological knowledge for successful solution of their problems. The list includes architecture-engineering, medicine-psychiatry, eugenics, education, military-defence, speech-music-fine arts, journalism-public service, and social work. The list is comprehensive but not exhaustive. Like normal probability curve it shall never entail all the instances of application of psychology.

The contributors to this volume are the distinguished psychologists from different parts of India who participated in the Asian and XXXII Conference of Indian Academy of Applied Psychology held in Aligarh in February 1996. However, the papers which have been included in this volume are not the same as presented in the different academic sessions of the conference. It was realized that a book of reading should have papers which are more in the format of chapters useful for psychologists, scholars, students and those who have keen interest in this field. Most of the papers that are presented in academic conferences have a brief introduction, a section on methodology, statistical details and discussion of results. This format is more useful for the evaluation of methodology than for giving information that would be useful for those who are interested in becoming familiar with the conceptual network useful for reorientation of applied psychologists towards unchartered avenues. However, sometimes it is more important that a budding and aspiring applied psychologist be told how he can find his way in the criss-crossing labyrinths of real-life situations. We have to illuminate his way and guide him to have a simplified representation of complex reality so that he can proceed step by step towards his goal of finding solutions to real life problems in different settings. We have, therefore, retained certain contributions in their original forms so that young colleagues may know how they can create new knowledge in psychology.

The papers that were presented in the conference were scrutinized by many prominent psychologists including Prof. S. Sultan Akhtar, Prof. K.V. Kaliappan, past and present president, respectively, of Indian Academy of Applied Psychology; Prof. D.M. Pestonjee, Vice-President of the Academy and Professor of Organizational Behaviour at Indian Institute of Management, Ahmedabad, and M. Habib Ahmad, Editor, *Journal of Indian Academy of Applied Psychology*. My own colleagues in the Department of Psychology also helped me in reading the manuscripts and drawing attention to errors that had unwittingly creeped in the manuscripts submitted for the presentation in the conference. It will not be proper for me not to express my gratitude to them, but it will also not be proper for me to list the names of all of my colleagues whose active support was available to me in organizing the conference. We have included in the present volume the paper contributed by many faculty members of the Department of Psychology to highlight what we are doing in the Department which is one of the oldest Departments in northern India.

When we think of those whose contributions to psychology have brought good name to our Department, we remember Prof. Afzal Kureshi as one of them who suddenly left for his heavenly abode a fortnight before the dates of the conference. We missed him very much during the conference and also cherish his memory to this day. The present volume is, therefore, dedicated to his memory.

With deep sense of gratitude I express my thankfulness to all those who accepted my request to revise and rewrite the papers to give them the form I wanted them to assume. It is a matter of great satis-faction to me that they could find time for revision and repose trust in me to put their valuable works in the form of this book of reading.

Qamar Hasan

Introduction

Applied psychology is an amalgamation of psychological research directed towards understanding human behaviour in real-life setting and transferring the understanding of human behaviour into paradigms programmes, routines, concrete steps, instructions, and techniques that are helpful in dealing with the problems of life. Besides availability of problem-specific prescriptions which have been tried and found useful in other societies, progress in the application of a field of knowledge in solution to real-life problems depends on many other things: awareness that a problem exists; the belief that scientific methods rather than ritualistic folk solutions can be effective in finding solution of the problem; the importance assigned to the problem in comparison to other problems that might exist in the society; and allocation of resources for perfecting the method and procedures dealing with the problems. The history of application of psychology in military selection programmes and waging psychological warfare led Prof. H.J. Eysenck to observe "the only way in which psychology could gain a foothold in an established organization like army was through the obvious and catastrophic breakdown of traditional procedure." Germany was first to realize that one of the important reasons of its defeat in World War I was recruitment of inefficient soldiers and officers in armed forces, and low morale of the troops. He also observed that psychologists should avoid the temptation of making use of face-valid procedures which appear to be more relevant and appropriate to the consumers of psychological services but are not really effective.

Psychology can have an impact on life in two ways: First it can bring radical changes in attitudes, beliefs, and the total prospective that lead to paradigm shift in search of a solution to a real-life problems. Examples of this kind of applications are 'sex revolution' set in motion by Freudian psychoanalysis, changes in approach to industrial relations following Hawthorne studies and Maslow's enunciation of the theory of motivation, the symptom-removing rather than conflict-resolving and insight-inducing treatment of maladaptive behaviour following Skinner's work on shaping and successive approximation, and the importance of communication of teacher's expectations of children in influencing school achievement following the work on the experimenter's bias and communication of expectations.

The change in the strategy of dealing with a problem begins with the professional and is gradually percolated to the common man through popular literature, mass communication, and social interaction. However, the change in people's outlook (and even that of professional's) is not without resistance. Those who are afraid of loosing their moorings shall cling to any thing which gives them positive self-esteem.

The second way in which psychology has been applied to deal with real-life problems is direct reliance on the conceptual systems, methods, procedures, techniques, and strategies developed by psychologist in either laboratory or the field. The best example of this direct application is use of psychological tests and other assessment devices for personnel selection and diagnosis. One can also refer to different kinds of psychotherapies; techniques of behaviour modification; transactional analysis; sensitivity training; brain storming sessions; methods of determining effectiveness of commercial and social welfare communications; Human Resource Development (HRD) programmes based on principles of learning and motivation; surveys that give information needed for formulation and implementations of policies and plans; social audit and evaluation studies as some of the examples of direct application of psychology by professionally trained psychologists.

The articles collected in the present volume represent the contributions of Indian psychologists in applying psychology to real-life problems of our people but it is never asserted that psychology is being applied by only those who have contributed to this volume and also that all kinds of applications of psychology to the problems of individuals and organizations have been illustrated and covered. From the point of view of areas of application, this volume could have been divided into many sections, namely, Clinical and Health Psychology, Organizational Behaviour and HRD, and Social Psychology. It is to be observed that categorization can never be rigid and it may lead to controversy regarding proper placement of the things to be classified. We are, therefore, inviting readers to go through the chapters in whatever order they like and make use of the presented material to equip themselves better for application psychology by garnering the concepts, methods and procedure presented in different chapters.

The opening chapter of the book is written by Prof. Durganand Sinha, a doyen of Indian psychologist, and the golden link between psychological researches in the foreign countries and India. He is the most competent person to do critical evaluation of psychological researches conducted in India and suggests the topic of research which need utmost interest of Indian applied psychologists. The neglected areas, according to Prof. Durganand Sinha are rural communication, family dynamics, social justice and equality. He observed that researches in applied psychology in the country are bogged down by their urban middle class prejudices and are closely oriented to the urban scenario, they have become blind to the rural issues of great importance for the development of the country.

The second chapter of the book is contributed by the most distinguished clinical psychologist, Prof. G.G. Prabhu. He provides a historic perspective on Clinical Psychology in India. Sir Ashutosh Mookerjee was first to realize the importance of psychology. He inspired Prof. N.N. Sen to establish the Department of Psychology in early years of the twentieth century. Prof. Prabhu divides the development of clinical psychology into three phases: 1905-55, 1956-75, and post-1975 period. He started his career when the second phase was on but as an insider, he had an opportunity to familiarize himself with what happened in the past, and what happened in the early days of his career. He is, therefore, the most competent clinical psychologist to show the path and inform us about the opportunities and challenges that would be thrusted upon the new crop of clinical psychologists.

The contribution of Dr. K. Krishna Rao is unique as it underscores the importance of helping those who have psi experiences that make them disturbed, fearful, and confused. It is, therefore, imperative to have a different approach to the counselling of those who encounter: poltergeist phenomena, out-of-the body experience (OBE), apparitions, near-death experience, and other psi experiences.

Of late health psychology emerged as an independent field of research and application. Prof. Qamar Hasan and his collaborators trace the progress of research that led to the paradigm shift in medicine and the realization of the importance of psychological factors associated with health and illness. As a consequence of this realization emerged the field of health psychology. Having discussed the evolution of this branch of psychology and highlighting important foreign contributions to this field, Prof. Hasan and co-authors have presented an account of the contribution of Indian psychologists towards the extension of our knowledge of the role of psychological factors in drug abuse, gynaecological complications, medical-care seeking/avoidance and other topics that have become the focus of attention of Indian psychologists.

The chapter on health psychology coming before a number of articles on stress and stress management, prepares a suitable background for what to follow. The problem of contemporary living which has entangled both the health psychologists and organizational and management psychologists, is individual's exposure to different kind of stressful situations. In addition to exposure to unavoidable stressful situation, one has to invite difficult situations so as to have a sense of accomplishment by surpassing the adversaries. While 'braving' the stress, a person is likely to exhaust his resources and suffer from physical and mental ailments. In contemporary psychological research, attempt to understand the nature of stress, measurement of stressful events at different points of time in the life of a person, significance of stress for well-being, and coping styles and process have become the main focus of attention.

Prof. Hamida Ahmad in her chapter Stress and Disease has discussed in detail the methodological problems in conducting research for establishing unconfounded role of stress in the etiology of physical and psychological diseases. In addition to drawing attention to the shortcomings of retrospective studies and reliance on memory, emphasis is placed on the necessity of measuring initial health status, morbidity, and comorbidity, because if disregarded, these factors may place havoc with the conclusions. Ignoring the course and stage of development of the disease is the greatest methodological pitfall towards which attention is drawn by her. She referred to the fact that in some diseases, role of stress is more potent during the progress of the disease, while in other diseases stress may be more relevant to recovery and recuperation. The emerging field of psychoneuroimmunology which provides a casual link between acute stress and acceleration of tumour growth and chronic stress and inhibitory effect on tumour growth, has also been referred to for inspiring Indian psychologists and medical scientists to make more significant contributions.

The stress that is generated during playing the role assigned to a person by virtue of employment in an organization has a determinant consequences not only for the person but also for his job performance. Psychologists are, therefore, called upon to deal with the problem of prevention and minimization of role stress. Prof. D.M. Pestonjee is the most competent person to discuss the nature of role stress, the problems of its assessment, and the strategies to cope with role stress. Systematic exposition of the steps involved in the proactive intervention for stress management is the most important section of the chapter contributed by Prof. D.M. Pestonjee.

With the employment of women in different organizations and the job demanding mobilization of different kind of personnel resources, and the conflict of home-keeping and professional responsibilities, the study of differential stressfulness of occupations has become a legitimate problem of research. Dr. Patiraj Kumari and Dr. A.P. Singh bring us face to face with the desirability of being more concerned with gender and individual differences along with the variation in job requirement and job-specific stressors. The work is also a good example of method and procedure to be followed in research on stress.

Prolonged exposure to stress peculiar to a job and work

environment leads to what psychologists call "burnout". The onset of burnout can be delayed or avoided by the availability of social support. While there is need to discover the factors which may give rise to burnout in different professions, Prof. Neelima Misra has taken initiative in this direction by studying burnout in medical professionals, who are required to work for long hours, have to witness emotional scenes, and to face the patients suffering from different diseases, attendant charged with feeling of fear, despair, and anger. An important finding of the study is that different components of jobs have different relationship with aspects of work and family stress.

Researches on stress and burnout give us knowledge that can be utilized for creating the circumstances for preventing the onset of their adverse impact on the person. However, more important are the strategies of management of stress mentioned by Dr. A.K. Srivastava. In addition to cognitive, behavioural, and organizational interventions, Dr. Srivastava has identified certain specific coping styles which are expected to be effective in stressful situations peculiar to our culture.

Hardship and cruelty of life, barriers, frustrations, and threat to personal security are the kind of stressors that have been with us from the dawn of civilization, but, pollution is a new source of stress to which we are being exposed to in modern times. As man's physical and psychological health is being adversely affected by the delicate imbalance between his psychological and physiological adaptability on the one hand, and level of pollution in his surrounding on the other, the emergence of behavioural toxicology was the natural consequence of the concern with this injurious imbalance. We have in this volume a chapter contributed by a young psychologist prepared under the able guidance of Prof. Mukta Rani Rastogi which discusses in detail the entry of injurious substances into our system through skin-contact, inhalation, and ingestion to cause morphological changes and a variety of clinical signs and symptoms. In addition to presenting a history of behavioural toxicology, post absorptive effect of toxic agents, the authors have presented an empirical study of deleterious effects of exposure of workers to toxic substance in dying and printing departments of cottage industry. The work shows the way for future studies and underscores the importance of taking effective steps in dealing with exposure to different kinds of solvent agents.

Illegitimate use of performance enhancing drugs gets attention of media when action is taken against some famous sportspersons for abusing such drugs. Dr. Akbar Husain and Dr. Jawed Ali in their article on Drug Abuse in Sports have mentioned the cases of death due to regular use of the performance-enhancing drugs. In addition, they have given a three-category classification of abused drugs and listed different kinds of drugs with their Indian trade names. They have also suggested the steps to be taken to prevent drug abuse by sportspersons.

Certain social problems of contemporary life have been the focus of attention of the next three chapters which show that Indian psychologists are taking a bold initiative in suggesting steps to deal with the problem which different sections of our society are encountering. With the increasing life-expectancy and erosion of conventional family values, the senior citizens have to bear not only rude and cruel behaviour of those who have been their dependents a few decades ago, but also to find ways and means to keep intact their self-esteem and utilize their unimpaired knowledge and skills for the benefits of others. Dr Akbar Husain has presented a scheme of welfare programme for the elderly in which their services are to be utilized for the execution of welfare programmes for other sections of society.

Dr Asiya Aijaz addresses the question as to what can be done to shield our young generation from going astray due to problems of getting suitable employment and the delay in getting foothold in life. She suggests that successful learning of vocational skills commensurates with developmental tasks of different ages, and the youth can equip themselves to open the door of opportunities. The author insists that HRD should not be a programme of limited duration and purpose; it should be continuous and concerned with the all round development of the individual.

A keen observer of changes related to political, economic, social, and work life can foresee the kind of society that would be established in a developing country like India after the crystallization of the process of change. While changes can be expected to open new opportunities for all, including the less empowered sections of society like women and the youth, the burden of readjustment will be greater than for the well-entrenched social groups. Dr. Mani K. Madala in her article "Strategies for Preparing Women and Youth for Future Societies" has not only given a detailed account of what would be demanded from these sections in the future society but has also laid down the parameters of policy and macro level strategies for the survival and growth of these groups. The recommendations also include launching of programmes for developing enterpreneural skills between these two groups, i.e., women and the youth.

Women as a group are underprivileged, backward, and oppressed, many steps including their empowerment and restoration of their equality with men are being taken. Nevertheless, they face sexual harassment even at places of worship. Prof Vidhu Mohan and Shabnam Priyadarshani have conducted a well-planned and well-executed study on dynamics of eve teasing and also discovered the strategies adopted by women to deal with this kind of harassment. The study is included in the present volume as an example of the kind of contribution psychologists are making to deal with evils that are prevailing in our society. The reasons of eve teasing given by male and female respondents show the prevalence of gender biases in our society. It is to be noted that women prefer to be passive victims of eve teasing and that reporting the matter to the police is the least preferred coping strategy.

The article contributed by Dr Naval Karrir deserves special attention as it is contributed by a person who is a psychologist by his academic background and an organizational man by his managerial position. We have, therefore, an inside appraisal of the concept of quality of worklife (QWL) and the significance of ensuring high quality of worklife for those who make a synergetic effort to promote the interest of organization to which they are affiliated. A comparison of quality of worklife of managers serving in public and private and corporate sector organizations and the implications of the difference obtained is the empirical contribution of Dr Naval Karrir.

Though not considered much important, good interpersonal relationship among the coworkers is definitely an aspect of QWL.

However, in the interest of better productivity, the importance is unwittingly undermined by an emphasis on performing better than others. In the chapter, "Cooperation and Competition among Industrial Employees", Dr Chittranjan N. Daftuar and Anjuli Srivastava presented a good survey of literature on group dynamics and sociometery before discussing in detail the study conducted by them on industrial workers to explore the effect of cooperation and competition upon interpersonal relationship. The findings of the study led them to conclude that works which need better efficiency, speed, and creativity are to be designed and based on cooperation.

In India we have to meet many challenges and have to tackle different kinds of social problems including provision for education to the disadvantaged, helping children to overcome learning disabilities, and social prejudices. All of these problems are entangled with poor quality of life of the majority of our people. The only alternative which remains available for educating socially disadvantaged children and preventing them from being exploited as cheap labour and candidates for recruitment in criminal and anti-social gangs, is the provision of distant education. Prof Shamshad Hussain who has first hand experience of organizing distant education programmes in his capacities as Director Correspondence Courses, Patna University and Vice-Chancellor, Nalanda Open University has given an insider's account of the different aspects of "educating socially disadvantaged".

Learning disabilities can be observed in children belonging to any social category but the rate of dropout in the disadvantaged groups indicates that children belonging to such groups may suffer more disabilities. Ms Neeta Rani and Dr S.P. Singh have discussed the learning problems of children that arise out of interplay of psychological factors, child rearing practices, and absence of quality teaching matched with the individual's special needs. They have focused on children showing of discrepancy between intelligence and achievement and found that such children are unable to decide when and how different strategies of learning and memory are to be utilized. Thus, there remains the possibility of training of the disabled and helping them to overcome their defective strategy of learning.

The greatest social evil which causes the interruption of daily life, disruption of productive activity, and law and order problems, is intergroup prejudice. Different theoretical stances and approaches have been proposed to explain and manage this sickness. Dr Saeeduzzafar and Dr Rama Sharma in their collaborative work "Role of Implicit Memory in the Development of Prejudice" have tried to understand the phenomenon in terms of the influence of prejudice-generating information to which a person is unconsciously exposed and which has temporarily enhanced the availability of this category of information and, thus, influence impression about the community to which one belongs and the community to which one does not belong. The information-availability approach is helpful in explaining as to why tolerant and tender minded people succumb to prejudice under certain circumstances. It also suggests that one can reduce intergroup hostility by making a prejudiced person aware of his history of exposure to the kind of information and to the fact that the wickedness of the member of an outgroup is not his real wickedness but is due to attribution of certain trait names available in one's memory without personal awareness and responsibility.

It must be evident that Indian psychologists have been making wide applications of psychology. However, much is to be done for reorientation of Indian psychologists to make more effective use of the knowledge they have and to generate knowledge that would be more fruitful and easy in its application. The first step towards the reorientation is getting rid of methodological rigidity. Giving up methodological rigidity does not mean shedding scientific rigour. What is being insisted upon is that the association among scientific rigour and experimental control and theoretical sophistication is not to be regarded as strong as it is supposed to be at present. We have to avail any opportunity to test hypotheses in real world and to strengthen external and construct validity of our prepositions. This will also be helpful in a escaping from decontextualization of research. Nevertheless, problem-based research is not to be guided by politics and whims; it should definitely be designed with the help of theoretical formulations. It is to be noted that problem-based research is not an impediment to construct validation; it rather enhances the construct validity of theoretical formulations because it depends upon, clear and unconfounded operationalization of the construct. In social experimentation in which the independent variable is a social action programme and experimental manipulation is making a social programme available to randomly selected groups, has been successfully employed in developing "Seasame Stress" educational television programmes (Ball and Bogatz, 1971) and "city police patrol" experiments (Kelling *et al.*, 1976). The problem of "kitchen sink" in such studies have been highlighted by Cook and Campbell (1979). Kitchen sink is the problem of sorting out from among a large number of factors involved, the factors responsible for a particular effect. Indian psychologists need increased opportunity for conducting real-world experiments; such opportunities are more easily available to the psychologists who are members of "experimenting society". Even at present psychologists have a definite role to play which can be that of methodological design consultant, devising measures of social behaviour, and interaction with policy makers, and others interested in different sources of impact on human behaviour.

REFERENCES

Ball, S. and Bogatz, G.A., 1971, *The first year of Seasame Street: An evaluation*, Princeton: N.E. Educational Testing Service.

Cook, T.D. and Campbell, T.D., 1979, Quasi-experimentation: design and analysis issues for field settings. In M.D. Dunnette (ed.), *Handbook of Industrial and Organizational Psychology*, S Kokie, IL: Rand McNally.

Kelling, G.T., Pate, T., Dieckman, D., and Brown, C.E., 1976, The Kansas city preventive patrol experiment. A summary report. In G.V. Class (ed.), *Evaluation Studies Review (Vol 1)*. Beverly Hills, C.A.: Sage Publications.

List of Contributors

Durganand Sinha has been a National Fellow of the UGC and the ICSSR; Professor and Head of the Department of Psychology, Allahabad University; Director, A.N.S. Institute of Social Studies, Patna. He has also for short periods been the Nehru Professor in the Department of Human Development and Family Studies, M.S. University of Baroda, and Visiting Professor in the Department of Psychology, University of Hong Kong, and in some other Indian and foreign institutions. He has been a Past-President of the IACCP, and was member of the Executive Committee of the International Association of Applied Psychology (IAAP) and the International Union of Psychological Science (IUPS). His current research interests include cross-cultural psychology, indigenization of psychology, psychology and national development.

Dr G.G. Prabhu had been on the faculty of All India Institute of Medical Science (1964-81); New Delhi. Later (1981-95), he was the Professor and Head of Clinical Psychology, at the National Institute of Mental Health, Bangalore, and Dean, Faculty of Mental Health & Neuro Sciences, Bangalore University. Prof. Prabhu was the founder Secretary-General (1968-71) of the Indian Association of Clinical Psychologists; member (1984-90) of the expert advisory panel (Mental Health) of the World Health Organization (Geneva) and a member of the Central Mental Health Authority of India (1992-94) on its being constituted. Currently he is a member of the General Council of the Rehabilitation Council of Indian and Chairman of its professional group on mental disability.

K. Krishna Mohan is a Research Fellow at the Department of Psychology and Parapsychology, Andhra University, Visakhapatnam. He is primarily interested in Parapsychology, Health Psychology, and Indeginization of Psychology. His numerous research papers have been published in many reputed journals. He recently founded Indian Young Psychologists Association for professional development of psychology in India.

Dr Qamar Hasan is Professor of Psychology and also at present Chairman of the Department of Psychology, Aligarh Muslim University, Aligarh. He is well-known psychometrician and exponent of empirical research in psychology. Dr. Hasan directed three research projects sponsored by the Indian Council of Social Science Research. *Dogmatism and Personality* (1976); *Muslims in India: Adjustment and Reactions* (1987); and *Personality Assessment — A Fresh Psychological Look* (1997) are his distinguished literary works. Dr. Hasan founded and edited a Journal, *Advances in Psychology*, for a couple of years. He is on the panel of refrees of some important journals and is member of Board of Studies and Faculties of certain Indian universities.

Syed Humaira Siddiqa is a Research Scholar in the Dept. of Psychology, A.M.U., Aligarh. Presently she is doing Ph.D. in the area of Personality under the supervision of Prof. Qamar Hasan. She is also working as Research Officer in a Project, "Intergroup Communication : A Psychological Analysis of Indian Press Reports", sponsored by the ICSSR.

Ms Rizwana Nawab is a Research Scholar in the Department of Psychology, A.M.U., Aligarh. She has completed her M.Phil and currently is working for her doctorate in the area of Health Psychology under the supervision of Prof. Qamar Hasan. She has also got published a few papers on the subject of health and illness.

Dr (Mrs) Hamida Ahmad is Professor of Psychology and a senior member of the teaching faculty of the Aligarh Muslim University, serving in the Department of Psychology since 1968. Her areas of interest are Cognitive and Clinical Psychology. She plays an active role to promote the education of female. She is also Director of the Centre for Distance Education of the Aligarh Muslim University. She has received the singular honour of being appointed member of the UGC.

Dr D.M. Pestonjee is presently the L&T Chair Professor of Organizational Behaviour and Chairman of the Organizational Behaviour Area at Indian Institute of Management, Ahmedabad. Professor Pestonjee has been temporary advisor to international organizations like WHO, USAID, OXFAM. He has served on several national bodies like the ICSSR, AICTE and the ICMR. He has been associated with public and private sector organizations, NGOs, MNCs, and joint sector organizations.

Dr Patiraj Kumari is currently Lecturer in the Faculty of Management, Gurukul Kangri University, Haridwar. Her area of research interest includes women studies, stress and coping.

Dr Ashok P. Singh is currently Reader and Head of the Department of Psychology, Banaras Hindu University. He is the member of International Association of Applied Psychology, International Association for Cross-Cultural Psychology, Indian Science Congress Association and the Indian Academy of Applied Psychology. His areas of research interest includes stress, leadership, women studies, work-family conflict, and social support.

Dr Neelima Misra is presently Professor of Psychology and Head at the Department of Psychology, Lucknow University. Currently she is engaged in research work on stress, burnout and stress management. Another area of her research interest is Environmental Psychology, especially the built environment. She is member of various academic bodies such as Indian Science Congress, Indian Academy of Applied Psychology, National Academy of Psychology, and member of the editorial board of Indian Journal of Clinical Psychology.

Dr A.K. Srivastava is Reader in Psychology at Banaras Hindu University since 1985. Job anxiety, occupational stress and mental health have been the focal areas of his research for the last two decades. Thrust areas of current research of Dr. Srivastava are stress and health, and stress-management. Development of the measures of occupational stress and psychosocial stress (under a Task-Force Project of the ICMR) is a significant contribution of Dr. Srivastava to stress-research in India.

Ms Bhavana Gulati is a meritorious ex-student of the Department of Psychology, Lucknow University and has keen interest in the problems of environmental pollution.

Dr Mukta Rani Rastogi, Professor, has been working in the Department of Psychology, Lucknow University since 1967. Political Psychology, Personality Growth and Behavioural Toxicology are the areas of her interest. Development of Self Concept Scale, Family Scale, and Political Efficacy Scale are her significant contributions to the field of Psychology. She has more than 30 papers to her credit. She is associated with Abhigyan, an NGO. She has also worked in the field of child prostitution.

Dr Akbar Husain, Reader, has been serving the department of psychology since 1980. He is the author of two books. He has contributed more than 60 research papers in the reputed national and international journals and has attended several national and international seminars, symposia and conferences. At present he is Regional President of the Indian Academy of Applied Psychology. His major contributions are in the fields of personality, social psychology, and addictive behaviour.

Dr Jaowad Ali is Reader and Chairman of the Department of Physical Health and Sports Education, Aligarh Muslim University, Aligarh. He had been associated as coach with the Indian Universities' Hockey team for a decade during 1980-1990. He was appointed coach of the Indian Universities' Hockey team which toured Germany in 1986. In 1990, Dr Jaowad Ali attended the International Olympic Committee solidarity course in Hockey organized by Pakistan Hockey Federation at Karachi. At present the author is working on several projects related to the Hockey players and trying to explore the psychological parameters that influence their performance.

Dr Vidhu Mohan is a Professor of Psychology at the Panjab University, Chandigarh since 1984. She was also selected as Professor of Behavioural Science at Haryana Institute of Public Administration in 1984. She specializes in the areas of guidance and counselling, criminal psychology, organizational behaviour and personality. She has more than 160 research publications in journals of International repute to her credit. She is on the panel of the UGC and advisor to a number of institutes of higher learning. She is associated with various NGOs as advisor. She is also a trainer and facilitator of various Organizational Behaviour labs.

Ms Shabnam Priyadarshini is a UGC Senior Research Fellow in the Department of Psychology, Panjab University, Chandigarh. She is currently engaged in working for her Doctorate under the supervision of Prof. Vidhu Mohan. The topic of her doctoral dissertation is "A Study of Eve Teasing as Related to the Perception of Feminine Worth". She has a number of papers published on the subject of Eve Teasing in renowned journals.

Dr (Ms) Mani K. Madala is Associate Professor at NITIE, Mumbai. She has experience of 22 years in HRD, IR, and allied areas. She was the coordinator of Indo-Yugoslav Research Project, "Self Management and Worker Participation in Management". Her interest in upliftment of specific sections of society dates back to her college days when she was awarded prize by the then Prime Minister Mrs. Indira Gandhi for her contribution "The Role of Indian Women in the Process of Development" in the competition instituted by Indian Committee for International Women's Year.

Dr (Mrs) Asiya Aijaz is working as lecturer in the Department of Psychology, Aligarh Muslim University since 1992. Dr Asiya Aijaz has contributed ten research papers in the reputed journals. Her current academic interest is in the area of Personality, Social Psychology, and Educational Psychology.

Dr Naval Karrir is M. Tech, Ph.D. from IIT Delhi and has a managerial experience of about twelve years in public and private sector organizations. Presently he is on deputation to Ministry of Petroleum from M/s Hindustan Petroleum Corporation Ltd. He is also visiting faculty to a premier management institute.

Dr Chittranjan N. Daftuar, Head of the Department of Psychology, M.S. University Baroda. He was trained in the technology of psychological test construction in cross-cultural settings with particular reference to underdeveloped countries at the Free University, Amsterdam, Holland. He has long experience and expertise in the area of Industrial/Organizational Psychology and is one of the few experts of Human Factors Engineering in the Third World. He has had the privilege of presiding over a session on a topic related to applied experimental psychology in the 3rd Conference of the International Association of the Cross Cultural Psychologists held at Tilburg (Holland) in 1976.

Dr Anjuli Srivastava (Gold Medalist), Lecturer Department of Psychology, M.S. University Baroda, has also written papers for reputed psychological journals. Her field of specialization are social psychology and industrial psychology.

Dr Shamshad Hussain is Professor of Psychology at the University of Patna and simultaneously Vice-Chancellor of Nalanda Open University. His field of specialization is Counselling, Social Psychology, and Distance Learning. Prof. Hussain has a lot of experience in organizing distance education programmes. He is a member of U.G.C. standing committee and the recipient of Vijay Shree Award from Indian International Friendship Society, New Delhi. He has been nominated as International Man of the Year by IBC Cambridge (UK) and ABI, USA (1993-94 & 95).

Miss Neeti Rana, is a research fellow of Bureau of Police Research & Development, Ministry of Home Affairs and has the assignment of conducting doctoral research in Criminology & Police Sciences in the Department of Psychology, Dayalbagh Educational Institute, Dayalbagh, Agra. Other areas of her research interest are Cognitive Psychology and Applied Psychology.

Dr (Miss) S.P. Sinha is serving as Head, Department of Psychology, Dean, Faculty of Social Sciences, Coordinator Management Programme, Dayalbagh Educational Institute, Dayalbagh, Agra. Cognitive Psychology and Environmental Psychology are her favourite research topics.

Dr Saeeduzzafar (Gold Medalist) is a senior most Reader in the Department of Psychology, Aligarh Muslim University, Aligarh. He specializes in the area of experimental psychology and has extended his interest in the areas of social and applied social psychology during the last half a decade.

ONE

Current Status of Applied Psychology in India

DURGANAND SINHA

During the last two years, I had the privilege of participating in two annual conferences of the Indian Association of Applied Psychology (IAAP) an all-India body which has been regularly organizing annual conferences for over three decades that focus on applications of psychological knowledge to different fields. The first one was the Asian and XXXII IAAP conference with focal theme "Emerging Horizons of Applied Psychology" held in Aligarh Muslim University from February 27-29, 1996 and the other was the 2nd Asian and XXXIII IAAP International Conference with the focal theme of "Developing Human Relations and Ethnic Understanding" organized by Gurukul Kangri University, Hardwar, from February 26-28, 1997. Both the conferences were well attended by scholars applied and psychologists from different parts of the country and a few from abroad. I attended as many sessions as was possible, and could gather a fairly good idea of the state of applied psychological research and concerns. The attendance in both the conferences was impressive and participation in various sessions — in spite of parallel sessions — was surprisingly good. People not only stayed till the last session — something unusual in our conference — but also displayed keen interest and occasionally raised important issues. As gathered from the Souvenir and Abstracts (1996) of the Aligarh Conference, a total of 111 abstracts were listed, divided into six sections, namely, perspective papers (5 papers), psychological aspects of human resource development (HRD) (24 papers), psychological health and well-being (20 papers), psychological interventions (12 papers), psychology for the welfare of special groups (28 papers), and psychology in social context (22 papers). The souvenir (1997) of the Gurukul Kangri Conference lists 136 abstracts classified under ten sub-themes of studying human relations: theoretical issues, ethnic understanding through effective communication, cultural ethos: human relations and ethnic understanding, psychological health: personality adjustment and mental health in the context of social and ethnic understanding, class conflict : regional affiliation and group harmony, role of management system in human relations and ethnic understanding, social pollution and human relations, religious conflicts, political behaviour and communal harmony, nationalism and international understanding, and family dynamics and ethnic understanding. Besides, there were two workshops on applications of somatic inkblot series in understanding inner cry and promoting human relations, and organizational citizenship. Soon after the conference in Hardwar an impressive volume of proceedings under the title *Developing Human Relations and Ethnic Understanding* edited by Dr. S.K. Srivastava (1997) was published comprising fifty papers.

A quick perusal of these sources provides an idea of the nature and directions of applied psychology in India. I am aware of the risk involved in making generalizations simply by the perusal of summaries and abstracts and participating in a few sessions only. However, I must point out that I was impressed by the number of papers and the variety of topics covered, and the interest displayed by the participants throughout the two conferences. However, looking at the problems investigated, the variables analysed, the general design of the studies, and the results and conclusions, the feeling that inevitably got generated is that the work in applied psychology in the country over the years had remained more or less static and rarely touched problems that are vital at the present time.

I have been in this game of research since early 1950s. I have not only conducted specific investigations but have been a careful analyst of the research scene that has been unfolding for nearly five decades. The impression that I get is that while some new topics have come on the menu of applied psychology, by and large the state of the subject can best be described as "old wine in a new bottle". Sometimes even the bottle is not new. More or less the same problems with same set of variables were still being investigated that had been done earlier. Studies on job satisfaction and job involvement illustrate the point. One also tends to get the feeling that researchers were generally not aware of the previous studies so that everything seemed to be done *de novo*. The work suffers from being repetitive and replicative. Science is a collective endeavour. Knowledge has to be built step by step. An individual researcher builds upon, improves, and modifies the existing structure, or makes necessary deviations. If the researcher is not aware of or ignores what already has been done on the topic by the investigators who have preceded him/her, neither any specific progress in knowledge is possible nor a healthy and scientific tradition is built up.

Further, I could not avoid the impression that research in applied psychology — or for that matter, in psychology generally — was largely toeing the western line and following the American "fashion" in the selection and treatment of topics to be investigated. There was hardly any evidence that investigators undertook for studying the problems that were important and of immediate societal relevance to the country. Studies on various aspects of stress like occupational stress and management of stress, organizational climate and work culture, HRD, women and deprivation studies in psychology, quality of life, social disadvantage, sports and a few others were exceptions. But it must be remarked that the way the topics were conceptualized and studied indicated overwhelming influence of the West. In fact, issues and problems that really mattered on the contemporary scene but did not constitute "fashionable" themes for research in the mainstream psychological literature were generally ignored. I shall discuss this point at some length later.

It is not necessary to make a detailed content analysis of the abstracts of the papers of the two conferences. Only a few overall impressions and observations are mentioned that bear on the state and status of applied psychology in the country. Firstly, the variety and diversity of topics covered almost the entire range of applications of psychology in the conventional sense. Favourite topics seemed to be stressed and its management, anxiety, job satisfaction and job involvement, adjustment, mental health, psychological correlates of disease, burnout, communication, organizational climate and work culture, HRD, motivation and aspiration, factors in academic adjustment, quality of life, rural-urban differences in children, beliefs and attitudes, and social conflicts. Sports psychology suddenly has become a prominent area. Behaviour modification training and its impact on academic achievement, and memory strategy training programme for children constituted two good intervention studies. There were a few other intervention studies indicating that such studies were becoming popular.

It is to be noted that the areas like anxiety and job satisfaction had been in prominence since the 50's and early 60's. The studies reported appeared to be routine in character without any new approach, ideas or variables investigated. They were entirely replicative. It was amusing to note that Spranger's classification of six values, and construction and standardization of conventional type of verbal test of intelligence still interest the researchers. In any case, studies reported were mostly correlational, conducted on small incidental samples with very little theoretical content. They were "one shot" affair and not a part of any ongoing, systematic and sustained programme of research. As a consequence, they appeared to be ad hoc in nature, being an outcome of isolated and sporadic effort.

Secondly, a perusal of abstracts revealed that a large number were discursive in character discussing in general terms the importance of topics like the role of a counsellor, HRD, employment restructuring, communication, environmental stress and health, mental health care, welfare of the elderly, strategies for the development of youth and women in the context of developing countries, management of literacy campaign, human relations and conflict, ethnic understanding — to mention some of them. Discussions were of very broad nature with little psychological input. They neither provided any insight into psychological processes involved in the phenomena nor suggested new directions for investigation.

Thirdly, compared to the situation in the 50's, many significant topics like deprivation, conflicts and violence, stress management, HRD and the like have come on the research agenda of psychology. But the manner in which they were studied were too narrow and reflected the overwhelming influence of American ethos. The orientation appears to be almost entirely microcosmic, placing disproportionate emphasis on narrow aspects of the problem. Structural variables were ignored so that one could hardly get an overall picture of the issues. As such, though the findings were often interesting, they were hardly of any help in application or in devising intervention programmes. In this context, the observation made by the first Review Committee of the ICSSR (1972, p. 44) on the nature of social psychological research in India is very pertinent. It was remarked that "most of the researches done in social psychology laid disproportionate stress on narrow aspects of large social problems and in consequence, the information gathered lacked in organization, synthesis and integration." (p. 44)

Lastly, as indicated earlier, studies reported were mostly along the lines of western ethos in psychology which is reflected in the job description of a psychologist provided by International Labour Office (ILO, 1969) in its International Standard Clarification of Occupation as follows :

> Studies human behaviour and mental process and investigates, and recommends treatment for, psychological problems in such fields as medicine, education and industry; plans and carries out experiments and observations on human beings and animals to measure mental and physical characteristics; analyses effect of heredity, environment and other factors on individual thought and behaviour; undertakes diagnosis, treatment and prevention of emotional and personality disorders and problems of maladjustment to social and occupational environment; develops and administers tests to measure intelligence, abilities, aptitudes, attitudes and other human characteristics, interprets data and makes recommendations as appropriate.

Many specialise in particular applications of psychology such as diagnosis and treatment of mental abnormalities, psychological problems arising during education and social development of children, or industrial and occupational psychological problems such as those associated with personnel selection, training and vocational guidance.

The job description restricts the activities of applied psychologists to individual emotional and personality problems and making contributions towards more efficient functioning in certain institutions like industries and work organizations educational institutions, clinical and military spheres and the like. Indian researches in applied psychology have generally followed this disciplinary ethos of the west with regard to the choice of topics and determining their priorities without reexamining them in the light of the needs of their own country (Sinha, 1986, p. 111). This has resulted in a shift in the Indian psychologists' focus of attention away from larger societal issues of immediate concern and problems that really matter. It is noteworthy that in spite of the fact that India lives in the villages and their problems should be of major concern not only to planners and administrators but also academicians who are interested in human development and human well-being, applied psychologists have generally neglected the rural issues. Hardly four studies pertaining to rural sector were listed. They related to (i) attitude towards family planning among rural women; (ii) comparison of beliefs and attitudes on some social issues of urban and rural people; (iii) child in urban, tribal and rural communities; and (iv) a new look at rural HRD. Excepting the last one which highlights specific aspects of developing and managing human resources in rural areas and need for supplementing management by objectives (MBO) by "management by relationship" (MBR) and provide some information about applications of such programmes in Orissa, the other three papers were commonplace and stereotypical hardly touching upon social and psychological problems of rural people caught in the process of large-scale social change in the country.

Neglect of psychological issues pertaining to rural areas is surprising especially in the context that some far-reaching pioneering researches on rural communication (Pareek & Singh

1968; Kivlin, Roy, Fliegel & Sen, 1968), psychological factors in agro-economic development (Sinha, 1969, 1974; Sinha & Chaubey, 1972; Hundal & Singh, 1975; Singh, et al., 1970) have been conducted and widely reported during the 60's and 70's. It appears that researchers in applied psychology in the country are bogged down by their urban middle class prejudices and are so closely oriented to the urban scenario that they have become blind to the rural issues which are of equal, if not greater, salience for the development and well-being of the country.

Psychological research into family dynamics was another significant area that was grossly neglected. Hardly five papers during the two conferences pertained to the topic, namely, (i) joint family disintegration and social imbalance; (ii) child in the family; (iii) effect of family environment on mental stress among working women; (iv) role of television in improving the mode of family relationship; and (v) child, family and adjustment. Two of them were general while others touched upon the area only peripherally.

Family in India has some unique features and has a pivotal role in the life and well-being of individuals. Rapid changes that it has undergone have brought to the fore many new dimensions having far-reaching psychological repercussions on adjustment and mental health, interpersonal relationships, and even organizational functioning. Transition and change have become its essence. A book entitled *Family Measurement in India* edited by Shalini Bharat (1996) has been recently published which brings out elaborately the psychological importance of family dynamics and discusses many researches. It is surprising that the topic has not attracted the researchers in applied psychology, though it is well-known that family therapy has come to be prominent and family councellors are fast mushrooming, especially in the metropolis and large cities. To put it figuratively, family in transition constitutes a "gold mine" of research which is located just at the doorstep but has been largely ignored by applied psychologists.

A problem that is vital and is churning the long stagnant Indian society is that of social justice and social inequality. The papers reported under the heading of social conflict and ethnic relations and understanding hardly touched upon the problem in any significant manner. They were in the mould of conventional research and failed to shed much light on its vital dimensions. It has rightly been pointed out that the policy of protective discrimination instead of helping those for whom it is meant was actually harming them (Tripathi, 1988, p. 143). The impact on both the 'beneficiaries' and the 'sufferers', on individual as well as the group level requires careful analysis. As Tripathi (1988, p. 143) observes, there is need for a second look at the national policy of education and employment for individuals belonging to the socially disadvantaged groups. The aberrations that the policy has produced, required careful analysis not so much as its narrow critique but for evolving strategies and programmes to prevent its negative psychological consequences and for forging interventions so that those belonging to the disadvantaged groups realize their full potential and get integrated in the mainstream of Indian society. The problem once again provides a 'gold mine' for investigations for applied psychologists.

Apart from areas indicated above, there were many other significant gaps. Increasing incidence of violence and lowering threshold for aggression despite the long tradition of *ahimsa* (non-violence); intergroup tensions and conflicts; alienation of the youth; sudden erosion of basic social values; and mounting incidence of social delinquencies mark the contemporary Indian society. These are problems that deserve the immediate attention of applied psychologists not just to analyse some of their dimensions but also to provide 'data' that would help combat these undesirable trends. Further, change and development constitute the most salient features of our present-day scenario not simply confined to economic and political planes but of all facets of our functioning. Applied psychologists have generally neglected the dynamics of change and their psychological consequences. A well-designed psychological analysis of developmental changes in a village or in a small town is likely to yield results that would enhance our understanding of the processes of change and at the same time provide insights for intervention strategies to make the process smooth and without deviating from the desired direction.

Mention has to be made of the relative neglect of studies on psychological concomitants of poverty and deprivation. The area has for sometime occupied a significant position on the agenda of applied psychologists. But the few papers presented during the two conferences were largely replications of what had already been done. Neither any new aspect of the problem was investigated nor new intervention programme suggested. One tends to agree with Udai Pareek's (1980) observation made in the preface to the ICSSR second survey of research in psychology that "in spite of the fact that poverty remains to be the foremost problem of India, there seems to be a general negligence on the part of behavioural scientists in studying it with researcher's rigour (p. xiii-xiv). This is especially true of applied psychologists in the country."

Despite these gaps, there were some hopeful trends. Though the overall number was small, some papers provided evidence of utilization of indigenous concepts and processes and the rich heritage of psychological thinking that India possesses for designing their studies. There were abstracts on interesting topics like new look at rural HRD, the Indian system of HRD, an insightful discussion on Indian perspective on human relations, studies on occupational stress, organizational commitment and job involvement in *sattva* (quintessence), *rajas* (luxuriousness-merry making-exhibitionism), and *tamas* (the quality of darkness or ignorance) personality types, yogic coping strategy for stress and interpersonal relations, and a pilot study an Swadhyay Pariwar's strategy to promote human relations. There was also a general paper on yoga as a means of reviving ancient values and promoting human relations.

Indigenization of research psychology is a significant trend. It is especially so for applied research, because for application, issues and problems have to be conceptualized in specific sócio-cultural context using indigenous categories and theoretical models. Contextualization is not only desirable but essential if research is to be utilized for enhancing our individual and social functioning.

Before concluding I would examine the findings of the researches reported along the lines of the exercise that Norman Sartorius, the then Director-General of Mental Health of the WHO, made to us during a consultation session for the preparation of the edited volume entitled *Health and Cross-Cultural Psychology : Towards Application* (Dasen, Berry & Sartorius, 1988). After we had prepared the draft papers on the specific themes allocated to us, each one of us was asked to prepare a tabular presentation of 'facts' and 'principles' contained in the papers each being rated according to: (1) its contribution to general knowledge without specific possibility of application; (2) conducive to being 'translated' into behavioural and other interventions after further work; and (3) already applicable. Analysing the abstracts and the findings reported along the line, the overwhelming impression that one got was that most of the contributions belonged to the first categories, i.e., contributing only to our general understanding, and hardly any could be categorized as already applicable. It is of no consolation to think that the same is true of applied psychology research generally. Operating in a developing country with acute scarcity of resources, the responsibility of a researcher is far greater. For psychologists in the affluent parts of the western world, doing research is often a luxury and a pastime often engaging in trivialities. For a psychologist in a developing country, research should not be merely for obtaining a doctoral degree enhancing one's curriculum vitae. It should be regarded as a kind of privilege for using meagre resources which could otherwise have been utilized for ameliorating the lot of at least a few of the disadvantaged people. As Jahoda (1975) has remarked in the context of cross-cultural psychology, the developing countries will not for long tolerate the activities of psychological researchers "without at least some prospect of tangible return". The lack of public support that we face is an evidence in support of Jahoda's contention.

I will not discuss at length the reasons for this state of affairs in applied psychological research in the country. I have outlined the same in my keynote address to the Asian Pacific Regional Conference of Psychology held in Guangzhou, China, in August 1995, which was subsequently published in the *Chinese Journal of Applied Psychology* (Sinha, 1995). As discussed in detail in my earlier publications (Sinha, 1986, 1995) certain features of modern psychology as a discipline stand in the way of its application to problems of developing countries. Besides, there are others that are specific to the development of the subject in this country.

The overall position is that application of psychology is very limited and has made hardly any impact on the societal issues and larger problems facing the country. The consequence of it, as stated very mildly by Ganguli (1971, p. 176), is that "... association of psychologists with government effort in planning and implementation of national development programmes is less than of social scientists of other disciplines". Pareek (1980, p. ix) is more forthright when he comments that there are "signs of growing crisis in psychology .... Psychology has failed to make a thrust in the national life". It is essential that research in applied psychology is 'relevant' and makes an impact not only on certain microlevel institutions like industries, educational institutions and in hospitals and clinics, but to quote Udai Pareek (1980), "it has to share with other social sciences the task of contributing to solutions of national problems, both in terms of conceptual and intervention insights." Modifying the observation of Kurt Lewin (1948) made fifty-five years ago, psychological research must accomplish social good. Research that produces nothing but books and papers will not suffice. This applies to the kind of researches conducted in the field of applied psychology today in our country.

REFERENCES

Bharat, S. (ed.), 1996, *Family measurement in India*. New Delhi: Sage.

Dasen, P.R., Berry, J.W., and Sartorius, N. (eds.), 1988, *Health and Cross-cultural Psychology: Towards application*. Newburg Park, CA: Sage.

Ganguli, H.C., 1971, Psychological research in India: 1920-1967, *International Journal of Psychology*, 6, 165-177.

Hundal, P.S., & Singh, S., 1975, Structure of Personality Characteristics and Motive Pattern of Farmers, *Indian Journal of Psychology*, 50, 33-43.

ICSSR, 1973, *A Report on Social Science in India*, Vol. I, New Delhi: ICSSR Review Committee Report.

ILO, 1969, *International Standard Classification of Occupations*, Geneva, International Labour Office.

Jahoda, G., 1975, Applying cross-cultural psychology the third world. In J.W. Berry & W.J. Louner (Eds.), *Applied Cross-cultural Psychology*, Amsterdam: Swets & Zeitlinger.

Kivlin, J.E., Roy, P., Fliegel, F.C., and Sen, L.K., 1968, *Communication in India: Experiments in inducing change*. Hyderabad: National Institute of Community Development.

Lewin, K., 1948, *Resolving Social Conflict*. New York: Harper & Raw.

Pareek, U. (ed.), 1980, *A survey of research in psychology, 1971-1976, Part I*. Bombay: Popular Prakashan.

Pareek, U., and Singh, Y.P., 1968, Sociometry and Communication Network in an Indian village, *International Journal of Psychology*, 3: 157-65.

Singh, N.P., 1970, Risk-taking and anxiety among successful and unsuccessful traditional and progressive agricultural entrepreneurs of Delhi, *British Journal of Social and Clinical Psychology*, 9: 301-308.

Sinha, D., 1969, *Indian villages in transition : A motivational analysis*. Delhi: Associated Publishing House.

———, 1974, *Motivation and rural development*. Calcutta: Minerva Associates.

———, 1986, *Psychology in a Third World Country: The Indian Experience*, New Delhi: Sage.

———, 1995, Application of psychology in developing countries, *Chinese Journal of Applied Psychology*, 1 (2), 9-16.

Sinha, D., and Chaubey, N.P., 1972, Achievement motive and rural economic development. *International Journal of Psychology*, 7: 267-72.

Souvenir, 1997, 2nd Asian & 33rd IAAP International Conference on Developing Human Relations and Ethnic Understanding, Hardwar, Gurukul Kangri University, February 26-29, 1997.

Souvenir & Abstracts, 1996, Asian & 32nd IAAP Conference on Emerging Horizons of Applied Psychology: Asian Perspective, Aligarh, Aligarh Muslim University, February 27-29, 1996.

Srivastava, S.K. (Ed.), 1977, *Developing Human Relations and Ethnic Understanding*, Hardwar, Department of Psychology, Gurukul Kangri University.

Tripathi, R.C., 1988, Applied social psychology, in J. Pandey (Ed.), *Psychology in India: The state-of-the-art*, pp. 95-157. New Delhi: Sage.

TWO

Progress of the Clinical Psychology in India

G.G. PRABHU

The history of modern psychology begins with the establishment of the psychology laboratory by Wundt in 1879 at Leipzig. Following this a spate of laboratories came up in Europe and the USA. It took nearly three decades for this movement to reach India.

The Genesis

In Wundt's laboratory the study of applied aspects was discouraged and at times totally prohibited. Lightner Witmer who received his doctorate in 1892-93 was one of the early groups of Americans to obtain it under Wundt. In his dissertation on the aesthetic values of varying proportions, Witmer studied in the main, the basic theoretical issues, but in addition managed to include the applied aspect of individual differences, and the determinants of such differences. On his return and starting of his professional career at Pennsylvania University, he was the first to enunciate that the emerging discipline of psychology, if appropriately utilized can be the basis for a helping profession. Based on this conviction he deliberately and consciously defined, established and nurtured the early development of clinical psychology. As Garfield (1965) records, if anyone has a claim to the title *Founder of Clinical Psychology* it is undoubtedly Lightner Witmer. His interest was in being of help to people to bring about their maximal functioning by the optimum utilization of whatever psychological knowledge and skills that existed. He felt that this can be provided not only by a profession independent of both medicine and education but which is closely attuned with basic scientific psychology. His contribution thus, was an idea that psychology which was in its initial phase of excitement as an experimental science may also be of direct help to people. His contributions can, thus, be criticized as nothing original and only a suggestion that psychologists should discover new uses and applications for already available knowledge and methods.

The role thus suggested by Witmer was far different from the one considered appropriate at that time for psychologists. Individuals had been studied by psychologists before but always with the aim of formulating scientific generalizations and generation of new knowledge. His signal innovation as a psychologist was to suggest and practice the application of psychological principles and techniques in the diagnosis and treatment of individual cases. His ideas came in conflict with the Zeitgeist in 1896 itself at the time of the Boston meeting of the American Psychological Association. He presented his ideas and described his work regarding the organization of practical work in psychology wherein he used the concept of psychological clinic for the first time. He declared that his clinic is an institution of social service, for original research and for instruction of students in psychological orthogenics — a concept evolved by him to include vocational, educational, correctional, hygienic, industrial and social guidance. Witmer felt that he is proposing something important, new and exciting, "the clinical method of psychology and diagnostic method of teaching". As Brotemarkle (1947) records "his talk stimulated the elevation of some of his colleagues eye brows but little else". In retrospect it is clear that the man was ahead of his times (Prabhu, 1992).

During the period 1896-1907, the new profession was gradually coming into being but it lacked a name. Witmer, just as he had established the first psychological clinic at Pennsylvania in 1896, founded the first journal devoted exclusively to the new profession being nurtured by him. The first issue of the journal — *The Psychological Clinic* — was published on 15th March 1907 and in its first article Witmer proposed that the new profession be named as Clinical Psychology.

Garfield (1965) records that such an unusual pioneer and innovator as Witmer did not have a greater impact on subsequent developments in clinical psychology. Witmer got clinical psychology moving but seemed to have succeeded very little in steering it. Watson (1953) opines that "Witmer turned his back on almost all that was to predominate in the later days of clinical psychology and became of historical significance only". Witmer always seemed to sail against the current. During the early part of the century when intelligence testing constituted the centre piece of most clinical work, Witmer decried it. He was not in tune with Freudian dynamic model which was on the rise. Witmer worked with children and continued to do so even after clinical psychology started being interested in therapy with adults. Even among children, his interest was in children with mental retardation and those with disabilities rather than those with behaviour disorders. His therapeutic approach was pedagogical and not dynamic, affective or motivational.

Witmer's influence was not felt directly at any time in the development of clinical psychology in India. Scientific disciplines and professional orientations do not get confined by geographical boundaries though in each set-up they have a history, development and pattern of their own. In his article in the first issue of the Psychological Clinic, Witmer (1907) had said "In the final analysis the progress of Clinical Psychology, as of every other science, will be determined by the value and amount of its contributions to the advancement of the human race" and the principles of scientific psychology can and are the basis of this helping profession. Clinical Psychology in India hinges on this philosophy and will be evaluated within its framework.

The Roots

At the turn of the present century, Sir Ashutosh Mookerjee, saw the immense possibilities of studying psychology at the highest academic level. As early as in 1905, he took initiative to enter experimental psychology as an independent subject in the list of postgraduate courses (Basu, 1976). The first department of psychology in India was established in Calcutta University in 1915 in the faculty of Science under the chairmanship of Dr. N.N. Sengupta.

For the purposes of a comprehensive coverage of the history and development of clinical psychology in India we have to go back to the year 1905. The developments of the last 92 years can be divided into three phases of fifty, twenty and twenty years respectively though perforce one may find certain amount of overlap of these phases.

An account of the development of psychology in India is to be gathered from several sources (Mitra, 1937, 1955; Sinha, 1963; UGC, 1968; ICSSR, 1972; Mitra, 1973; Basu, 1976) as it has not been compiled in a single source. It is clear from these sources that before independence the centres of psychology were established only in five major cities of India, i.e. at Calcutta, Mysore, Patna, Lucknow and Madras. Even before the Indian Psychological Association (IPA) came into being in 1925, the IPA was started at Calcutta in 1921 by Dr. Girindra Sekhar Bose who was a student of Dr. N.N. Sengupta. This society opened an institution in 1930, called the Indian Psychoanalytical Institution for analysing the prospective members of the society. *Samiksha* the Journal of the society was started in 1947. From the very inception when modern psychology was introduced in India it inherited a strong tradition of Freudian psychoanalysis along with a tradition of experimental psychology and psychological measurement. This was very much unlike what Whitmer evolved in the USA. Unluckily, in the West the three stands existed separately in a tension ridden set-up. But, in India it is a harmonious *triveni sangam;* there is no room for tension which is the important past in West.

The First Phase

During the first phase (1905-55) the rate at which the overall growth of psychology and within this framework that of clinical psychology occurred was slow, yet there were some identifiable merits. The dynamic approach (Eysenck 1968) with its emphasis on projective techniques, interpretation and psychotherapy was adhered to both by the University departments of psychology and the clinical psychologists engaged in rendering service to the community. Carl Jung's visit to Calcutta in 1938 at the time of the silver jubilee session of the Indian Science Congress generated further interest in Analytical Psychology.

During this phase we find the original contributions of Dr. G. Bose (1886-1959) about repression, defiance, ambivalence, free association, opposite fantasies and a new theory of mental life. Since 1911, Bose was working with his own analytical concepts. On many basic issues there was close correspondence between the thinking of Freud and Bose but on some important aspects Bose differed from Freud. Bose (1933) had developed his theory of "Opposite Wishes" and had treated his patients on these lines. He did not agree with Freud regarding Oedipus situation. The initial phase thus was characterized by serious attempts at theory building.

During this period the relationship between psychology and psychiatry is worth noting. At that time psychiatry was neither developed as a profession nor as a medical subject (Varma 1953). It hardly provided anything more than custodial care to the severely ill psychotics in mental hospitals, the state of which as per Taylor (1946) was disgraceful with "the making of a major public scandal"; psychiatric services on an out patient basis were hard to come by. Compared to this psychology was in a position to render therapeutic assistance and enjoyed a respectable status as a discipline and a profession. It is this that made Dube (1953) point out that "Psychology has now become a password and an order of the day. Psychologists are being employed right and left. Psychological Bureaus (sic) are being set up. The word has now acquired almost mystical power, vocational guidance, selection through psychological testing is strongly advocated.....". All this was said in a presidential address to the Indian Psychiatric Society where Dube (1953) pointed out that "in our country we seldom hear the voice of a psychiatrist who is being constantly ignored". Probably none would have thought or visualized at that time as to what was round the corner; for like the rise and fall of civilizations the "distress of Psychiatry" was about to end and the enviable position of psychology was not to last much longer. Despite such an evaluation of the relative status of the two professions, as has been recorded by Prabhu (1983) a fairly congenial and cooperative attitude existed between the two.

In the first phase of development of psychology, the academic and professional leadership was in the university departments of psychology. The phase was characterized by slow but steady development of psychology including clinical psychology; contributions to and interaction with international thinking of the day; a predominantly therapeutic orientation based on analytical concepts and an enviable professional status for psychology which lead to a virtual gold rush of job opportunities immediately after the end of World War II.

The Second Phase (1956-75)

From the early fifties, the whole field of psychology in India was characterized by a spate of growth with a simultaneous turmoil characterized by internal contradictions.

In the post-independence period when the ministry of defence started advertising for jobs in research laboratories and the selection boards, university departments of philosophy started introducing postgraduate courses in psychology; psychology courses which were available in about 19 universities in 1968 (UGC, 1968) spread over and were available in 51 universities by 1975 (Mitra 1973; Basu 1976) indicating a 168 per cent growth in seven years. Unfortunately this was at the expense of quality, as the programmes became examination and degree oriented with scant respect for contemporary scientific trends and functional relevance.

In 1915, psychology was introduced in Calcutta University, a lead which did not get followed extensively in other centers. During the goldrush, psychology was increasingly introduced in the "Arts" faculties and "harder modules with a sound scientific base" like experimental psychology, physiological psychology, etc., were left out. All this was happening at a time when in the international arena psychology was getting established on sound scientific foundations.

During this period, cheap editions of American books started flowing in. What initially looked like a boon turned out to be a bane. "Indian production of books for the postgraduate level in any branch of psychology is practically nil. British and American books are generally prescribed as texts or reference books" says Krishnan (1972). The mind set of the postgraduates was so distorted that they hardly looked for socio-cultural relevance of the subject they were studying. As Shanmugam (1972) records "The research in personality are at present mainly confined to the applying of the theories of Rosenzwig, Allport, Murray, Maslow, Eysenck, Cattell and McClelland" which made Agrawal (1975) muse whether Indian psychology is synonymous with "Adaptology". Prabhu (1975) felt that psychology in India was turning out to be "uncritical transplantology" devoid of scientific temper and rigour. All this made for a poor foundation on which to build sound professional programmes in clinical psychology.

The founding of the Indian Psychoanalytical Institution in 1930 in a way introduced training programmes in the clinical area. In 1945, the University of Calcutta started a certificate course in applied psychology which provided for an option to specialize in advanced abnormal psychology. A formal training programme of one year's duration in clinical psychology was introduced at the Banaras Hindu University in 1951. From the late seventies, a clinical psychology programme has been in existence at the Kashi Vidyapeeth. An applied psychology programme at the Aligarh Muslim University and clinical psychology programmes at the Karnataka University and the SNDT University existed for a few years. All these programmes remained low profile and though they made efforts at providing exposure to clinical situations and material they did not have extensive supervised internship. Generally they existed for a short time and had a chequered history. In England and the USA clinical psychology programmes have evolved predominantly within the framework of university departments. The inability of the clinical programmes to take firm roots in the Indian university setting needs to be looked into in-depth; for logically they have the maximum desirable potential to build robust and socio-culturally meaningful programmes within a psychosocial model.

In 1954, the Government of India established the All India Institute of Mental Health (known as National Institute of Mental

Health & Neurosciences (NIMHANS) since 1974). From 1955, it started offering a two-year post MA diploma programme in medical psychology (DMP). Currently, the programme is known as M.Phil. in clinical psychology. This programme has been incorporated as full time, structured and has built in supervised internship. Financial support to all the trainees during their apprenticeship is the biggest attraction which helps them to learn sincerely. This economic help must be continued to students. The setting is that of a mental hospital with a progressive philosophy. At the inception the orientation was predominantly British and the emphasis has been on the medical model though an adherence to as yet not clearly defined multidisciplinary philosophy is claimed. Simultaneously, a two-year post MBBS programme (DPM) was also introduced to train Psychiatrists. In 1962, the postgraduate training centre (currently known as Central Institute of Psychiatry, (CIP) was established at Ranchi. This again was in the overall setting of a model mental hospital. This centre started the same programmes as in Bangalore. Later, from 1973 a third programme with limited intake and a differing training philosophy was introduced at BM Institute Ahmedabad. The last programme has not been exclusively for students with postgraduate qualifications in Psychology and has faced a chequered progress.

At Bangalore and Ranchi, each centre has a capacity to train 12 clinical psychologists per year. Those trained in these centres during the earlier years (1955-75) espoused a psychometric approach (Eysenck, 1968) with its emphasis on evaluation and classification. Sinha (1963) points out that in the first phase clinicians had a "preoccupation with Rorschach and TAT" but Mitra (1973) records that "one finds a movement away from preoccupation with Rorschach and TAT to objective tests like Cattell's 16 PF and Eysenck's measures....." All this was adhered to within the framework of the medical model. The setting of the two training centres being psychiatric facilities, to be precise hospitals for mental diseases, and not centres of scientific psychology seems to be the main reason for this graft. The trainees were influenced more by the medical model rather than a professional pyscho-social model made meaningful for use in the clinical area. The predominant exposure of the trainees is to the problems of the severely mentally ill. The Bangalore centre provides certain amount of exposure to those with neurological and neurosurgical problems. The trend of psychologists working in collaboration with other health specialities could not take roots because of the limitations inherent in the settings. The role of a clinical psychologist as an independent care giver went understressed and gradually clinical psychology in India started embracing most of the trends and beliefs of psychiatry which perforce minimized the using of principles, laws and methods of scientific psychology. As a result, clinical psychology looked more like a contributory profession in the field of mental health than a complimentary one.

If one perceives normality-abnormality along a continuum, the psychologist works from the "normal" end while a medically trained person from the "pathological end" towards the centre. Adequately trained professional persons are those who are competent, sensitive and capable of giving care to a range of problems as perceived according to the tenets of their own fields. Clinical psychology can play a complimentary role in the mental health setting, which is bound to be utilitarian to the psychiatrist and satisfying to the clinical psychologist not by duplicating the role of a psychiatrist at a subordinate level but by making contributions unique to them because of their training in socio-behavioural areas and scientific experimental methodology.

In the west, the clinical psychologists moved from an earlier diagnostic role to the later role of a therapist. In India this process was temporarily reversed, as the therapeutic role adhered to by the psychologist was replaced by the diagnostic role and a magnified diagnostic role (Ramalingaswami 1976, 1977) got clamped to the image of the clinical psychologist.

In addition to the above, there were other developments which generated an identity crisis among clinical psychologists. In the West university departments resisted the dynamic approach and its acceptance was gradual and guarded. They gave it up much earlier than practicing clinical psychologists. In India psychology began in the universities with a dynamic approach and university departments hold on to projective techniques and analytical concepts as sacrosanct. On the other hand, professional psychologists have increasingly questioned their validity and utility leading to lesser reliance on them since the early seventies. Gradually, thus, a cleft has occurred between university departments and professional clinical psychologists resulting in decreasing interaction among them.

Of the two centres for training in clinical psychology, the Bangalore centre (NIMHANS) has merits of its own. Over the last forty years it's infrastructure has developed. The laboratory and library facilities are good. The strength of the faculty and the scientific staff with staff student ratio of 1:1.5 provides good scope for clinical supervision. The academic programme has been monitored and undergone changes over the years. The postgraduate diploma (DMP) was converted into DM and SP (Diploma in Medical and Social Psychology) in 1960 and for the last decade and a half is made into the M. Phil degree programme. A three years Ph.D (Clinical Psychology) programme is also available. Despite all this, its very history and setting became major constraints. The difficulties to be faced because of the setting have been highlighted earlier. It's history and associated institutional goals put severe constraints on the possible choice and flexibility that can be incorporated in the training programmes. The number of patients seeking help at the centre is enormous and the primary institutional goal is that of providing clinical services. Training and research come next in the order of priority. As the trainees are financially supported, heavy demands are made on their time to provide routine clinical services. The placement of the trainee in other centres like a general hospital setting becomes difficult, if not impossible, as any such placement would create a void in the parent institution. In 1955, with the limited concept of care of the mentally ill the mental hospital setting was adequate for providing training facilities. The last forty years have brought about a sea change in the concept of mental health care. Training programmes have to diversify. The Bangalore programme can bring about minor modifications which are far from adequate to keep in step with fast changing times and trends. Unfortunately, the Ranchi centre did not bloom much after the initial years. For the last 2 years the centre had no faculty member in clinical psychology yet the programme has been on the go.

Training programmes in psychiatry which started in mental

hospital settings in 1955 and 1962 moved over to the general hospital setting by 1964. Their number increased over the years and currently there are 32 such centres. On the other hand, training centres in clinical psychology have neither moved out of their original settings nor their number increased. For the purposes of a better professional role perspective; as a simulation to their job placement subsequent to the completion of their training, for the utilization of psycho-social model, and an exposure to a wider variety of clinical problems it was essential that clinical psychology programmes had moved out of the mental hospital settings much earlier than similar programmes in psychiatry (Prabhu, 1975).

The Present

As clinical psychologists started feeling that they have to face some specific problems. The "Indian Association of Clinical Psychologists" came into being in 1968. The Association has been fairly active and celebrated its silver jubilee. The Journal of the Association; *The Indian Journal of Clinical Psychology* which started publication in 1974 has been coming out regularly. If one scans the literature, a variety of material is available as to who is a clinical psychologist (Prabhu, 1974, 1976, 1977; Ramalingaswami, 1977; Sen Muzumdar, 1976; Krishna Dutt, 1993) the work they do (Sharma *et al.*, 1974, 1975) their role (Prabhu, 1974, 1975, 1976, 1977a; Ramalingaswami, 1976, 1977; Sen Muzumdar, 1976; Ghosh, 1977; Murthy, 1982; Bharathraj, 1984; Dube, 1985; Paintal, 1987) the past and desired future of clinical psychology (Prabhu, 1974; Sen, 1975; Basavanna, 1981) development and evaluation of training programmes (Prabhu, 1974, 1975a), Human resource planning (Prabhu, 1977), and registration and licensing (Prabhu, 1974, 1977; Gupta, 1988).

The research carried out in India in the field of clinical psychology has been well documented in three research surveys commissioned and published by the Indian Council of Social Science Research since 1972.

The kaleidoscopic picture presented by the wide variety of views is not to be taken as an index of confusion but as a reflection of the complexity of the issues involved.

Sen, Muzumdar (1976) and Ghosh (1977) stressed that clinical psychologists in India should take greater responsibility in the care and therapeutic management of the client. Ramalingaswami (1976, 1977) strongly advocated the diagnostic functions. In the West, clinical psychologists spend nearly 50 per cent of their time in therapeutic activities, about 25 per cent of the time in teaching, about 20 per cent of the time in research and less than 10 per cent of the time in diagnostics and administration. In India, emphasizing the diagnostic role that came up in the second phase would be an archaic and counter productive move, though diagnostics would continue to be one of the minor responsibilities. The increasing emphasis now being given to therapeutics — both psycho-social and behaviouraly based — during the training period seems fully justified. Prabhu (1977a, 1983) pointed out that in the Indian set-up the number of working clinical psychologists is around 350. The settings where they work, the characteristics of the clients they serve and the professional functions demanded from them because of the overall institutional goals varies so widely that a search for that "the most widely recurring combination" which evolves and finally defines the role is very elusive. Depending on the setting where one works the clinical psychologist has to be innovative in his functioning. It is this that makes one very skeptical about mental hospital based training centres in clinical psychology. Subsequent to the completion of their training, a young clinical psychologist hardly gets an appointment in the mental hospital setting as the pattern of delivery of mental health care has grossly changed over the last four decades. The new type of setting, a clientele with totally different type of characteristics and new type of professional functions demanded may make a young clinical psychologists work feel paralysed.

To answer the question as to how many clinical psychologists are there in the country with a population of 940 million, one has to first answer the question as to who can be classified as a clinical psychologist. Working clinical psychologists have to take on care giving responsibilities and hence it is mandatory that they adhere to a prescribed or self-imposed code of conduct and ethics and do not exceed the boundaries of the skills to discharge which they have been trained or they have acquired them subsequently by way of continuing professional education (Prabhu, 1996). It is gratifying to note that the Indian Association of Clinical Psychologists have brought out a draft code of conduct and ethics for its members. This is an important issue as unlike in the seventies or prior to that, during the last decade and a half the Consumer Protection Act, the Mental Health Act, the Rehabilitation Council of India Act and the People with Disabilities Act have become operative. A recent judgement of the Honourable Supreme Court of India is a pointer. It held that a medical practitioner trained in a particular system of medicine is competent and is justified to practice what one is trained for. One going beyond the boundaries of the recognized training undergone, is accountable, as it amounts to professional negligence and malpractice. In view of this, it is necessary that while conducting applied psychology programmes in general and clinical psychology programmes in particular the concerned departments must clearly state the aims and the objectives of the programme; the details of the programme content with specification of theoretical, research, practical and supervised training inputs; the functions such a qualified person is entitled to discharge; and the service that can be rendered. Even a single instance of litigation, like those being now faced by the medical profession or going against the profession would create difficulties and bring disrepute to psychology and psychologists.

The days when anyone with a Masters or doctorate degree in psychology could call themselves as 'clinical psychologists' and claim that they have 'some required considerable or extensive' training in clinical psychology are gone. A minimum basic requirement would be one where after one has obtained a Masters degree in psychology one undergoes a two-year full time structured programme with built in supervised internship leading to a diploma or degree awarded specifically in clinical psychology by a recognized university. This is similar to the recommendations made by the Trethowan (1977) Committee Report in England two decades ago. The conditions laid down in the USA are more stringent as one has to undergo 4/5 year APA approved doctoral programme before one can seek a license and registration to function as a clinical psychologist. This does not mean that there is no scope for having different types and grades of professionals to provide psychological services like counselling, psychometric services, etc. The Rehabilitation Council of India registers Rehabilitation Professionals and Workers separately. The important aspect is to state the training objectives in detail and lay down the role responsibilities.

Going by the standard suggested above, over the last four decades a little over 600 clinical psychologists have been trained in India. Of these, 365 are from NIMHANS, nearly 220 from CIP and the rest from Ahmedabad. Migration, misplacement, and matrimony in a female dominated profession lead to considerable drainage from the total number trained. It is difficult to say as to how many of these are actively working as clinical psychologists in this country. "Guestimates" put it around 300 to 350 which is grossly inadequate in a country of the size of India. The need in the immediate future is to start standard programmes in clinical psychology and other allied care giving areas. The Indian universities have to come forward to meet this challenge — a role they effectively played in the first phase which bestowed psychology with glory.

The Immediate Future

If one visualizes professional programmes in applied psychology as post MA programmes, it virtually means that from the time of taking up graduation a student would put in a minimum of 6 to 7 years or 9 to 10 years of study in the field of psychology, to obtain the M. Phil or the Ph. D. degree respectively. If curriculum and training is carefully planned at each stage it should be possible to turn out a first rate clinical psychologist (or for that matter any type of applied professional psychologist) at the end of this period. It is to be remembered that IIT's; IIM's or standard medical colleges produce a professional in much less time. It is not a happy commentary about education in psychology in this country if similar results cannot be obtained. Wastage of time for professional training is to be avoided by getting rid of stereotyped repetition and by building up sequential modules of training.

The applied psychology programmes should be conducted, to the extent possible, in the university departments of psychology so that a scientific temper is maintained and one does not loose sight of laws and methods of scientific psychology. More than these it would encourage the imparting of the training within the appropriate framework of the psycho-social model with emphasis on the independent complimentary professional role the trainee has to discharge subsequent to the training. Programmes carried out in medical settings run the risk of failing to provide a proper professional identity and may well create identity diffusion if not a distorted identity of a subordinate paramedical professional.

There is also a need to implement programmes which are of socio-cultural and contemporary relevance. Visualized and implemented in the mid-fifties the NIMHANS, programme was excellent but it served certain limited objectives and goals towards which it was geared. The developments that have occurred in the field of psychology and the changes that have come about with regard to socio-cultural realities make it necessary that newer programmes are considered. The counsellors programme that is being conducted at the Maharashtra Institute of Mental Health, Pune for the last three years and a diploma programme in clinical psychology the Applied Psychology Department of Bombay University is planning to implement are worth mentioning. The latter is being planned with an emphasis which differs considerably from the Bangalore and Ranchi programmes. A recent report on manpower development (RCI, 1996) indicates that in the light of the developments that are occuring in the field of disability and in view of recent legislation like the People With Disabilities Act of 1996 the number of Rehabilitation psychologists needed during the 9th and 10th plan would be 2000 and 4000 respectively. As financial constraints may not permit the implementation of some of the projects, the figures given may turn out to be on the higher side. Yet it cannot be denied that the new profession of Rehabilitation Psychologist has arrived. Arya's (1990) thought provoking editorial on this issue has gone unnoticed and one finds that — leave alone implementing professional programmes in Rehabilitation psychology extensively, Indian Universities have not even introduced it as a subject.

During the last two decades health psychology has established itself as an independent and robust speciality of psychology. The role played by psycho-social factors in health, well-being and illness, the role of lifestyles in maintaining health and the need to change faulty lifestyles; and the concepts of well-being and quality of life have revolutionized the thinking and practice in the field of health. Specialization in health psychology should be provided for on a priority basis. If one looks around one finds that substance abuse; clinical neuropsychology; child and adolescent mental health; school psychology, the area of AIDS programmes, to mention just a few, are areas of national concern wherein psycho-social inputs are required. These never challenges have to be addressed. Maintaining a single track mind and continuing to perceive and conceive programmes as done in the mid-fifties would be hazardous if not foolhardy. The time to diversify and specialize has long arrived. Witmer might have sailed against the current; but Indian Psychologists would do well to sail with Witmer's statement and remember his words that psychology would be ultimately judged by the value and amount of its contributions to the advancement of human race.

REFERENCES

Agrawal, K.G., 1975, Psychology or Adaptology? Book Review: Review Article, *Social Scientist*.

Arya, S., 1990, Editorial : Emerging trends in Rehabilitation Psychology, *Ind. J. Clin. Psychol.*, 17, 56.

Basavanna, M., 1981, Twenty-Five Years of Clinical Psychology in India, *Ind. J. Clin. Psychol.*, 8, i.

Basu, C.K., 1976, A brief look at Psychology in India, Souvenir, *IPA Golden Jubilee Celebrations*, pp. 13-14.

Bharathraj, J., 1984, Presidential Speech., *Ind. J. Clin. Psychol.*, 11, i.

Bose, G., 1933, A new theory of mental life, *Indian J. Psychol.*, 8.

Brotemarkle, B.A., 1947, Fifty Years of Clinical Psychology: Clinical Psychology 1896-1946, *J. Consult. Psychol.*, 11, i.

Dube, B.L., 1985, Presidential Address, *Ind. J. Clin. Psychol.*, 12, i.

Dube, K.C., 1953, Presidential Address Psychiatry in Distress, *Ind. J. Neurology & Psychiatry*, 4, 101.

Eysenck, H.J., 1968, The Contributions of Clinical Psychology to Psychiatry, In Howells J.G. (ed.), *Modern Perspectives in World Psychiatry*, London: Oliver & Boyd.

Garfield, Sol L., 1965, Historical Introduction, In Wolman B.B. (ed.), *Handbook of Clinical Psychology*, New York: McGraw Hill.

Ghosh, A., 1977, Role of a Clinical Psychologist: A Psychiatrist's point of view, *Ind. J. Clin. Psychol.*, 4, 198.

Gupta, S.C., 1988, Registration of Clinical Psychologists—A profession under identity crisis, *Ind. J. Clin. Psychol.*, 15, i.

ICSSR, 1972, *A survey of research in Psychology*, Bombay: Popular Prakashan.

Krishnan, B., 1972, Clinical Psychology in India: A trend report, In ICSSR, *A survey of research in psychology*, pp. 1-55, Bombay: Popular Prakashan.

Krishna Dutt, 1993, Clinical Psychologist in India, *Ind. J. Clin. Psychol.*, 20, i.

Mitra, S.C., 1937, History of Psychology Department of University of Calcutta, *Ind. J. Psychol.*, 12, (3).

———, 1955, Progress of Psychology in India, *Ind. J. Psychol.*, 30, 93.

Mitra, S.K., 1973, A decade (1963-72) of Science in India, Progress of Psychology, Calcutta, Indian Science Congress Association.

Paintal, H.K., 1987, Expanding Horizons for Clinical Psychologists in India, *Ind. J. Clin. Psychol.*, 14, 5.

Prabhu, G.G., 1974, Clinical Psychology in India—in retrospect and prospect, *Ind. J. Clin. Psychol.*, 1, 3.

———, 1975, Training Programmes in Clinical Psychology, *Ind. J. Clin. Psychol.*, 2, 7.

———, 1975a, Clinical Psychology in India: A Review of Clinical and Research Trends, Souvenir. VI All India Convention of Clinical Psychologists, Varanasi, Dept. of Psychology, BHU.

———, 1976, New Perspectives in Clinical Psychology, *Ind. J. Clin. Psychol.*, 3, 203.

———, 1977, Editorial, *Ind. J. Clin. Psychol.*, 4, 1.

———, 1977a, Letter to the Editor, *Ind. J. Clin. Psychol.*, 4, 91.

———, 1983, Clinical Psychology Then & Now, *Ind. J. Clin. Psychol.*, 10, i.

———, 1992, Lightner Witmer: Recognition delayed or totally Denied? *NIMHANS Journal*, 10, 75.

———, 1996, Time to Act, *Ind. J. Clin. Psychol.*, 23, i.

Ramalingaswami, P., 1976, Clinical Psychology in India: Need for a new perspective, *Indian J. Clin. Psychol.*, 3, 53.

———, 1977, Letter to the Editor, *Ind. J. Clin. Psychol.*, 4, 87.

Rehabilitation Council of India, 1996, *Report of Manpower Development*, New Delhi, RCI.

Sen, N.N., 1975, Clinical Psychology of the Eighties, *Ind. J. Clin. Psychol.*, 2, i.

Sen Muzumdar, D.P., 1976, A Profession in search of its image, *Ind. J. Clin. Psychol.*, 3, i.

Shanmugam, T.E., 1972, Personality: A trend report, In ICSSR. *A survey of research in Psychology*, pp. 226-337, Bombay: Popular Prakashan.

Sharma, V.P., Ojha, K. N. and Vagrecha, Y. S., 1974, Clinical Psychology in India, *Ind. J. Clin. Psychol.*, 1: 98.

Sinha, S., 1963, Fifty Years of Science in India : Progress of Psychology, Calcutta: Indian Science Congress Association.

Taylor, M., 1946, *Report of the Health and Development Committee*, Vol. III, Simla: GOI Press.

Trethowan, W.H., 1977, *The Role of Psychologists in Health Services*. London: Her Majesty's Stationery Office.

U.G.C., 1968, *Psychology in Indian Universities*, New Delhi: University Grants Commission.

Varma, L.P., 1953, History of Psychiatry in India & Pakistan, *Indian J. Neurology & Psychiatry*, 4, 27.

Vinoda, N. Murthy, 1982, New Directions in Clinical Psychology, *Ind. J. Clin. Psychol.*, 9, iii.

Watson, R.I., 1953, A Brief History of Clinical Psychology, *Psychol. Bull.*, 50, 321.

Witmer, L., 1907, Clinical Psychology, *The Psychological Clinic*, 1, i.

THREE

Parapsychological Experiences and Psychopathology: A Counseling Approach

K. KRISHNA MOHAN

M. Ullman (1973) has described a close relationship between parapsychological experiences and psychopathology, the two modern concepts of psychology, in a beautiful way. Interest among parapsychologists towards parapsychological experiences and psychopathology has grown up in recent times due to farfetched implications in parapsychological research findings to psychotherapeutic process and also to counseling individuals with troublesome psi experiences. The terms psi experiences and parapsychological experiences are synonymous and refer to a person's experience of clairvoyance, the extrasensory awareness of objects or events; precognition, the knowledge of a future event which could not have been predicted or inferred by normal means; telepathy, the extrasensory awareness of another person's mental content or state, or psychokinesis, the influence of mind on external objects or process without the mediation of known physical energies or forces.

Surveys conducted by Palmer (1979), Harldson and Hontkooper (1991) indicate that more than half of the general population says that they have had a psi experience. The case study literature on these experiences confirms that there are often emotional reactions or psychological problems associated with these experiences. And those who have been upset or disturbed by their psi experiences and who sought professional psychiatric help have often encountered frustrating responses. What they have reported honestly and out of conviction is rarely accepted as such. More often it is either discounted or worse yet, labelled as a psychotic symptom. Most of the therapists are unable to realize that a person may have a history of severe mental disorder and yet experience bonafide psi effects from time to time (Ullman, 1980).

In a study conducted by Julie Milton (1992) on the effects of "Paranormal" experiences on people's lives, respondents showed that the range of emotional reactions during and immediately following the respondents experiences included the predictable amazement, surprise, curiosity and puzzlement, and less predictably, for this perhaps unusual group of people. It is also found that responses vary from fearfully telling no one, to immediately rushing to all people. Respondents wanted someone to talk to them, advise them, explain to them, believe or understand them. Wanted "counseling" from someone who was knowledgeable, unprejudiced and accepting.

Undoubtedly, the claim of psi experiences is out of and develops from psychopathology. But enough of empirical data show that some individuals really have spontaneous psi experiences. Greeley (1991) survey research conforms that "normalcy" of the paranormal should be assured, that spontaneous experiences are neither unusual nor they are sign of mental problems and disturbances.

Given the magnitude of this problem and the relative absence of knowledge among the mental health professionals about psi experiences, there is need for work in these lines, first into separating true from false claims for psi in individuals and second, into finding that there is a typical pattern of responses to spontaneous psi experiences that individuals display. This will help the counselors to deal with psi experiences for better understanding of the reality and dynamics of spontaneously occurring psi and the same time more emphasis will be given to potential mental health problems.

An urgent need exists for psi counseling approach for individuals who are disturbed, fearful, and confused by their psi experiences, such as pre-cognitive, dreams, verdical hallucination, out of body experiences (OBE), poltergiest phenomena, and possession. The aim of this study is to illustrate how a counselor who has knowledge of psi process and therapeutic skills, can serve an important need in helping persons relate themselves to experiences in a balanced way.

Studies on Psi and Psychopathology

The purpose of the review of the studies is to show the existing close relationship between psi experiences and psychopathology. Since the beginning of the twentieth century, investigation were carried out into the possibility of psi linkage to altered states of consciousness. The earliest investigations were carried out in the cases of hysteria, multiple personality and paranoia (Mitchell, 1921, 1922; Prince, 1915-16, 1927). Myer's Classic study (1903) not only outlined the evidence for survival but also provided a comprehensive survey of what was known at that time, the relationship among disordered internal states, including hysteria and insanity and man's superaliminal (the term used to connote psi ability) capacities.

Ehrenwald (1948, 1971) undertook a serious assessment of the significance of the telepathy hypothesis for understanding of paranoia and schizophrenic psychosis. Telepathic sensitivity, according to him, plays its most significant role at the onset of a psychotic process and during the later, more deteriorated phases of the disorder. He also developed his ideas on the relationship of psi phenomena to hysteria drawing upon similar dissociate tendencies in mediumship and conversion hysteria. Some time there is a possibility of telepathy in family patterns of neurotic interaction as well as in the tendency of marital partners to be involved often in complementary neurosis (Ehrenwald, 1955). In his review of parapsychology and psychopathology Alberti (1974) re-examined the long held belief of the close relationship between psi to dissociated states such as one seen in hysteria, and psychosis, conforms the association between certain hysterical features such as the tendency to dissociation states and the occurrence of various automatisms and psi phenomena.

Studies on psi experiences and psychotic disorders was initiated by Mahler (1969) who described early symbiotic period as the source of psi and from that starting-point has traced the role played by psi in origin of paranoid hostility. Ullman (1973) study suggests the possibility that precognition would be more characteristic of schizophrenia, telepathy or clairvoyance of the manic state and retrocognition of the depressive psychosis. Rogo (1974a) while examining the issues with regard to the relationship of psi to the psychotic process, suggested that not only do psi factors emerge initially in the early symptomatology but are also often seen to emerge after the cure of the disorder. Based on his clinical observation, Ullman (1949, 1952) reports that patients who function close enough to psychotic break were aware of its possible immence do manifest psi ability in the therapeutic context more frequently and more consistently than do other patients.

In the lines of relationship between psychosomatic symptoms and psi conditioned responses, Eisenbed (1970) described several cases of what seemed to be psychosomatic symptoms initiated as psi conditional responses. Other observers, notably Schwaz (1967) and Stevenson (1970), suggest that the effect is more frequent than is generally suspected. Based on his studies of telepathic impression, Stevenson feels it is reasonable to assume that somatic symptometalogy, ranging from obscure physical symptoms to identifiable psychosomatic syndromes may come about as physical analogies of a telepathic message.

The convergence between psi and psychopathology lies in the still unexplored area of the interpersonal milieu in which potergeist phenomena is alleged to occur. Almost all modern authors writing on the subject such as, Owen (1964), Roll (1972), and Rogo (1974b) have followed Fodor's (1959) lead in viewing the phenomena themselves as externally displaced paranormal manifestation of repressed agression.

It was evident from these studies that the close relationship between psi and psychopathology presents an important problem in therapeutic setting. It is noteworthy that some amount of help for those troubled by psi experiences is beginning to be available from research organizations in only some countries. Keeping this in view, organizations working in this area should develop counseling procedures to meet the needs of the individuals who are troubled in their lives with psi experiences and also attempt to educate the public about these experiences. The second part of this study presents a model counseling approach for those who counsel the individuals with troubled psi experiences.

Model of Counseling Approach to Psi Experience

In contrast to emotional and psychopathological disturbances, individuals who have faced disturbances due to psi experiences should be counseled with a different approach in helping them to cope with their problems. According to Arthur Hastings (1983), the focus of the counseling, given therapeutic purpose, should be to assist the person to a state of balance, integration and judgement relating to apparent or genuine psi experiences.

Reality of Psi

The first step in meaningful counseling of emotionally disturbed individuals due to psi experiences, is initial presumption of the reality of psi on the part of the counselor. It is also found that clinicians interested in parapsychology have been more ready to see it as a part of the personality process (Ehrenwald, 1966; Eisenbud, 1970). In doing so, they have been able to show their relation to motivation, emotion, interpersonal relations, therapeutic process and other psychological process.

Normal or Paranormal

The second task of the counselor is to conform to the experiences as normal or psychopathological, because some psi phenomena can be mimicked by psychopathology even closely associated with them. For example, a schizophrenic may have a genuine psi experience and be troubled by them, and hence gain reality control by identifying their nature as psychic and separating them from fantasy and hallucination.

Reality Testing

The next job of the counselor is to test reality of the psi experience as real or imaginary. To determine whether psi is actually involved, clinicians should be familiar with the literature on case study investigations of spontaneous psi experiences and laboratory work. They should also have good knowledge of clinical psychology and parapsychology, and should understand how psi experience and pseudo psi experiences interact with motives, needs, emotion, self-concept, belief system, personality and other psychological elements.

Clinical Issues

The next step is to look into the clinical features of an individual. Stevenson (1970) in his review of studies on telepathic impression found that, individuals at the time of the experience had felt fear, dread, anxiety and depression. It would not be surprising for persons having spontaneous psi to have generalized fear or depression. Any one who is dealing with people and has a spontaneous psi experience needs to know that the person is very likely to be afraid of the event or may be mentally disturbed, and is uncertain about what is happening.

At this stage basic counseling principles along with attentive and emphatic listening to the experience will help in bringing a close connection between the counselor and the person, and usually reduce emotional fears and also brings rationality and calmness to the client. A psi experience, *per se* is not an indicator of mental disturbance. However, the counselor should always be careful to identify if any psychological problems are present, e.g., paranoia, dissociation, emotional repression, or physical problem including medication that might produce hallucinations, vision or healing impairment that might contribute to a misinterpretation of the experience since ESP information comes in a two-step process, first unconscious and processed to the conscious (Rhine, L.E., 1962), the counselor must be attentive to unconscious as well as conscious process of the psi experience.

Further step that gives individual some way of handling the experience is to describe what is known about the type of case. This reduces the cognitive confirmation that is often associated with violation of consensual reality produced by a psi event. To handle the question on whether precognition will come true? For this counselor should take apparent precognition at a reality level and if they are negative, give an attempt to change the circumstances to prevent danger and also warns others who are involved in the event.

Poltergeist Phenomena

Another type of spontaneous case frequently encountered by clinicians are poltergeist. This phenomena usually take place in a house, object move, noises are heard, bottles pop their lids, things break or malfunction, and other physical effects occur. Without apparent physical courses (Owen, 1964; Roll, 1972). The general belief among parapsychologists is that the phenomenon comes from a human agent and is unconscious feelings of frustration, fear, anger or blocked psychokinesis, motivated by repressed impulses (Hestings, 1983). Most of the contemporary investigations have found human agents rather than spirits as the focus of the phenomenon (Sevenson, 1972).

The clinical counseling approach to a poltergeist case should begin with a description of the situation by the person, how the person felt, what action was taken and how the individual attempted to understand or explain it. After the initial recounting of the incidents, the counselor should consider if they appear to be normal events, misinterpreted (or a hoax, fabrication, or prank), or if they appear to be paranormal. If the disturbances appear to arise from normal causes, the task of the counselor is to explain this to the persons involved. If at all the event seems to be paranormal, the quickest route to an understanding, is to explore the emotional side, where there are strong emotional changes like there may be motivation for discharge of energy in the form of a poltergeist manifestation.

From the emotional interaction the counselor can infer possible function of the poltergeist effect — as expressions of feelings by the individual, as the persons cannot for some reason express themselves overtly and directly, so it occurs physically in the environment through psychokinesis. However, the counselor need not, interpret the event to the participants, but considers the possibility for his own information in working with the situation. As with spontaneous psi cases, persons in poltergeist situation are often confused, frightened, and want to know what is going on. The basic approaches of careful listening with sympathy and understanding, and reassurance that this is a real occurrence are very important here. A description of poltergeist cases, and their typical nature, may be useful.

Out of the Body Experience

The counselor usually comes across common reaction to OBEs as fear, primarily the elementary fear of survival. A second aspect of fear is that of mental illness. The most direct way to reassure individuals is through explanation of the experiences. The counselor should well attend the OBE experiencing individuals emotional, psychological and spiritual aspects to have an insight into the experience.

The clinical psychologist should learn to distinguish between genuine OBEs and vivid dreams, lucid dreams and states of dissociation. For assisting individuals experiencing OBEs the counselor should suggest that the person is in good physical health and not having major psychological problems. Hastings (1983) suggests training in conscious, centering awareness, and focused attention would seem to be valuable along with methods of leaving the OBE state and returning to an IBE (In the body-experience).

Psychic Channeling

This is an another form of psi experience in which, persons who believe they are receiving messages or creative material from the "other side" from discurnate beings or spirits. In this situation the counselor should look at the content of the material itself and should ask the client to evaluate it on its own merits. Usually these messages may link with the needs of the individual, but often they create dissonance that counseling can resolve. The counselor may explain how a suppressed feeling can come out in devious ways and counsels the individuals to change towards a better relationship with himself or herself in responding to psi experiences.

Other Psi Experiences

Several other psi experiences are likely to be presented to the counselor: appearance of apparitions, cases of alleged possession, near-death experiences, alleged psychic healers, aura readers, past life memories, and various occult practices, for all these experiences, some of the same principles and procedures of counseling mentioned earlier will be appropriate. For each type of experience it will be useful to develop an understanding of its characteristics, emotional reactions, personality — psychic interaction that occur and specific counseling approach that can be applied.

To be an affective counselor in dealing individuals with psi experiences, one should be versed in basic counseling techniques, including listening and communication skills, working with emotions, intervention processes and a balanced fluid ability to respond. The second important aspect one should be familiar with is research studies and findings in parapsychology. Importantly, the counselor should have an indepth understanding of psychodynamics and personality of the individuals who are troubled with psi experience.

Conclusion

In India, psi experiences are a common phenomena Rao, R.K. (1994) a leading parapsychologist shares similar views that our tradition does not regard psi phenomena as anomalous. Consequently there is no priori resistance in our ethos that engenders instant disbelief in them. Such openness is good, but it is not without its problems.

Lack of right prospective and understanding among mental health professionals regarding the close relationship and their line separating between bonafide psi experiences and psychopathology is posing problems of adjustment to the individual who had that psi experience but could not distinguish from psychopathology. This leads to problems of adjustment in normal life which would be eased by intervention of mental health professionals who have adequate understanding of the nature of our socio-religious culture.

The goal of the counselor working with different types of troublesome psi experiences is to assist the persons to move towards an integrated response to the experiences and to perhaps incorporate it as a balanced part of the total personality. There is a need for responsible counseling of this nature and it can draw on the body of knowledge already accumulated in parapsychology. In turn, proper counseling can contribute information and ideas, and questions for further scientific understanding of psi experiences. Effective counseling may provide ways of integrating the psi processes into a healthy personality as well as reducing the disruptive effects that often occur as people encounter psi experiences.

REFERENCES

Alberti, G., 1974, Psychopathology and parapsychology: Some possible contacts. In A. Anoff and B. Shapin (eds.), *Parapsychology and the Sciences*, pp. 225-33. New York: Parapsychology Foundation.

Ehrenwald, J., 1948, *Telepathy and Medical Psychology*. New York: W.W. Norton.

———, 1955, *New Dimensions of Deep Analysis*. New York: Grune and Stratton.

———, 1971, Mother-Child symbiosis: Cradle of ESP, *Psychoanalytic Review*, 58, 455-66.

Eisenbud, J., *Psi and Psychoanalysis: Studies in the psychoanalysis of Psi-conditioned behaviour*. New York: Grune and Startton.

Fodor, N., 1959, *On the Trail of the Poltergeist*. London: Arco.

Greeley, A.J., 1991, The paranormal is normal: A sociologist looks at parapsychology, *Journal of the American Society for Psychic Research*, 85: 367-374.

Haraldwon, E. and Houtkooper, J.M., 1991, Psychic experiences in the multinational human values study: who reports them? *Journal of the American Society for Psychoic Research*, 85: 145-65.

Hastings, A., 1983, A counseling approach to parapsychological experience, *The Journal of Transpersonal Psychology*, 15: 143-67.

Mahler, M., 1968, *Human symbiosis and the vicissitudes of individuation*. New York: University Press International.

Milton, J., 1992, Effects of Paranormal experience on people's lives: An unusual survey of spontaneous cases, *Journal of the Society for Psychic Research*, 58: 314-323.

Mitchell, J.W., 1921, The Doris Fischer case of multiple personality, *Proceedings of the society for psychic research*, 31: 30-74.

Mitchell, J.W., 1922, *Medical Psychology and Psychic Research*. New York: Dutton.

Myers, F.W.H., 1903, *Human personality and its survival of bodily death*. London: Longmans, Green, 2 Vols.

Owen, A.R.G., 1964, *Can we explain the poltergeist*? New York: Garret/Helix.

Plamer, J., 1979, A community mail survey of psychic experiences, *Journal of the American Society for Psychic Research*, 73, 221-51.

Prince, W.F., 1915-16, The Doris case of multiple personality, *Proceedings of the American Society for Psychic Research*, 9, 1-700, 10, 701-1419.

Prince, W.F., 1927, The cure of two cases of paranoia, *Bulletin of the Boston Society for Psychic Research*, 6, 36-72.

Rao, K.R., 1994, Anomalies of consciousness: Indian perspectives and Research, *Journal of Parapsychology*, 58: 149-187.

Rhine, L.E., 1962, Psychological Process in ESP experience. I. Waking Experience. II. Dreams, *Journal of Parapsychology*, 26, 88-111: 171-199.

Rogo, D.S., 1974a, Psi in the clinical framework of abnormal psychology. In A. Angoff and B. Shapin (eds.), *Parapsychology and Sciences*, pp. 52-65. New York: Parapsychology Foundation.

Rogo, D.S., 1974b, Psychotherapy and the poltergeist, *Journal of the Society for Psychical Research*, 47: 433-46.

Roll, W.G., 1972, *The Poltergeist*. New York: Doubleday.

Schwarz, B.E., 1967, Possible telesomatic reactions, *Journal of Medical Society of New Jersey*. 64: 600-603.

Stevenson, I., 1970, *Telepathic impressions: A review and report of thirty-five new cases*, Charlottesville, University Press of Virginia.

———, 1972, Are poltergeists living or are they dead? *Journal of the American society for psychical research*, 66: 233-52.

Ullman, M., 1949, On the nature of psi processes, *Journal of Parapsychology*, 13: 59-62.

———, 1952, On the nature of resistance to psi phenomena, *Journal of the American Society for Psychical Research*, 46, 11-13.

Ullman, M., 1973, Psi and Psychiatry: The need for restructuring basic concepts. In W.G. Roll, R.L. Morris, and J.D. Morris (1972) (eds), *Research in Parapsychology*, pp. 110-113, Metuchen, N.J.: Scare Crow Press.

Ullman, M., 1980, Life history and psi events: Significance for counseling, *Research in parapsychology*, 1979: 45-45.

FOUR

Psychology of Health and Illness

QAMAR HASAN, S. HUMAIRA SIDDIQA
and RIZWANA NAWAB

The relationship between mind and body and the effect of one upon other has long been a topic of interest amongst philosophers, psychologists and physiologists. Among philosophers it was Hippocrates of COs (460-357) BC, Greek Physician, known as the father of medicine and believed to have authored medical writings and established medical schools who first speculated about the source of relation between mind and body. He postulated that temperament is determined by relative dominance of four humors in body, i.e., blood, phlegm, black bile, and yellow bile. Fechner (1860) in his treatise on 'psychophysics' reported a quantitative relationship between mind and body. Sigmund Freud founder of psychoanalysis, is regarded as the first contributor towards the understanding of physical symptoms in terms of psychodynamics by studying the cases of conversion hysteria and postulating that it was the result of unfulfilled desires rather than that of wandering of uterus in the body. This led to the development of the study of psychosomatic disorders in the discipline of psychology.

Paradigm Shift in Medicine

With the identification of physical diseases which do not have any organic physiological bases for the symptoms associated with them, the role of psychological factors was realized in the etiology of certain diseases. Such diseases were classified as psychosomatic diseases. Psychosomatic disorders are characterized by physical symptoms that are caused by or can be worsened by emotional factors.

The accidental discovery of general adaptation syndrome (GAS) by Dr. Hans Salye (1986) is an important landmark in bringing medicine and psychology closer. While attempting to isolate a new sex hormone by injecting ovary extracts to rats, Selye observed that the injection gave rise to a reaction pattern different from the effect of any known sex hormone. He reported that the pituitary — adrenal axis, which is a physiological pathway underlying the GAS, gives rise to the following three phases: alarm reaction, stage of resistance and stage of exhaustion.

Medical scientists were also compelled to have a new outlook at conscious and unconscious functioning that emerged from a neurophysiological model suggested by Sperey and his colleagues (1969). The model explains as to how emotional thoughts outside awareness influence attitudes, behaviour, and physiology. The work of two cardiologists is to be referred because it recognizes the role of a particular personality type in the increasing frequency of heart disease. Friedman and Roseman (1959), proposed that a particular style of behaviour places individuals at risk for early coronary heart disease (CHD) even in the absence of traditional risk factors of CHD. This specific behaviour pattern is called coronary prone behaviour of 'Type A Behaviour Pattern' (TABP). 'This is characterized by a number of behaviours such as competitiveness, ambitiousness, time urgency, restlessness, and annoyance. On the contrary, the behaviour of Type B individuals is characterized by easy goingness, not feeling guilty, working without becoming irritated, and having no excessive sense of responsibility. Type B individuals lack a sense of urgency with its accompanying impatience and they are not easily aroused to anger.

Gradually, these approaches to study psychological disorders were replaced by a more behavioural and biological approach which seeks to employ interventions derived from behavioural medicine. The increased cooperation between psychologists and physicians became wider with the realization that the role of psychological factors is not confined to the etiology of psychiatric symptoms and psychosomatic manifestations. It was realized that when a physician or doctor treats a patient he does not treat the symptoms or a disease, but he treats a human being, an individual who has the disease. This change in viewpoints regarding illness and health led to the development of a distinct field of study, namely, 'health psychology'.

Health Psychology as an Area of Study

Health psychology was given recognition as a separate field of study in a convention held by American Psychological Association (APA) (1978). Health psychology subscribes to the view that both body and mind are important determinants of health and illness. Specifically, health psychologists assume that our beliefs, attitudes and behaviour contribute significantly to the onset and prevention of disease (Engel, 1980). A very comprehensive definition of health psychology as a field is proposed by Joseph Matarazzo (1980):

"Health psychology is the aggregate of the specific educational, scientific and professional contribution of the discipline of psychology to the promotion and maintenance of health, the prevention and treatment of illness, the identification of etiology and diagnostic correlates of health, illness and related dysfunction, and the analysis and improvement of the health care system and health policy formation".

The above mentioned definition describes four goals of health psychology.

1. Promotion and maintenance of health;
2. Prevention and treatment of illness;
3. Finding the causes and detection of illness;
4. Improvement of the health care systems and policies.

The three main concerns of health psychology are discussed below:

(i) Preventive behaviour,
(ii) Health care seeking,
(iii) Psychological factors involved in health and illness.

Health psychology has interest in the study of topics such as why people do or do not smoke cigarette, use and do not use safety belts in cars, consume alcohol and eat particular diets. Harris and Guten (1979) in a study asked the subjects to report the three most important things they do to protect or maintain their health. They were also asked to rate certain health related behaviours. Cluster analysis of the data produced the following categories of preventive health practices.

1. Sleeping sufficiently, eating healthy food, and exercising regularly to remain healthy;
2. Repairing tools and vehicles, keeping ready first-aid kits and telephone directory with emergency telephone numbers at a safety measure;
3. Periodical check up of some body parts such as teeth and eyes, as a preventive measure;
4. Avoiding of environmental hazards such as areas of pollution and crime;
5. Avoiding harmful substance such as smoking or drinking.

This research finding suggests that people's health habits are not interdependent or stable. For example, Leventhal et al. (1985) reported that people practice some habits, such as sleeping enough and having regular breakfast to promote health but engage in other health related behaviours, such as limited use of alcohol and cigarette. Berg (1976) pointed out that being aware of several unhealthy practices, people sometimes continue to engage in the activities which they know to be harmful to their health. Another reason for low stability includes the fact that people change as a result of experience, e.g., they do not avoid smoking until they have a heart attack.

Besides promotion and maintenance of health, the task of health psychology also includes the prevention and treatment of disease. This can be achieved by informing people about the risks that certain behaviours (or non-behaviours) can endanger. Psychologists with clinical training can help people to adjust their current conditions, and future prospects such as reduced working ability. Breslow (1983) pointed out that the greatest opportunity for health promotion probably lies in influencing behaviour, such as by reducing cigarette smoking, excessive alcohol use and unhealthy dietary practices. In general, three levels of prevention are identified, namely, primary, secondary, and tertiary prevention.

Primary Prevention: Primary prevention refers to adopting basic health habits to avoid a disease. It can begin for an individual before his/her birth or even conception.

Secondary Prevention: Secondary prevention involves people taking action in the primary stage of disease to identify and treat an illness or injury with the aim of stopping and reversing it.

Tertiary Prevention: Tertiary prevention involves taking some action when the disease progresses in an advanced stage. For instance, tertiary prevention includes doing exercise for physical therapy and taking medicines to control inflammation and pain in the case of having severe arthritis.

Although the preventive measures adopted by an individual are good for the maintenance and prevention of his health, certain problems may impair his effectiveness.

1. One problem is that people are reluctant to setting limits on their unhealthy behaviours because healthy behaviours are less pleasurable.
2. Another problem is that it becomes very difficult for people to change longstanding behaviours into wellness behaviours because they have become habitual smokers and drunkards.
3. Living in a family also poses certain problems in an individual's effort to promote wellness behaviours. For example, one family member cannot stop eating less cholestrol diet if he wanted to do so because other family members are not willing to stop eating high cholestrol diet.
4. One more problem that prevents one from taking preventive steps is associated with financial problems. Due to this problem people are not able to take periodical check-up and remain unaware about the malignancies building up in the system.

Health-Care Seeking Behaviour

We have noted that the primary aim of health psychology is to determine important relationship between psychological variables and health. The psychological factors are learning, perception, cognition and social and emotional factors which determine to some extent the health-related behaviour of an individual.

When an individual gets sick, a number of social, cultural,

psychological and financial factors determine his or her decision about the health-care seeking and recovery from illness. Suchman (1965) has described number of stages which intervene between the person's decision to consult a competent physician or do self-treatment. These stages are: (i) symptom experience stage; (ii) assumption of sick role, (iii) medical care contact; (iv) dependent patient role; and (v) recovery.

In the first stage an individual perceives that something is seriously wrong with him, and decides that he is sick and enters the second stage. In the second stage, sick person adopts the sick role and is excused from his regular duties, initial contacts are often made by the sick person with spouse or family and friends. Sick person leaves lay care system and enters the third stage in which he usually resumes his normal roles or goes to other physicians, until he achieves the diagnosis he wants and comes into the next stage which is dependent patient role. This stage is fraught with problems. In this stage the patient must wrestle between his child like dependence upon the physician and the normal state of adult independence. This is also a stage in which physician and patient work together to commence recovery to normal physical state. Recovery is the last stage in which pain subsides and individual resumes his normal routine.

It is to be observed that the time taken by a sick person to enter into different stages and the duration of each stage depends upon a number of physical, psychological, financial, social and cultural factors. It is not necessary that in every case of illness all the stages come one after another following a rigid pattern. Depending upon painfulness, fear and other factors, some of the stages may be circumvented and the person may enter into a stage without undergoing some or all of the preceding stages. Other problems in which health psychologists have been interested are the phases and processes involved in the medical health-care seeking behaviour. There are several models which have been proposed in this context.

Barker et al. (1953) has described five basic psychological forces that operate on the person who feels he or she may require physician's medical treatment and guidance. These forces are S (generated by pain and discomfort), RH (anticipation of returning to health), H (concept of himself as a healthy person), I (anticipation of possible illness), and DT (diagnosis and treatment).

Another model, the health belief model, was originally proposed by Rosenstock (1966) and later on modified by Becker and Maiman (1975). This model suggests that the perception of a personal threat is influenced by our health values, specific beliefs, perceived susceptibility to illness perceived benefits, expenses and trouble in getting medical care and beliefs concerning the seriousness of the illness.

The self-regulation model of illness was proposed by Leventhal and Cameron (1987). This model defined three stages which regulate behaviour:

(a) cognitive representation of the health problem, which includes the dimension of perceived symptoms, causes and effects;
(b) formulation and implementation of a plan of action to change the current state; and
(c) the person's utilization of specific techniques or rules to assess the progress of action, and the modification of the health-restoring actions if they are perceived to be ineffective.

Health psychologists play a very vital role in the prevention of various fatal diseases for which there is no cure such as AIDS (Baldwin & Baldwin, 1988; Kegeles et al., 1988; Phillip, 1989; Hingson et al., 1990); cancer (Hirayama, 1981; Ashton & Stepney, 1982; Russell, 1989); cardiovascular diseases (Rosenman, Brand, Sholtz & Friedman, 1976; Harpanen et al., 1989; Humble et al., 1990). To illustrate the role of health psychologists in health care we are describing what they do to minimize and ultimately eliminate the hazardous habit of smoking.

Preventing Smoking

Health psychologists suggest some of the following treatments for the cessation of smoking:

1. Using cognitive coping strategies to remind oneself of negative consequences of smoking and benefits of creation.
2. Using social skills in rejecting offered cigarette and asking others not to smoke.
3. Learning alternative strategies for dealing with stress such as, relaxation training and other tension-reducing techniques.

4. Using behavioural training techniques which include deep and frequent inhalation leading to nicotine overdosing. As a consequence of overdosing the smokers begin to fell ill and then stop smoking — aversive conditioning generates negative feeling towards cigarettes.

Besides behavioural techniques recent research has set its focus on multicomponent programme (Using pharmacological and psychological approaches in combination). These programmes have been emphasized both due to the relatively high clinical success of these programmes, and the recognition that smoking is multidetermined and relatively unaffected by any single intervention.

Public health approaches have involved increasing the price of cigarette through taxation, launching health awareness campaigns through media and putting a ban on smoking at public places.

Psychological Factors Involved in Health and Illness

Among many determinants of health and illness, stress is one which has been studied largely nowadays. The stress of modern living have played havoc with the mental state of man, making him not only the master of his environment but also slave to it. The change in modern societies such as the demands and pressures of modern living, the information and technology explosion, increasing consumerism and the urbanization of societies all have brought pressures and stress that the hardiest of us find difficult to cope with.

Stress reflects the inability of the human mind and body to cope with the demands of the external world imposed on it. In fact it is the first visible sign of some physical or mental affliction that a person might suffer from. It could be the primary cause of something as ordinary as insomnia or something as serious as chronic heart disease. Needless to say that stress impairs the ability of the human body to function properly.

Stress produces illness in an organism in two ways: directly, from the changes produced by it in the body's physiology; or indirectly, affecting health through the person's behaviour. Weibe and McCallum (1986) demonstrated that people who experience high levels of stress tend to perform behaviours that increase their chances of becoming ill or injured. People under stress usually consume more alcohol, cigarettes, etc., that may give rise to various illnesses. Moreover, effects of alcohol, such as carelessness, often result in high rate of accidents.

Changes produced by stress in the body's physiology also impair health. Schnall et al. (1990) reported a greater association between high stress and high blood pressure and abnormally enlarged hearts. The release of catecholamines and corticosteroid during arousal, affects health as some of these hormones impair the functioning of the immune system. Sometimes stress becomes incompatible with the defensive potentialities of the organism and in turn, produces certain deficiencies in the organism making it vulnerable to many kind of stress-related diseases.

A variety of environmental situations can produce stress, for example, family atmosphere, school atmosphere and work atmosphere. Among the most important of these are stressful life events and hassles of daily life taking place in all these situations. Recent studies and theories suggest that stressful life events are a primary source of any disease (Dohrenwend and Dohrenwend, 1974; Gunderson and Rahe, 1974). Holmes and Rahe (1967) studied major changes that take place in day to day life which are highly stressful (death of a close friend or relative, trouble with inlaws, family problems or problems at work and moving from one place to another) and are likely to be associated with the onset of illness and recovery.

Broadly, life events can be divided into three major categories: positive/benign, irrelevant, or stressful. Further, stressful life events can be classified into the following main types — harm/loss, threat or challenge (Coyne and Lazarus, 1980). For a given individual, for example, marriage might be a benign/positive event; moving to a new apartment close to the work place as an irrelevant life event; parental death as a harm/loss situation; problems with an employer as a threat; and birth of a first child as a challenge.

Research on stressful life events has shown that different types of events are associated with different diseases. Evans (1926) suggested that one of the leading causes of cancer was the loss of a love object or an important emotional relationship.

It is also to be noted that all events are not equally stressful for all individuals, e.g. events such as the death of a spouse may not produce stress, but may primarily produce a sense of relief. The important thing for a person is the perceived meaning of an event. Cultural differences are also found to play a significant role in the perception of an event as highly stressful. Jahan and Hasan (1987) in one study found that due to cultural differences, an event which is highly stressful in one society is not experienced as such in another society and vice versa. Other factors such as the relative ability to cope with or adopt to stressful conditions, genetic predisposition to a disease and the presence of a disease agent in an individual's environment may affect his proneness to illness.

Hassles of Daily Life

Not only major events of our lives but minor repetitive events may also have detrimental effects on health. This is evident by the findings of several studies conducted by Lazarus and his colleagues (DeLongis, Folkman & Lazarus, 1988; Kanner et al., 1981; Lazarus et al., 1985). High scores on the Hassles Scale are associated with poorer psychological well-being (Lazarus et al.; 1985) and poor physical health. Weinberger, Hiner and Tierney (1987), conducted a study on elderly arthritis patients, found that the more hassles reported by their patients, the more severe the pain of their arthritis.

Social and Personal Resources Against Illness

The research work on stressful life events and illness has clearly shown that stressful life events are a major source of somatic and psychological diseases. However, in some of the studies the correlation between stress and illness could not exceed beyond 0.30 (Rabkin and Struening, 1976). These research findings led investigators to conclude that all individuals are not equally susceptible to stressful life events. Some people are likely to develop chronic diseases and psychiatric disorders after exposure to stressful situation, while others do not. These circumstances motivated researchers to identify various moderating variables which interact with stress and decrease its debilitating effects. Johnson and Sarason (1978), Antonovsky (1979), Kobasa (1979), and Lefcourt (1980) tried to find out how a single resource, or pair of resources, helps the individual in times of stress. A number of moderator variables that resist the debilitating effects of stress have been identified to be personality traits, social support and coping mechanisms.

Personality Factors as Stress Moderators

A number of personality factors or traits have been cited as stress-resistance resources. One such variable is 'hardiness'.

The term hardiness was introduced by Kobasa (1979) to refer to the personality style which keeps the person healthy even after prolonged exposure to stress. Hardy people are hypothesized to possess three general characteristics:

(i) *Commitment:* Hardy people show deeper involvement in whatever they do and have a tendency to perceive these activities as worth doing.

(ii) *Control:* They have a tendency to feel and act in an influential manner in the face of varied contingencies of life.

(iii) *Challenge:* Hardy people tend to perceive change as a challenge, for them anticipation of changes are interesting incentives to growth rather than threat to security. Together, these characteristics mitigate the potential unhealthy effects of stress and prevent the organismic strain that often leads to illness. In contrast, non-hardy or less hardy individuals easily succumb to ill effects of health as they find their environment boring, meaningless and threatening. They have a belief that life is best without change and allow external forces to impinge upon them and do not try to transform the events by taking decisive actions. Kobasa (1979) demonstrated the link between hardiness and health in a study of high stressed executives. She identified two groups of individuals through questionnaire, a group of those who experienced high levels of stress and severe illness, and another group who had experienced high level of stress but little illness. Hardiness scale was used to assess the hardiness level of both the groups. Kobasa found that, although, both groups had experienced high levels of stress, low illness group was more hardy as compared to the high illness group. The high stress/low illness executives reported a greater sense of control, commitment and challenge than the high stress and high illness individuals did.

Hardiness reduces unhealthy effects of hardiness in two ways: (a) it improves health by acting as a buffer to stressful life events (Kobasa and Puccetti, 1983) and (b) it directly reduces the strain by decreasing the use of unsuccessful coping strategies (Kobasa, 1982).

External Factors as Moderators

Like personality factors, psychologists have also identified certain external or social factors that reduce unhealthy effects of stress. Caplan (1974) suggested that existence of loving and caring relationships provide a sort of protective web around the individual, hence reducing his likelihood of falling ill. Schachter (1959) pointed out that persons seek to associate with others, rather than remain alone, when threatened by stressful conditions. Since then, a number of research studies demonstrate the effectiveness of other individuals, groups and organizations in fostering health (Cassell, 1976; Cobb, 1976). People who interact closely with friends and relatives are better able to avoid illness, and if illness occurs, they recover from it earlier than those who are interpersonally isolated. This helpful cushion from others is termed as 'social support'.

Cohen and Wills (1985) distinguished two major aspects of social support, i.e., structural and functional. Structural social support refers to a person's status and number of friends. Functional social support is concerned more with the quality of relationship, e.g., does a person believe he or she has friends to call on in time of need? Both types of social supports have been related to disease onset. Higher levels of functional support were found to be related to lower rates of clogging of arteries (Seeman and Syme, 1987). Structural support has been found to be related to various aspects of cardiovascular diseases (Read et al., 1983).

How social support effects health? This has been a focus of research. Researchers have produced two theories — the "buffering" and the "direct effect" hypotheses. According to buffering hypothesis, social support affects health by protecting the person against bad effects of high stress. This protective function is effective when the person encounters a stressor. The direct effect hypothesis maintains that social support is beneficial to health and well-being regardless of the amount of stress people experience.

Beneficial effects of social support on health are demonstrated by James Lynch (1990) who found that widowed, divorced and bachelor individuals have far higher death rates from heart disease than married people. There is also research evidence regarding the impact of social support in reducing the likelihood of illness and speeding up recovery. Kulik and Mahler (1989) showed that heart disease and surgery patients with high levels of social support recover more quickly than comparable patients with less social support.

Coping

Coping is a process through which people try to combat the emotional and physical strain. People cope with stress through continuous cognitive and behavioural transactions with the environment. Lazarus and Folkman (1984) have described two ways of coping with the stressful situation: (a) emotion-focused coping; and (b) problem-focused coping. Emotion-focused coping is aimed at controlling the emotional response to the stressful situation. People use certain cognitive and behavioural approaches to regulate their behaviours. Behavioural approaches include using alcohol or narcotic drugs, seeking social support from significant people or engaging oneself in leisure activities to distract one's attention from the problem. Cognitive approaches involve changing the meaning of the situation, for example, by deciding that "it could have been much worse". The point to be noted here is that people use this kind of approach when they believe that things are out of their control and they cannot do anything to change them.

Problem focused coping aims at reducing stress through problem solving, decision making and or direct action. People tend to use problem-focused coping approaches when they believe that their resources or demands of the situation can be changed.

Effective copers tend to use both kinds of techniques. Feeling of control toward outcome, social support and optimistic outlook of life are some of the variables which are related to effective ways of coping. Less effective copers, on the other hand, may solve the immediate problem at a high cost in terms of their emotional and physical well being and may escape into a way of thinking that makes them feel better but do not do anything to change the basic source of their stress.

Regarding individual differences in the coping process, two different approaches have been pursued by different investigators. Some researchers e.g., (Byrne, 1964; Goldstein, 1973) have emphasized coping traits, styles or dispositions, while the other, (Cohen et al., 1973; Katz et al., 1970) investigators preferred to study the active coping strategies in a particular stress situation.

There are a number of psychophysiological and psychosocial routes by which coping can affect health and well-being of an individual. The three main routes through which the coping process might adversely affect somatic health are as follows:

First, it can influence the frequency, intensiry, duration and patterning of neurochemical stress reaction in one of three ways :

1. By failing to prevent or ameliorate environmentally noxious or damaging condition.
2. By failing to regulate emotional distress in the face of uncontrollable harm or threat.
3. By expressing a set of values and corresponding lifestyles that are continuing to mobilize internal resources in a harmful way.

Any mode of coping can have mixed outcomes, positive in some respects and negative in others.

Secondly, coping can negatively affect health by increasing the risk of mortality and morbidity. When it involves excessive use of injurious substances such as alcohol, narcotic drugs and tobacco or when it involves the persons in activities of high risk to life.

Thirdly, emotion focused modes of coping can impair health by adversely affecting the management of stress. For example, Holahan and Moos (1986) reported a prospective study conducted over a period of one year in which subjects who experienced a high degree of stress and employed avoidance coping strategies dealing with it had more psychosomatic symptoms such as headaches and acid stomach.

Health Psychology in India

Indian psychologists have made significant contributions in the field of health psychology. Addiction and drug abuse are the problems which have been extensively studied by Indian psychologists.The studies of drug abuse can be divided into three main categories :

(i) studies of demographic variables associated with addiction and substance preference (Deb & Jindal, 1974; Khan, 1978; Ahmad & Verma, 1987; Sethi and Trivedi, 1979; Advani 1981; Veeraraghvan, 1981; Kanappan & Cherian, 1989);

(ii) studies of relationship between personality characteristics and drug abuse (Singh & Chopra, 1979; Shanmugan, 1979; Mohanty & Saraswat 1982; Ahmad, Ramalingam, & Ahmad, 1984; Sahasi, Chawla, Bhushan & Kakkar, 1990; Vadra & Hussain, 1991); and

(iii) the studies of relationship between substance preference and personality and demographic variables.

Although it is difficult to draw a distinction between studies falling in the third category and other two categories, we have treated substance preference studies as a separate category because studies falling in this category assume that the personality characteristics of the individual affect the reaction of drugs and thus determine preference for depressants, stimulants or hallucinogens. A good example of this kind of study is the work of Meyen (1994), inspired by the findings of Di Mascio, Rinkel & Liberman (1961) and Eysenck (1957, 1960, 1963) that personality type influence the way a person reacts to drugs. Meyen (1994) conducted a study to find whether choice of a drug is a mere accident or it is an outcome of personality dynamics. Implying a sample of 200 drug addicts from Jagriti, a deaddiction clinic, Meyen divided the addicts into three groups: depressant users; stimulant users; and hallucinogen users. The subjects were administered the 16-PF questionnaire. Information was also collected regarding the change in drug, the reason for change and the demographic background of the addicts. The discriminant function analysis of the data showed different groups can be discriminated with the help of discriminant function comprising different personality factors. It was also found that the dissatisfaction of a particular drug accounted for a changeover from one category of drug to another irrespective of the availability of the drug. Among demographic variables, socioeconomic status, education and marital status were found to influence the substance preferred by the adults.

In a study of drug dependence and drug abuse among senescent,

Khan (1996) administered a checklist of reasons for taking drugs and a list of psychological consequences of taking drugs. The subjects were 25 males and 25 females in an age group of 65-95 years. The majority of subjects were found taking psychotropic drugs. It was found that the frequency of different reasons represented in percentage was not the same for male and female senescents. The reasons given by males may be ordered as below:

Chronic physical pain (66%), anxiety (51%), fatiguability (48%), depression (44%), loneliness (40%), headache (40%), insomnia (39%), tension (33%), can't relax (31%), palpitation (17%), loss of control (15%) and nervousness (13%).

The reasons given by females are :

Headache (83%), chronic physical pain (75%), insomnia (50%), fatiguability (56%), semantic preoccupation (51%), tension (51%), depression (43%), anxiety (41%), can't relax (24%), palpitation (24%), nervousness (20%), boredom (13%), and loss of control (13%).

Indian psychologists have done a lot of work on stressful life events, situational stress, and coping styles. It was natural for them to pay attention to the role of stress and other psychological factors in the etiology of dreadful diseases like cancer and heart diseases. Important contributors to research on association of stress and cancer are Shrivastava & Baroota, (1987), Bose and Mukhopadhyay, (1993). Mahendru, Seth and Agrawal (1976) reported the prevalence of neuroticism in Coronary Heart Disease (CHD) patients. In another study Shukla (1995) could not find difference between CHD patients and population norms on neuroticism.

Poor strategies of coping with stress and lack of social support were also found to be associated with MI. Srivastava (1990) in a study found the loss of mother and lack of closeness of patients to their mothers as a major cause of cancer. The type of life changes which were found by Shukla (1989) to be related to CHD were deficiency of money, problem of daughter's marriage, family conflict, and unemployment of son. A study conducted by Upinder and Hooda (1991) on stress among patients of ischemic heart disease (ISD) showed that ISD was accompanied by distress in almost all areas.

Indian researchers also paid attention to the involvement of stress in psychosexual, psychoneurotic, psychosomatic and affective disorders. Rao & Nammalvar (1976), Chaudhri, (1971), Sahaney & Merchant (1977), Shirali & Bharti (1986), Dang & Agrawal (1995) are the main contributors to this kind of research.

Work on hardy personality has also been extended by Indian psychologists. Singh & Ramadhar (1985) conducted a study in which it was found that the executives who remain healthy in the face of stressful situation have dispositions of control, commitment and show preference for challenging situations. Siddiqa (1996) conducted a study to find the development of components of hardy personality. Since longitudinal study is time taking and is beset with a number of practical and methodological problems, Siddiqa tried to understand the development of components of hardiness with the help of life experiences recalled by hardy and non-hardy persons. It was found that hardy persons recall events showing that there has been purpose in their lives and they take interest in their assignments. Evidence of feeling of control and effectiveness were also present in the events recalled by the hardy persons. Moreover, hardy persons rated greater impact of the events which contributed in making them committed, self-controlled and challenge preferring.

Indian studies on health-care seeking behaviour are also available. Nawab and Hasan (1994) carried out a study to find out difference in medical health-care seeking behaviours of the subjects differing in their self-assessment of finding how strenuous are their day to day activities. It was found that the option for medical-care was related to individual's evaluation of strenuousness of day to day activities.

In another study, Nawab and Hasan (1996) studied the delay and reporting to the hospital for medical-care. Physician's rating regarding the painfulness and seriousness of disease was used to group diseases into different categories. The finding of the study shows that irrespective of painfulness and seriousness of the disease, patient's delayed reporting to hospital till the illness reached a moderate level of deterioration.

The discussion of the role of certain psychological factors in recovery from illness must have created an impression that the same psychological factors are important for recovery irrespective of socioreligious belief system of the patient. This impression is to be removed as attribution-based strategies of coping are dependent upon the attribution of ill health to our beliefs about the world and causes of disease, and the factors that are believed to be contributing to the recovery. Dalal and Singh (1987); Dalal and Pande (1988); and Agarwal and Dalal (1993) have shown that in the case of Hindu patients with different kinds of physical problems, recovery is related to beliefs about the world, beliefs about causes of disease, and beliefs about the factors that contribute to recovery. Among hospitalized Hindu accident victims, attribution of accident to karma was to be positively correlated with the psychological recovery of the patient, more so, in the case of permanently disabled (Dalal and Pande, 1988). Belief in karma was also found to be significantly correlated with psychological adjustment of tuberculosis patients (Dalal and Singh, 1992). There is also evidence that socioreligious beliefs about the world and cause of disease and recovery may not have same kind of relation with the recovery that has been observed at different intervals from the occurrence of the problem. Agarwal and Dalal (1993) reported that indices of recovery of Hindu Myocardial patients obtained after 4 to 5 days heart attack (Time I) and a month after (Time II) have different degree of correlation with the patient's world beliefs, causal beliefs, and recovery beliefs concerned with karma, God, and just world (self).

Studies have also been conducted on menstrual problems and psychological factors and complications during pregnancy. Dysmenorrhea, (pains during menstruation) is one of the most common complaints which is best explained in terms of a combination of physiological and psychological problems (Paulson and Wood, 1966). Some of the important psychological factors involved in dysmenorrhea are attitudes, beliefs, tensions and stress and fear associated with menstruation and sexual contact. A study of spasmodic and conjustive menstrual symptoms in married and unmarried women was conducted by Mathur and Jain (1988). Spasmodic dysmenorrhea is related to part of body controlled by the uterin or ovarian nerves and the pain is similar to labour pain; in conjustive Dysmenorrhea there is a dull aching pain that often begins before menstruation. Employing a sample of 100 married and 100 unmarried women in age group of 16-45 years and collecting data with the help of Menstrual Symptom Questionnaire developed by Chesney and Tasto (1975), Mathur and Jain (1988) found that the six most dominant symptoms are: weakness and dizziness, abnormal pain and discomfort, knowing menstrual date by calendar only, and cramps. In general, married women were found to have more menstrual problems than unmarried women. However, spasmodic symptoms were more in the unmarried women while conjustive symptoms were more prevalent in married women. Further, around the age of 25 years there is reduction in the spasmodic symptoms.

Studies conducted by Rahman and Kureshi (1990) and Draboo (1993) are the good examples of the study of relationship between demographic variable and menstrual disturbances. Draboo (1993) reported that menstruation is more disturbing for Aligarh women than for Srinagar women and that married rather than unmarried women are most susceptible to stress and they also find it more difficult to cope with stress created by menstrual disturbance.

In another study Aleem and Hussain (1993) tried to determine a link between self-consciousness and social support (i.e., actual and ideal) among menopausal women. The sample was divided into pre-menopausal (N=50); transitional menopausal (N=50); menopausal (N=50); and post-menopausal (N=50) women. All four groups were administered Self-Consciousness Scale (SCS) and Significant Others Scale (SOS). The results revealed a positive and significant relationship between self-consciousness and actual and ideal social support scores among different groups of subjects.

An outstanding contribution is the study of psychological factors involved in complications during pregnancy carried out by Jahan (1985). The period of pregnancy was divided into three trimesters and complications specific to each trimester were identified. The term complication denoted physical symptoms as well as subjective experience of troublesome symptoms. The two aspects of complication were taken care by reliance on physician's diagnosis and self-report of the patients. For the study of complications during first trimester of pregnancy three groups were employed — Normal pregnancy group (N=30); Vomiting group (N=30); and Threatened abortion group (N=30). Complications during second trimester were studied by using normal pregnancy group (N=30) and threatened abortion group (N=30). For the study of complications during the third trimester the groups were: Normal group (N=30); Vomiting group (N=30); Antepartum Hameorrhage group (N=30); and Pre-eclamutic Toxamia group (N=30). Data were collected by using Personal Data Sheet, Symptom Checklist, Cornell Medical Index and Hindi version of questionnaire for measuring presumpted stress. Bivariate and multivariate statistics of the data showed that women suffering from threatened abortion during the first and second trimesters, and antepartum hamorrahage (bleeding) during the third trimester as compared to women with normal pregnancy, have higher accumulation of stress and tension, and have a history of previous abortion or still births. The following pattern was observed in regard to the role of stressful life event in complications: stressful life situations give rise to emotional tension, due to lack of necessary personality resources, pregnant women find it difficult to manage the dissipation of tension and as a consequence of this pregnancy for them becomes a state of sickness. The model which seems to be effective in explaining complications during pregnancy is that of learned helplessness and learned resourcefulness.

In addition to making the above mentioned contribution to health psychology, Indian psychologists have developed a large number of questionnaires, inventories, checklists and rating scales for the measurement of variables like stress burnout, quality of life, quality of work life, psychological well-being, social support, coping mechanisms and other variables in which health psychologists are interested.

REFERENCES

Advani, G.B., 1981, Preliminary observation of research project, Alcohol abuse in rural areas of Ajmer district, In Mohan (ed.), *Current Research in Drug Abuse in India*, pp. 169-74, New Delhi: Gemini.

Agarwal, M. and Dalal, A.K., 1993, Beliefs about the world and recovery from Myocardial Infraction, *The Journal of Social Psychology*, 133: 385-94.

Ahmad, H., Ramalingom, S., and Ahmad, S., 1984, Drug abuse and personality: A cross-cultural study, *Indian Journal of Clinical Psychology*, 11: 33-39.

Ahmad, S. and Verma, 1987, A study of drug use behaviour among college students from different religious backgrounds, *Advances in Psychology*, 2: 29-33.

Aleem, S. and Hussain, A., 1993, A study of self-consciousness and social support among menopausal women, *Journal of Community Guidance and Research*, 1: 71-78.

Antonovsky, A., (1979), *Health, stress and coping*. San Francisco: Jossey-Bass.

Ashton, H. and Stepney, R., 1982, *Smoking: Psychology and Pharmacology*. London: Tavistok.

Baldwin, J.D. and Baldwin, J.I., 1988, Factors affecting Aids-related sexual risk-taking behaviour among college students, *Journal of Sex Research*, 25: 181-96.

Barker, G., Wright, B.A., Meyerson, L., and Gomick, M.R., 1953, Adjustment to physical handicap and illness, A survey of the social psychology of physique and disability, 2nd ed., Bull. 55, *Social Science Research Council*, New York.

Becker, M. H., and Maiman, L.A., 1975, Socio-behavioural determinants of compliance with health and medical care recommendations, *Medical care*, 13: 10-24.

Berg, R.L., 1976, The high cost of self-deception, *Preventive Medicine*, 5: 483-95.

Bose, S. K. and Mukhopadhyay, 1993, An attempt to trace the emotional maturity factor and its impact on stress among male and female cancer patients, Paper abstracted in the proceedings of the XXX IAAP Conference, II.

Breslow, L., 1983, The potential of health promotion, In D. Mechanic, (ed.), *Handbook of health, health care, and the health professions*. New York: Free Press.

Byrne, D., 1964, Regression-sensitization as a dimension of personality, In B.A. Mathur (ed.), *Progress in experimental personality research*, pp. 169-20, New York: Academic Press.

Caplan, G., 1974, *Support systems and community mental health*. New York: Behavioural Publications.

Cassel, J., 1976, The contribution of social environment to host resistance, *American Journal of Epidemiology*, 104: 107-23.

Chaudhri, N., 1971, Amenorrhea and psychic stress, Paper presented at the International Seminar on Stress in Health and Diseases, Banaras Hindu University, Varanasi.

Chesney, M.A., and Tasto, D.L., 1975, Development of the menstrual symptoms questionnaire, *Behavioural Research and Therapy*, 13: 237-44.

Cobb, S., 1976, Social support as a moderator of stress, *Psychosomatic Medicine*, 38: 300-14.

Cohen, E., and Lazarus, R.S., 1973, Active coping processes, coping disposition and recovery from surgery, *Psychosomatic Medicine*, 35: 375-89.

Cohen, S., Glass, D.C. and Singer, J.E., 1973, Apartment noise, auditory discrimination, and reading ability in children, *Journal of Experimental Social Psychology*, 9: 407-22.

Cohen, S. and Wills, T.A., 1985, Stress, Social support and the buffering hypothesis, *Psychological Bulletin*, 90: 310-57.

Coyne, J.C. and Lazarus, R., 1980, Cognitive style, stress perception and coping. In I.L. Kutash and L.B. Schlesinger and Associates (eds.), *Handbook on stress and anxiety*, pp. 144-58. San Francisco: Jossey-Bass.

Dalal, A.K. and Pande, N., 1988, Psychological recovery of accident victims with temporary and permanent disability, *International Journal of Psychology*, 23: 25-40.

Dalal, A.K. and Singh, A.K., 1987, Role of causal and cosmic beliefs in psychological recovery of chronic tuberculosis patients, Unpublished manuscript, University of Allahabad, Allahabad.

———, 1992, Role of causal and recovery beliefs in the psychological adjustment to a chronic disease, *Health and Psychology: An International Journal*, 6: 193-203.

Dang, R. and Agarwal, S., 1995, A study of life events in patients of unipolar depression, *Journal of the Indian Academy of Applied Psychology*, 21: 145-52.

Deb, P.C. and Jindal, R.B., 1974, Drinking in rural areas — A study of selected villages of Punjab, Monograph Ludhiana: Punjab Agricultural University.

Delongis, A., Folkman, S. and Lazarus, R.S., 1988, The impact of daily stress on health and mood: Psychological and social resources as mediators, *Journal of Personality and Social Psychology*, 54: 486-95.

Di Mascio, A., Rinkel, M. and Liberman, J., 1961, Personality and Psychosomatic Drugs, In Third World Congress of Psychiatry: Proceedings, Vol. II, Toronto, University of Toronto Press, pp. 933-36.

Dohrenwend, B.S. and Dohrenwend, B.P., 1974, Life, stress and illness: Formulation of the issues, In B.S. Dohrenwend (eds.), *Stressful Life events and their contexts*, New York: Prodist.

Draboo, S.R., 1993, Stress, Marital Status and Menstrual disturbance, *Journal of Personality and Clinical Studies*, 1: 99-102.

Engel, G.L., (1980), The clinical application of the biopsychosocial model, *American Journal of Psychiatry*, 137: 535-44.

Evans, E., 1926, *A Psychological study of cancer*, New York: Dodd-Mead.

Eysenck, H.J., 1957, Drugs and personality. 1. Theory and methodology. *J. Ment. Sci*, 103: 119-131 (a).

———, 1960, Level of personality, constitutional factors, and social influences: An experimental approach, *International Journal of Social Psychiatry*, 6: 12-24.

———, 1963, Personality and drug effect. In H.J. Eysenck (ed.), *Experiments with Drugs*, pp. 1-24, New York: McMillan.

Fechner, G.T., 1860, *Element der Psychophysik*, Breitkopf and Hartel, Leipzig.

Folkman, S. and Lazarus, R.S., 1980, An analysis of coping in a middle aged community sample, *Journal of Health and Social Behaviour*, 21: 219-39.

———, 1985, If it changes it must be a process: A study of emotion and coping during three stages of a college examination, *Journal of Personality and Social Psychology*, 48: 150-70.

Friedman, M. and Rosenman, R., 1959, Association of specific overt behaviour pattern with blood and cardiovascular findings: blood cholestrol level, blood clotting time, incidence of arcus senilis and clinical coronary artery disease, *Journal of the American Medical Association*, 169: 1286-96.

Goldstein, M.J., 1973, Individual differences in response to stress, *American Journal of Community Psychology*, 2: 133-37.

Gunderson, E. and Rahe, R., (ed.), 1974, Life, stress and illness. *Springfield;* III: Charles C. Thomas.

Harpanen, A., Koskenvuo, M., Kaprio, J., Kesaniemi, Y.A. and Heikkila, K., 1989, *Carotid arteriosclerosis in identical twins discordant for cigarette smoking circulation*, 80: 10-16.

Harris, D.M. and Guten, S., 1979, Health protective behaviour: An exploratory study, *Journal of Health and Social Behaviour*, 20: 17-29.

Hingson, R., Strunin, L., Berlin, B. and Heeren, T., 1990, Beliefs about Aids, use of alcohol and drugs and unprotected sex among Massachusetts adolescents, *American Journal of Public Health*, 80: 295-99.

Hirayama, T., 1981, Non-smoking wives of heavy smokers have a higher risk of lung cancer: A study from Japan, *British Medical Journal*, 282: 183-85.

Holmes, T.H., and Rahe, R.H., 1967, The social readjustment rating scale, *Journal of Psychosomatic Research*, 11, 213-18.

Holohan, C.J. and Moos, R.H., 1986, Personality, coping and family resources in stress resistance: A longitudinal analysis, *Journal of Personality and Social Psychology*, 51: 389-95.

Humble, C., Croft, J., Gerber, A., Casper, M., Hames, C.G. and Tyroler, H.A., 1990, Passive smoking and 20-year cardiovascular disease mortality among non-smoking wives, Evans County, Georgia, *American Journal of Public Health*, 80: 599-601.

Jahan, M., 1985, A study of psychological factors associated with certain complications during pregnancy, Thesis submitted for Ph.D. degree, Dept. of Psychology, A.M.U., Aligarh.

Jahan, M. and Hasan, G., 1987, A comparative study of stressfulness of certain life events for Indians and Americans, *Advances in Psychology*, 2: 1-6.

Johnson, J.H. and Sarason, I.G., 1978, Life, stress, depression and anxiety, internal/external control as a moderator variable, *Journal of Psychosomatic Research*, 22: 205-208.

Kanappan, R. and Cherian, R.R., 1989, Personality factors and alcoholism, *Journal of Personality and Clinical Studies*, 5: 43-46.

Kanner, D., Coyne, J.C., Schaefer, C. and Lazarus, R.S., 1981, Comparison of two modes of stress measurement, daily hassles and uplifts versus major life events, *Journal of Behavioural Medicine*, 4: 1-39.

Katz, J., Weiner, H.G., Gallagher, T. and Hellman, L., 1970, Stress distress and ego defense, *Archives of General psychiatry*, 23: 131-42.

Kegeles, S.M., Allen, N.E. and Irwin, I.E., 1988, Sexually active adolescents and condoms: changes over one year in knowledge, attitudes and use, *American Journal of Public Health*, 78: 460-61.

Khan, G., 1996, Use of psychotropic drugs and their psychophysical consequences in the alleviation of disorders among senescents, Dissertation submitted for the degree of M.Phil, Dept. of Psychology, A.M.U., Aligarh.

Khan, M.Z., 1978, *Social correlates of drugs use among college students in Jabalpur town*, Department of Criminology and Forensic Science, University of Sagar.

Khatri, S., Chansouria, J.P.N. and Udupa, K.N., 1977, Role of stress in malignant diseases, Paper presented at the international seminar on Stress in Health and Disease, Banaras Hindu University, Varanasi.

Kobasa, S.C., 1979, Stressful life events, personality and health: An inquiry into hardiness, *Journal of Personality and Social Psychology*, 37: 1-11.

Kobasa, S.C., 1982, Commitment and coping in stress among lawyers, *Journal of Personality and Social Psychology*, 42: 168-77.

Kobasa, S.C. and Puccetti, M.C., 1983, Personality and social resources in stress resistance, *Journal of Personality and Social Psychology*, 45: 839-50.

Kulik, J.A. and Mahler, H.I.M., 1989, Social support and recovery from surgery, *Health Psychology*, 8: 221-38.

Lazarus, R.S., Delongis, A., Folkman, S., and Gruen, R., 1985, Stress and adaptational outcomes: The problem of confounded measures, *American Psychologist*, 40: 770-79.

Lazarus, R.S. and Folkman, S., 1984, Coping and adaptation, In W.D. Gentry (ed.), *Handbook of behavioural medicine*. New York: Guilford.

Lefcourt, H.M., 1980, Locus of control and coping with life's events. In Staub, E., (ed.), *Personality: Basic issues and current research*, Englewood Cliffs, N.J.: Prentice Hall.

Leventhal, H. and Cameroon, L., 1987, Behavioural theories and the problem of compliance, *Patient Education and Counselling*, 10: 117-38.

Leventhal, H., Prohaska, T.R., and Hirschman, R.S., 1985, Preventive health behaviour across the life span. In J.C. Rosen and L.J. Solomon (eds.), *Prevention in health psychology*. Hanover, N.H: University Press of New England.

Lynch, J., 1990, The broken heart: The psychobiology of human contact. In R. Ornstein and C. Swencionis (eds.), *The healing brain: A scientific reader*, New York: Guilford.

Mahendru, R.K., Sethi, B.B., and Agarwal, A.K., 1976, Psychological correlates in Coronary heart disease, *Indian Journal of Psychiatry*, 18: 273-83.

Matarazzo, J.D., 1980, Behavioural health and behavioural medicine: Frontiers for a new health Psychology, *American Scientist*, 35: 807-17.

Mathur, C.N. and Jain, P., 1988, A study of Spasmodic and congestive menstrual symptoms in unmarried and married women, *Advances in Psychology*, 1: 47-52.

Meyen, Y.B., 1994, A study of personality and demographic variables in substance preference amongst addict, Thesis submitted for the Ph.D. degree, Dept. of Psychology, A.M.U., Aligarh.

Mohanty, B. and Saraswat, G.P., 1982, Attitude toward narcotic drugs as a function of some personality variables, *Asian Journal of Psychology and Education*, 9: 29-33.

Nawab, R. and Hasan, G., 1994, Medical-care seeking and self-assessment of health, *Journal of Indian Academy of Applied Psychology*, 2: 125-29.

———, 1996, Physician's assessment of patient's condition at the time of hospitalization, *Journal of Personality and Clinical Studies*, 12: 79-81.

Paulson, M.J. and Wood, K.R., 1966, Perception of emotional correlates of dysmenorrhea, *American Journal of Obstet. and Gynecology*, 95: 996.

Phillips, C.A., 1989, Rehabilitation of the patient with rheumatoid hand involvement, *Physical Therapy*, 69: 1091-98.

Rabkin, J.G. and Struening, E.L., 1976, *Life events stress and illness*, 194: 1013-20.

Rahman, S., and Qureshi, A., 1990, Regional differences in personality deviance among menstrually disturbed married and unmarried women, *Indian Journal of Community Guidance Service*, 7: 67-74.

Rao, V. and Nammalvar, M., 1976, Life changes and depressive disease, *Indian Journal of Psychology*, 18: 293-304.

Read, D., Mc Ghee, D., Yano, K., and Feinlab, M., 1983, Social networks and coronary heart disease among Japanese men in Hawai, *American Journal of Epidemiology*, 119: 356-70.

Rosenman, R.H., Brand, R.J., Sholtz, R.I. and Friedman, M., 1976, Multivariate prediction of coronary heart disease during 8.5 year follow-up in the western Collaborative Group Study, *American Journal of Cordinology*, 37: 903-10.

Rosenstock, I.M., 1966, Why people use health services? *Millbank Memorial Fund Quarterly*: 44-94.

Russell, M.A.H., 1989, The addiction research unit at the institute of psychiatry-II. The work of the unit's smoking section, *British Journal of Addiction*, 84: 853-64.

Sahani, S.M. and Merchant, P.C., 1977, Maternal and Fetal plasma cholestrol level in normal abnormal labour, Paper presented at the international seminar on Stress in Health and Disease, Banaras Hindu University, Varanasi.

Sahasi, G., Chawla, H.M., Bhushan, B. and Katkar, 1990, Eysenk's Personality Questionnaire, Scores of heroin addicts of Indians, *Journal of Psychiatry*, 22: 25-29.

Schachter, S., 1959, *The psychology of alienation*, Stanford, Calif, Stanford University Press.

Schnall, P.L., Pieper, C., Schwartz, J.E., Kārasker, R.A. Schlussel, Y., Devereux, R.B., Gannu, A., Aldermen, M., Warren, K. and Pickering, T.G., 1990, The relationship between "Job Strain" workplace diabetic blood pressure and left ventricular mass index: Results of a case — control study, *Journal of the American Medical Association*, 263: 1929-35.

Seeman, T.E. and Syme, S.L., 1987, Social networks and coronary artery disease: A comparison of the structure and function of the social relations as predictors of disease, *Psychosomatic Medicine*, 49: 381-406.

Selye, H., 1956, *The stress of life*. New York: McGraw-Hill.

Sethi, B.B. and Trivedi, J.K., 1979, Drug abuse in a rural population, *Indian Journal of Psychiatry*, 21: 11.

Shanmugan, T.E., 1979, Personality factors underlying drug abuse among college students, *Psychological Studies*, 24: 24-34.

Shirali, K.A. and Bharti, S.P., 1986, Life stress, demographic variables and personality (TAT) in eleven cases of possession (Trance-Medium) in Shimla Tehsil, *Personality Studies and Group Behaviour*, 6: 73-81.

Shukla, P., 1995, Personality traits and Coronary heart disease (CHD) patients, *Journal of Personality and Clinical Studies*, 11: 1-4.

Shukla, R.R., 1989, Life change events in coronary heart disease: A clinical study, *Journal of Personality and Clinical Studies*, 5: 249-51.

Siddiqa, S.H., 1996, Past memories of hardy and non-hardy individuals, Dissertation submitted for the degree of M.Phil., Dept. of Psychology, A.M.U., Aligarh.

Singh, S. and Chopra, N., 1979, Subject variables in drug use, *Indian Journal of Clinical Psychology*, 6: 149-52.

Singh and Ramadhar, 1985, Stress-resistant executives: The hardy personality, *Vikalpa*, 10: 463-65.

Sperey, R.W., Gazzaniga, M.S. and Bogen, J.E., 1969, Interhemispheric relationship, The neocortical commissures: syndrome of hemispheric disconnection, In P.J. Vinken and G.W. Bruyn (eds.), *Handbook of Clinical Neurology*, (Vol. 4), Amsterdam, North Holland.

Srivastava, S., 1990, Stress, personality and cancer, *Journal of Personality and Clinical Studies*, 6: 151

Srivastava, K.B. and Baroota, K.D., 1987, Stress and cancer, *Journal of Personality and Clinical Studies*, 3: 89-94.

Suchman, E.A., 1965, Stages of illness and medical care, *Journal of Health and Human Behaviour*, 6: 114-28.

Upinder, D. and Hooda, K., 1991, Ischemic heart disease and distress: An exploratory study, *Praachi Journal of Psycho-cultural Dimension*, 7: 64-70.

Vadra, P. and Hussain, A., 1991, Life attitude profile of In-patient and Non-patient alcoholics, *Journal of the Indian Academy of Applied Psychology*, 17: 45-49.

Varkey, L.P., 1988, A study of personality, stress and coping in individuals with coronary heart disease, (Unpublished paper), Bangalore University, Bangalore.

Veeraraghvan, V., 1981, Drug use among university students, In Mohan et al., (eds.), *I. Current research in drug use in India*, New Delhi.

Weibe, D.J. and McCallum D.M., 1986, Health practices and hardiness as mediators in the stress-illness relationship, *Health psychology*, 5: 425-38.

Weinberger, M., Hiner, S.L. and Tierney, W.M., 1987, In support of hassles as a measure of stress in predicting health outcomes, *Journal of Behavioural Medicine*, 10: 19-31.

FIVE

Stress and Disease

HAMIDA AHMAD

Psychologists and sociologists accept that stress is an inevitable part of human existence. It has always been with us and will undoubtedly continue to be our loyal companion in the journey of our lives. However, we were never as overwhelmed or overpowered by it as we are today, it has assumed such gigantic proportions that humankind feels threatened by it.

Why is it that stress is perceived today as the 'numero uno' danger for mankind? Looking back in history, we find that life was never smooth and easy for us. Wars and famines, poverty and lawlessness, cruelty and injustice dominate the canvas and must have affected human beings. No doubt, the sources of stress existed even then, but no one has written history with a psychological bias — history is primarily a chronological juxtaposition of events with some references to political, economic and social conditions. The thoughts, perceptions, anxieties and health status of the common man have no place in those annals. Stress must have been experienced but the relatively easy pace of living in contrast to today's razor-edged competition probably kept it within manageable limits. The awareness of stress and its implications is a phenomena of modern times.

Gradually, our society has evolved into an 'achieving society' with emphasis on high aspirations, material acquisitions and social success. And this is the way it was bound to be, because competition at the global level, explosion of knowledge and technological advancement of unimaginable magnitude have ushered an era in which new avenues for growth are within reach of those who are ready to run the race. To win, one has to use all the energy and wits at one's disposal and even then, everyone cannot win. Stress is inescapable — for the winner, for the loser and even for those who decide to bask in the sun and not run at all. In this competitive age, an insulated existence is a nonviable option and is in itself a likely source of stress.

What is this phenomena called stress and what makes it so awesome and frightening? It is frightening because it has been found to be related not only to poor quality of life but also with the occurrence of a large number of diseases including deadly diseases like cancer, coronary heart disease and to some extent even AIDS (Acquired Immune Deficiency Syndrome). It is well known that emotional, psychosocial and anxiety - stimulated stress produces increased plasma concentration of adrenal corticoids and other hormones through well known neuro endocrine pathways. These corticoid concentrations injure elements of the immunological apparatus and this may leave the subject vulnerable to the action of latent oncogenic viruses, newly transformed cancer cells or other incipient pathological processes that are normally held in check by an intact immunological apparatus (Riley, 1981). Thus, the various biochemical changes associated with stress increase the propensity to disease and stress becomes etiologically associated with a vast variety of diseases.

The answer to the question "What is stress?" is not easy, partly because the phenomena is experienced in a vast variety of situations, therefore different aspects stand for different observers. Thus, disturbing and disruptive aspects of the environment are emphasized by some theorists who take up the position that "it should be understood once and for all that stress is what happens to the man, not that which happens in him, it is a set of causes and not a set of symptoms (Symonds, 1947)". Yet another approach is concerned with the specification of the particular response or pattern of responses which may be taken as evidence that the person is, or has been under pressure from a disturbing environment. Selye (1956) wrote "stress is the non-specific (physiological) response of the body to a demand made upon it." His breakthrough work in the area has been widely acclaimed and has almost assumed the flavour of a classic. However, this has not prevented it from being criticized. A third viewpoint of stress which has emerged, expresses the view that stress arises out of a particular relationship between the person and his environment. It means different persons suffering from different types of stresses.

Thus, stress has been defined in three ways: (i) as stimulus (which focuses on events or circumstances which are 'stressors'); (ii) as response, (which concerns itself with the person's psychological and physiological response to the stressor and is often called 'strain'); and (iii) as process (which involves stressors and strain but also adds the important dimension of transactions between the individual and the environment). The third approach is being emerged by the new psychologists and research scholars as preferred position because unlike the machine, the human being is not a passive recipient of load with predictable responses to its pressure, but is an active participant in all stages of the process. An event becomes a stressor only if it is perceived as such by the person, and it is this evaluation of event as beyond coping potential of the person which results in psychological and physiological responses. This man-environmental interaction mode of stress suggests that stress can be most adequately described as part of a complex and dynamic system of transaction between the person and his environment. There are five recognizable stages in this system:

(i) The first stage is represented by sources of demands relating to the person and is part of his 'environment'.
(ii) The individual's 'perception' of the demand and of his own ability to cope form the second stage.
(iii) The third stage is of psychophysiological changes and represents the 'response' to stress.
(iv) The 'consequences' of the coping responses comprise the fourth stage and
(v) the fifth and last stage is that of 'feedback' which occurs at all the stages.

According to this system, the most important activity is

cognitive appraisal both of the situation and of the individual's own capacity to cope. Emotional breakdown is conceptualized as resulting from an imbalance between environmental stressors and resources.

By integrating ideas put forward by prominent researchers in the area (Cox, 1978; Lazarus and Folkman, 1984; Singer and Davidson, 1986; Trumbull and Appley, 1986) we may conclude that:

> Stress is a condition, involving psychological and Physiological responses resulting from transactions between the individual and his (her) environment which foster the perception and belief, sometimes even wrongly that his (her) bio-psycho-social resources are insufficient to meet the demand of a situation.

Let us visualize a concrete situation to understand this definition. X has to submit an important assignment and to secure good grades he/she must do it well and on time. Parents and family members have high expectations and X works hard. The nagging feeling that "I may not succeed" keeps cropping up and seeing other students finish their work while he/she is still half way through further lowers confidence. He/she becomes more and more tense, experiences severe anxiety and palpitations and falters through the work with difficulty. The student's pessimistic perception of resources (whether this self-evaluation was correct or incorrect does not matter here) in the context of societal expectations resulted in what may be termed as stress.

Another aspect of the definition is also important. Suppose we substitute "...foster the belief and wrongly so, that his/her biopsycho-social resources are sufficient to meet the demands of a situation." While this situation may not exemplify the experience of stress *per se*, it is an unhappy situation. Although perception of discrepancy between resources and demand is not apparent at the moment, the fact that transactions with the environment will continue to take place in the framework of wrong premises about capacities, a situation of severe stress is imminent.

It may be observed that a common factor in all approaches to stress is the indication of relationship between stress and disease. Whether it is the stimulus oriented definition in which permanent damage to the organism is visualized if the pressure is beyond a particular limit, or the response-oriented approach in which a state of collapse ensues at some point when the necessary energy for adaptation may be exhausted, or the process-oriented definition in which breakdown occurs due to imbalance between environmental stressors and resources, in all situations the advent of disease is heralded by stress. This aspect of stress is given so much importance that the whole disease paradigm has undergone a change. The 'germ theory' was the stronghold of the physical disease paradigm, but we observe that today stress is also given a position of prominence in the total configuration.

A lot of empirical evidences are quoted which illustrate strength to this contention. This stress-centered explanation of disease is so exciting and appealing that occasionally one wonders if it is after all being magnified. It is, therefore, important that we critically evaluate the evidence available in this regard.

The tendency to assign an unequivocal role to stress in the aetiology of disease has been questioned at many levels. Primarily, the methodology used in studies which suggest these conclusions has been exposed to criticism. To evaluate stress, the retrospective method is usually employed. Most instruments to measure psycho-social stress are on the lines of Schedule of Life Experiences and Life Events Scale which call upon the individual to recall past experiences together with judging the intensity of their positive or negative valences. There is no way to verify the authenticity of their recalls. While it may be argued that even if after passage of time the recall is not perfect and many experiences may have been forgotten or exaggerated, yet the meaning and priorities which they have for the individual is reflected in his responses. This would be a valid argument if our focal concern is to explore the individual's phenomenological world, but if we are interested in linking stress to disease, the exact status of events should be known, and the unique perceptions of the individual *vis-a-vis* the events should form another important parameter. Further since the interplay of biological and psycho-social risk factors both are important in the epidemiology of disease, retrospective studies do not furnish parallel information about biological risk factors. Prospective study designs are to be preferred because then it is possible to have information of psycho-social risk factors for a particular disease and also have in the initial data collection of an assessment of biological risk factors. Failure to include them may result in improper conclusion. At present, studies with such holistic designs are few in number. The problem is especially acute when one works, as is usual, with a diseased sample. Then, rather than biological risk factors, it becomes necessary to measure initial health status, morbidity and comorbidity, without which detecting the casual role of stressful life events or other psycho-social variables becomes nearly impossible. In well-controlled studies of this nature where adequate assessment of initial health status is made, it usually turns out to be a powerful predictor of subsequent health status and the intervening stressful life experiences seldom add much to the prediction, thus not confirming to the clear cut role that was being hypothesized.

Another direction of association is however being indicated. The role of stressful life events and other psycho-social factors can be more clearly delineated in the context of disease development. For example, in a study of infectious mononucleosis, it was found that the same psycho-social variable was either a positive or negative risk factor for IM, depending on the disease development process stage (Kasl, Evans and Niederman, 1979). In the same manner the role of stress in cancer relapse has been brought out. Studies of different psychologists already diagnosed with cancer have found that subjects who experienced more stressful life events or received less social support had significantly more relapses within a specified subsequent time than those who did not experience as much stress or received more social support (Rogentine and others, 1979; Sabbioni, 1991; Watson and Ramirez, 1991). This approach of studying stress at different stages of disease is eliciting valuable information. In the best of circumstances, causal relationships are difficult to formulate in psychological research and in such situations where the two major classes of factors being studied interact with such intimacy and intricacy that their effects are difficult to isolate, the task is an onerous one. In view of methodological limitations of researches, we should be content with concluding that stress is a likely risk factor at certain stages in the process of disease, and well-designed studies will bring out this position more clearly. It is more likely that the picture may be different for different diseases. In some diseases there may be a greater role of stress in the precipitation of diseases, but in some diseases it may be slightly less, in some diseases the role may be more marked during progress of diseases and in some diseases in recovery and recuperation. In view of the complex factors that may operate in aetiology such a picture may be conceptualized.

An interesting aspect of the picture has emerged from cancer and coronary heart disease research. While it has been impressively brought out by researches (again of retrospective nature) that life stress events frequently precede the appearance of certain forms of neoplasia, another noteworthy fact has been brought out in animal studies. It has been demonstrated that acute stress accelerates tumour growth and also exacerbates metastasis, whereas chronic stress has an inhibitory effect on tumour growth as well as on the formation and growth of metastases (Sklar and Anisman, 1981). They go on to say that these conclusions have a bearing on human beings because acute and chronic stress have remarkable parallels at the neurochemical, hormonal and immunological level. To quote:

> acute stress results in depletion of catecholamines and increases of A Ch, increased synthesis and secretion of hormones, and immuno suppression. Adaptation in these biological mechanisms is observed with chronic stress, such that normal levels of functioning or alterations opposite to those induced by acute stress are apparent.

Using the medical parallel, Eysenck (1983) calls this 'inoculation effect'. But the observations by many other researchers, particularly Levi and Kagan (1975) are that only if stress response is prolonged, intense or often repeated, it is accompanied by an increase of wear and tear in the person and produces structural as well as functional damage. Thus, chronic stress is considered contributory to disease by these researchers whereas it has been hypothesized to have a beneficial effect in cancer studies. It may be noted that Levi and Kagan studied diseases other than cancer, so once again we are led to conclude that certain findings may be disease-specific. Studies of different diseases, their stages and role of stress at different points need to be conducted. An order and system will be doubtless and discernible when all findings are placed on the canvas and evaluated.

Again from the area of cancer research some more observations of importance will see the light. A large number of studies have pointed that cancer patients are lower on neuroticism and higher on extraversion than controls (Kissen and Eysenck, 1962; Berndt, Gunther and Robte, 1980; Green and Morris, 1975). Further, a negative link between cancer and functional psychosis has been observed (Abse and others, 1974; Ure, 1969; Grece and Morris, 1975 and Bahson and Bahson, 1964). Eysenck (1983) has stated that several studies in different countries dealing with many thousands of cases have "confirmed this negative link beyond doubt". This has been explained on the basis of 'inoculation effect' by certain theorists who suggest that since psychotics are exposed to continuous stress, they are protected against cancer (chronic stress having an inhibitory effect on tumour growth).

However, we must give close attention to this observation from another point of view. It brings a major point into focus that individual differences and personal characteristics both have a vital role to play in stress and disease. It may appear exciting to explain the various configurations of stress and cancer through the medical analogy of 'inoculation effect' but since the applicability of the analogy still awaits experimental validation, it would not be wise to stretch it to such an extent as to lose sight of other important alternatives. If research indeed continues to support the finding that psychotics do not succumb to cancer, we may consider the alternative explanation that the susceptible and vulnerable part of the psycho-physiological system responds to stress, and thus in some persons either physical or mental diseases may be precipitated.

The need to study personality factors which are related to vulnerability of stress and disease is reiterated. More importantly it is necessary that factors which can buffer the effect of stress need to be understood.

Psychoneuroimmunology is an important source of understanding which is based on the observation that strengthening the immune system protects against disease. Psychoneuroimmunology has in its purview the study of psycho-social processes *vis-a-vis* their relationships with nervous activities and endocrine system which through neurotransmitter activities either increase or decrease hormones thus influencing the immune functions. In turn, cells of the immune system (through chemicals produced) collect information and passes it on to the brain.

Brain performs the crucial task of maintaining an equilibrium in the immune system. Too little and too much activities of the immune system are harmful to the psychological and biological systems of the human being.

It has been observed that emotions in general and stress related emotions (anxiety and depression) in particular disturb the immune balance critically. Heiden (1991); Kamen Siegel, Rodin, Seligman and Dwyer (1991) and many other eminent psychologists have demonstrated that pessimism, depression and stress from major and minor events are related to lowered immune functions.*

This has brought our discussion of stress and immune functions on a more optimistic and intervention-based note. While more researches are needed in this area, there is evidence that people who perceive high levels of social support have stronger immune systems as compared to those unlucky people who do not (Kennedy, Kiecolt Glaser and Glaser, 1990). The question does remain whether it is a strong immune system which contributes to positive perceptions like that of social support rather than vice versa, but even so, such questions do not undermine the role of social support. At the most, the possibility that the two processes are related to each other in terms of "feedback loops" may be contemplated. More important, social support is an experience that we can attempt to manage through appropriate measures and thus have with us a method of strengthening the immune system. The relationship between biological and psychological factors postulated by psychoneuroimmunology is suggestive that by strengthening certain psychological characteristics in the individual the possibility of his succumbing to disease will be reduced.

* Eye-opening researches in the area of stress and immune functions were conducted by Antoni and others (1990, 1991) which demonstrated that stress-reducing therapy, including aerobic exercises increased immune function in people infected by AIDS virus.

Some exciting results are forthcoming from animal studies. Ader and Cohen (1975, 1985) have demonstrated that immunosuppression can be conditioned and that conditioning can influence both antibody mediated and cell-mediated immune process to moderate degrees. While findings of animal studies cannot and should not be applied sweepingly to human beings it is important to note that a situation which is not originally a causative factor in immuno-suppression becomes so through association with a factor that had that characteristic. Human beings in whom cognitions are complex and a network of associations, unconscious conditioning operate, the role of perceptions and experiences becomes even more important and the possibility of conditioning to achieve immunological strengthening can be contemplated.

Psychoneuroimmunology is thus an optimistic development in the area of health psychology. It clearly declares in unequivocal terms that the holistic paradigm of biological and psychological integratedness in the individual and the greater likelihood that common laws and principles to explain all aspects of the individual — biological, psychological and social — will ultimately emerge. It is thus suggestive of a stage of high scientific understanding in the area, for parsimony undoubtedly brings greater order and interrelatedness in the universe.

There is thus a complex relationship between stress and disease. While the unique biological aspects of different diseases undoubtedly play the crucial role, the individual too has an important say in the matter. But since biological aspects of disease are less under our control and psychological factors more within intervention limits, the individual's role is more important for us. That is why psycho-social factors in disease have been highlighted, sometimes at the expense of biological causality. The individual is also a preferred aspect of the intervention because while the biological system operates within a specified framework, the human being has a greater and often unimagined range of adjusting, managing and coping. One is reminded here of the engineering analogy with stress. In the 1940's, Hookes law suggested that when load exceeded the elastic limit, there was deformation and damage of material and the same relationship was applied to environment and organism to explain stress. We know that materials have the capacity to retain their shapes much beyond elastic limit. After crossing elastic limits to enter plastic limits and then even after crossing plastic limits, materials survive through the process of 'strain hardening'. This is true of all materials except the brittle. By the same analogy, the human being who is not brittle has the capacity to withstand pressures and loads of life without breakdown. Psycho-social characteristics which contribute to the ability to withstand pressures and 'buffer out' these effects will act as shields to stave off (at least control to some extent) disease. And we are talking of all psychological and biological diseases, the psychoneuroimmunological paradigm encourages us to do so. Characteristics like enhanced feelings of personal control and hardiness, lowered hostility and type A behaviour have been found related to better management of adverse factors (Averill, 1973; Thompson, 1981; Kobasa and Maddi, 1977; Sheckelle and others, 1985; Monston and Vavak, 1991). The energy of stress-related emotions can even be sublimated and channelized to achieve difficult goals.

For stress has to stay with us and we with it. As Selye has said, "complete freedom from stress is death" and Shakespeares Hamlet, also realized that in order to escape "The heartache and the thousand natural shocks. That flesh is heir to", death is the only solution. But we will live, face, manage and even use stress to fight disease and attain a high quality of life. This should be our goal and evidence suggests that one day we will reach it.

REFERENCES

Abse, D.W., Wilkins, M.M., Castle, R., Buxton, W.D., Demars, J. Brown, R.S. and Kirschner, L.G., 1974, Personality and behavioural characteristics of lung cancer patients, *Journal of Psychosomatic Research*, 18: 101-13.

Ader, R., and Cohen, N., 1975, Behaviourally conditioned immunosuppression Psychomatic Medicine, 37: 333-40.

———, 1985, CNS immune system interactions conditioning phenomena, *Behavioural and Brain Sciences*, 8: 379-95.

Antoni, M.H., Schneiderman, N., Fletcher, M.A., Goldstein D.A., Ironson, G., and Laperriere, A., 1990, Psychoneuroimmunology and HIV-I, *Journal of Consulting and Clinical Psychology*, 58: 38-49.

Antoni, M.H., Baggeti, L., Ironson, G., LaPerriere, A., August, S., Kumas, N., Schneiderman, N. and Fletcher M.A., 1991, Cognitive-behavioural stress management intervention buffers, distress responses and immunologic changes following notification of HIV-I seropositivity, *Journal of Consulting and Clinical Psychology*, 59: 906-15.

Averill, J.R., 1973, Personal control over aversive stimuli and its relationship to stress, *Psychological Bulletin*, 80: 286-303.

Bahnson, C.B. and Bahnson, M.B., 1964, Cancer as an alternative to psychosis. In D.M. Kissen and I. LeShan (eds.), *Psychosomatic Aspects of Neoplastic Disease*, Philadelphia: Lippincott.

Cox T., 1978, *Stress Baltimore*, University Park Press.

Eysenck, M.J., 1983, Stress, Disease and Personality: The Inoculation Effect. In Cary L, Cooper (ed.), *Stress Research: Issue for the Eighties*, John Wiley.

Greer, S., and Morris, T., 1975, Psychological attributes of women who develop lung cancer: A controlled study, *Journal of Psychosomatic Research*, 19: 147-53.

Houston, B.K., and Vavak, C.R., 1991, Cynical hostility: Development factors, Psychosocial Correlates and health behaviours, *Health Psychology*, 10: 9-17.

Kagan, A. and Levi, L., 1975, Adaptation of the psychosocial environment to man's abilities and needs, In L. Levi (ed.), *Society, Stress and Disease*, 1971, Vol. 1, London: Oxford University Press.

Kasl, S.V., Evans, A.S. and Niederman, J.C., 1979, Psychosocial risk factors in the development of infections mononucleosis, *Psychosomatic Medicine*, 41: 445-66.

Kobasa, S.C. and Maddi, S.R., 1977, Existential personality theory. In R. Corsini (ed.) *Current personality theories*, Itaska, IL: Peacock.

Lazarus, R.S. and Folkman, S., 1984, *Stress, Appraisal and Coping*. New York: Springer.

Riley, V., 1981, Psychoneuroendocrine influence on immunocompetence and neoplasia, *Science*, 217: 1: 110-9.

Rogentine, G.N., Van Kammen, D.P., Fox, B.H., Docherty, J.P., Rosenblatt, J.E., Boyd, S.C. and Bunney, W.E., 1979, Psychological Factors in the Prognosis of malignant melanoma: A prospective study. *Psychosomatic Medicine*, 41: 647-55.

Sabbioni, M.E.E., 1991, Cancer and stress: A possible role for psychoneuroimmunology in cancer research, In C.L. Watson and M. Watson (eds.), *Cancer and stress: Psychological, biological and coping studies*. New York: Wiley.

Schachter and Singer, J.E., 1962, Cognitive, social and emotional determinants of emotional state, *Psychological Review*, 69: 379-99.

Shekelle, R.B., Hulley, S.B., Neaton, J.D., Billings, J.H., Borhani, N.O., Gerace, T.A., Jacobs, D.R., Lasser, N.L., Millelmark M.B., and Stamuler, J., 1985, The MRFIT Behaviour Pattern Study II, Type A behaviour and incidence of coronary heart disease, *American Journal of Epidemiology*, 122: 599-70.

Singer, J.E. and Davidson, L.M., 1986, Specificity and Stress Research. In M.M. Appley and R. Trumbull (eds.), *Dynamics of Stress Physiological, Psychological and Social Perspective*. New York: Plenum.

Sklar, L.S. and Anisman, H., 1981, Stress and Cancer, *Psychological Bulletin*, 89: 369-406.

Symonds, C.P., 1947, Use and abuse of the term flying stress, In 'Psychological Disorders in flying personnel of the Royal Air Force'. Investigated during the war, 1939-45, H.M. S.O. London.

Thompson, S.C., 1981, Will it hurt less if I can control it? A complex answer to a simple question, *Psychological Bulletin*, 90: 89-101.

Trumbull, R. and Appley, M.H., 1986, A conceptual model for examination of stress dynamics. In M.H. Appley and R. Trumbull (ed.), *Dynamics and stress: Physiological, Psychological and Social Perspectives*. New York: Plenum.

Ure, D.M., 1969, Negative association between allergy and cancer, *Scottish Medicinal Journal*, 14: 51-4.

Watson, M. and Ramirez, A., 1991, Psychological factors in cancer prognosis, In C.L. Cooper and M. Watson (eds.), *Cancer and Stress: Psychological, Biological and Coping Studies*, New York: Wiley.

SIX

Role of the Applied Behavioural Scientist in Managing Organizational Stress

D.M. PESTONJEE

Organizational Role Stress

In the past two decades empirical researchers on the theme of stress have increased manifold. One of the major area of interest in India appears to be organizational stress in general and role stress in particular. Researchers have focused their attention on causal factors of stress, stress manifestations, moderator of the stress-strain relationship, types of stress experienced by diverse work populations, and various coping strategies/relaxation techniques adopted by organizational entities to cope with stress.

Stress related activities pertaining to industrial settings are many and scattered. In most of these studies stress and related phenomena are studied in relation to particular job categories. Very little attempt has been made to study stresses experienced by all the job categories of a particular organization (Khanna, 1985; Bhaskar, 1986; Singh, 1987). Subjects in most of the studies varied from supervisors to top management, and scant attention has been paid to the stresses experienced by the lower level workers.

Measurement/Instrument of Organizational Role Stress:

Pareek developed and standardized the organizational role of stresses (1983b, 1983c). He noted that until recently researches were done only on the three role stresses, namely, role ambiguity, role overload, and role conflict. However, he found many other role stresses in the organizations. The earlier version of the tool, 'Your feeling about your role' measured eight types of role stresses. And a more refined version of this instrument, called 'Organizational Role Stress (ORS) Scale', measured ten types of role stresses which are mentioned below:

(i) Inter-role distance (IRD)
(ii) Role Stagnation (RS)
(iii) Role Expectation Conflict (REC)
(iv) Role Erosion (RE)
(v) Role Overload (RO)
(vi) Role Isolation (RI)
(vii) Personal Inadequacy (PI)
(viii) Self-Role Distance (SRD)
(ix) Role Ambiguity (RA)
(x) Resource Inadequacy (RIn)

The previous scale 'Your feeling about your role' consisted of forty items and measured only eight types of role stresses. The ORS scale by Pareek consists of fifty items and measures the ten above said stresses. It is a five-point scale indicating how true a particular statement is for the role. Sen (1981) calculated the test-retest reliability for a group of five hundred bank employees. However, this reliability is available for seven factors of role stresses as well as overall role stress.

According to Pareek (1983b), the ORS scale can be used for several purposes. It can be used to investigate the nature and dynamics of role stress in various organizations and to develop intervention for the use of individuals, groups, and organizations. In a comparatively recent publication, a large number of intervention strategies have been listed and explained by Pareek (1993).

Another Psychometric instrument is the Occupational Stress Index which was constructed and standardized by Srivastava and Singh (1981). This scale measures twelve types of role stresses and consists of fifty items, covering all the relevant components of job life which might cause stress in one way or the other. This scale has sufficient degree of consistency in assessing an individual's stress pertaining to his or her occupation.

Coping

The word coping has two connotations in literature. The term has been used to denote the way of dealing with stress, or the effort to master conditions of harm, threat or challenge when a routine or automatic response is not readily available (Lazarus, 1974).

Two different approaches for the study of coping have been pursued by various investigators. On the one hand some researchers (Byrne, 1964; Goldstein, 1973) have emphasized general coping traits, style or disposition. On the other hand, other researchers (Cohen and Lazarus, 1973; Katz, Weiner, Galigher and Hallman, 1970; Wolf and Goodell, 1968) have preferred to study the active ongoing strategies in a particular stress situation.

Coping trait refers to a disposition to respond in a specific way in situations that are stressful. Coping traits are thus, stable characteristics of persons that transcend classes of situations. Coping style implies a broader, more encompassing disposition. Traits and styles refer to a characteristic way of handling situations, they are stable tendencies on the basis of which inferences are drawn about how an individual will cope in some or all type of stressful situations. A person's coping style or disposition is typically assessed by personality tests, not by actual observation of what the person says or does in a particular stress situation.

Coping can be assessed in terms of three kinds of outcomes — psychological, social and physiological. From a psychological perspective, coping can have effects on the psychological morale, emotional reaction, e.g., level of depression, or anxiety or balance between positive and negative toned feeling (Bradburn, 1969), the incidence of psychiatric disorder and even performance. From a social perspective one can measure its impact on functioning effectiveness such as community involvement and sociability (Renne, 1974), the effectiveness of interpersonal relationship or the degree to which useful social roles are filled. From a physiological perspective, outcomes include consequences, such as the development and progression of a particular disease.

Coping Measurement

Coping refers to efforts to master conditions that tax or exceed adaptive resources (Monat and Lazarus, 1977). Lazarus (1974b) has emphasized the key role of cognitive processes in coping activity and the importance of coping in determining the quality and intensity of emotional reaction to stress. There are many ways to classify coping responses (Moos and Billing, 1982), most approaches distinguish between strategies that are active in nature and oriented towards confronting the problem, and strategies that entail an effort to reduce tension by avoiding dealing with the problem.

Pareek (1983b) has proposed two types of coping strategies which people generally use in order to handle stress, i.e., dysfunctional and functional coping styles. There is no clear consensus as to which coping strategies or mode of coping are most effective. Coping may either take the form of avoiding the situation (dysfunctional style) or confronting and approaching the problem (functional style). Combining the two aspects of each of the three dimensions yields there are eight possible strategies to cope with stress: (1) The dysfunctional or impunitive (M); (2) Intropunitive (I); (3) Extrapunitive (E); and (4) Defensive (D).

The four functional style are: (5) Impersistive (m); (6) Introperspective (i); (7) Extrapersistive (e); and (8) Interpersistive (n).

Thus, broadly speaking 'avoidance' and 'approach', are only two most effective coping strategies to control stress.

For researchers studying how people cope with job stress, a major empirical concern is the development of a coping measure. Latack (1986) presented construct validity evidence of three measures of coping behaviour related to job stress: control, escape and symptom management. He has also identified various measurement issues particularly in reference to coping scale development.

Pareek (1983b) has developed role of Projective Instrument for Measuring Coping Style (PICS) which involves a semi-projective technique to obtain profiles of coping style adopted by a person while dealing with role stress situations. The instrument depicts twenty-four situations, three each for eight type of role stress, he is experiencing the situation of another person, who is supposed to respond to the former's problem. The responses obtained on this instrument are scored in eight styles, which can be broadly grouped, as approach and avoidance modes of coping. The scores on approach and avoidance modes are bipolar — increase in avoidance score leads to decrease in approach score and vice versa.

The responses given by respondent can be scored by using a system of categorizing. The system is a 2*2 cube, having three dimensions which are as follows :

1. *Externality*: The feeling that external factors are responsible for role stress, resulting in aggression and blame on the external factors.
2. *Internality*: The feeling that the respondent himself is responsible for stress and therefore, may express aggression towards himself.
3. *Mode of Coping*: Coping may take the form of either avoiding the situation (reactive strategy) or confronting and approaching the problem (proactive strategy).

Both externality and internality may be low or high. Combining the two aspects of each of the three dimensions yields eight possible strategies to cope with stress which role PICS measures. These are as follows :

(i) Impunitive
(ii) Intropunitive
(iii) Extrapunitive
(iv) Defensiveness
(v) Impersistive
(vi) Introspersistive
(vii) Intrapersistive
(viii) Interpersistive.

Of these dimensions, the first four imply avoidance-oriented behaviour. They are perceived as dysfunctional styles of coping with stress situations. The remaining four dimensions are approach-oriented and are regarded as functional. Pareek has suggested that the role PICS scale has a wide range of uses such as, research, counselling, and OD intervention. And it can also be used as a feedback intervention.

Sharma (1988) while reviewing the literature on stress in India, has indicated the paucity of meaningful research on stress and coping strategies in different occupational groups.

Gupta and Murthy (1984) studied role conflict and coping strategies among Indian women, and they found the most popular coping strategy among them was personal role redefinition.

Ahmad, Bhatt and Ahmad (1990) studied stress and coping strategies among executive technocrats by using role PICS, and found that they used intropersistive style as the dominant style for coping followed by defensive and extrapersistive style.

Kaur and Murthy (1986) also studied the coping strategies of the managerial personnel at different organizational level in public sector. Their result indicated significant difference in the coping strategies adopted by individuals working at different organizational levels.

Stress Audit

Right from the time of birth till the last day of life, an individual is invariably exposed to various stressful situations for one reason or another. In all economies of the world, it has been found that people, specially business executives die of disorders created by stress. Stress, therefore, is considered a major killer and the consequent loss to organizations is often great (Pestonjee, 1984a).

> Organizational stress refers to a situation wherein job related factors interact in such a way that the worker experiences a disruption in his or her psychological or physiological conditions, so that he or she is forced to deviate from normal functioning.

Pestonjee (1984b) attempted to diagrammatically present the nature and consequences of the stress phenomena. He identified three important sectors of life in which stresses originated. These are: (1) Job and organization, (2) Social Sector, and (3) Intrapsychic Sector. Job and organization refer to the totality of the work environment (task, atmosphere, colleagues, compensations, and policies, etc.). The social sector refers to the social-cultural context of one's life. It might include religion, caste, language, dress, food habits, and such other factors. The intrapsychic sector encompasses those things which are intimate, personal, and specific to the individual, i.e., temperament, values, abilities, skills and health.

Research evidence indicates that besides the health-related problems, job stress also affects the smooth operation of the organizations. It has been found to be associated with absenteeism (Gupta and Beehr, 1979); with job dissatisfaction (Sharma and Sharma, 1984; Pestonjee and Singh, 1982).

When an organization decides to have a scientific peep in to the mental-cum-physical health status of its backbone group (executives) we call it 'Stress Audit'. Stress Audit refers to the attempt organizations make to study, explore and control the various types of stresses which the individual executives experience by virtue of their organizational membership.

In setting up a stress audit in an organization a distinction can be made among three categories of variables: causal stress variable (the stressors); mediating variable (the effect of personality, culture, and contemporary nonwork environment); and result variables of stress reactions. The data for the stress audit can be collected with the help of questionnaires, clinical diagnostic interviews and if possible physical examination.

Management of Stress

Each individual needs a moderate amount of stress to be alert and capable of functioning. Given that, the presence of more or less stress is inevitable. Many researchers sought to find out what could be done to counteract stress so as to prevent its negative consequences. Some researchers closely link stress and coping. Stress arises only when people find that they cannot cope with a difficult situation.

Normally coping is defined as an adaptive response to stress: a response intended to eliminate, ameliorate or change the stress producing factors or intended to modify the individual's reaction to a stressful situation in a beneficial way (Newman and Beehr, 1979).

Pestonjee (1989) stated that to overcome stress, effort may be required from both the organization and the individual. Some proactive interventions which an organization incorporates to alleviate stress are given as follows:

(i) Undertake a stress audit
(ii) Use scientific inputs
(iii) Check with the company doctor
(iv) Spread the message.

What can an Individual do to Alleviate Stress

Effective management of stress involves directing stress for productive purposes, preparing role occupants to understand the nature of stress, helping role occupants to understand their strength and usual styles and equip them to develop approach strategies of coping with stress (Pestonjee, 1989).

Gmelch (1982) suggested the following six strategies to overcome stress affliction :

(i) Take a hard look at yourself
(ii) Stay alert
(iii) Take risks
(iv) Avoid isolation
(v) Stretch for success
(vi) Overcome obsolescence.

Besides the above mentioned strategies to overcome stress all individuals possess stress safety values. A few safety values are suggested below:

(a) Changing gears
(b) Cutback on excessive hours
(c) Exercise
(d) Pamper yourself
(e) Warm up slowly
(f) Release pressure on the job
(g) Practise relaxation techniques.

In recent years there is a concern for analysis and categorizing the available inputs on management of stress. There are three different categories of intervention listed by Murphy (1988).

Employee Assistance Programme (EAPS)

This is a counselling programme in which organizations provide counselling services to their employees, to overcome their on the job and outside job problems. It is designed to deal with symptoms that have already emerged.

Stress Management Training (SMT)

These programmes refers to a training course designed to provide employees with improved coping (with stress) skills, including training in techniques such as meditation, bio-feedback, muscle relaxation and stress inoculation (Newton, 1992).

Stress Reduction or Intervention (SI)

It denotes interventions designed to change the level or form of job stress experienced by employees either through job redesign or job reform. Stress audit is one such strategy with the help of which organizations can understand, ameliorate and forestall the organizational stresses.

REFERENCES

Ahmad, S., Bhatt, D. and Ahmad, H., 1990, Stress and coping strategies among executive technocrat, Unpublished paper, (Personal Communication).

Byrne, D., 1994, Repression-sensitization as a dimension of personality, In B.A. Maher (ed.), *Progress in Experimental Personality Research*, pp. 169-220, Vol. 1, New York: Academic Press.

Bhaskar, S., 1986, Investigation into relationship between job stress and personality factors among police officers and constables. Ph.D. Thesis, University of Delhi, Delhi.

Bradburn, N., 1969, *The structure of u ell-being*, Chicago: Aldine.

Cohen, E. and Lazarus, R.S., 1973, Active coping processes, coping disposition and recovery from surgery, *Psychosomatic Medicine*, Vol. 35: 375-89.

Goldstein, M.J., 1973, Individual differences in response to stress, *American Journal of Community Psychology*, Vol. 2: 113-37.

Gupta, B.R. and Murthy, V.N., 1984, Role conflict and coping strategies — A study on Indian women, (Unpublished paper), Bangalore University, Bangalore.

Katz, J., Weiner, H., Gallagher, T. and Hallman, L., 1970, Stress distress and ego defences, *Archives of General Psychiatry*, Vol. 23: 131-42.

Kaur, G. and Murthy, V.N., 1986, Organizational role stress, coping strategies and locus of control in a major public sector industrial organizations, (Unpublished paper), Bangalore University, Bangalore.

Khanna, B.B., 1985, Relationship between organizational climate and organizational role stress and their impact upon organizational effectiveness — A case study, Ph.D. Thesis, B.H.U., Varanasi.

Latack, J.C., 1986, Coping with job stress: Measures and directions for scale development, *Journal of Applied Psychology*, Vol. 71(3): 377-85.

Lazarus, R.G., 1976, The psychology of coping: Issues of research and assessment. In G.V. Coelho, D.A. Hamburg and J.E. Adams (eds.), *Coping and Adaptations*, New York: Basic Books.

Monat, R. and Lazarus, R.S., 1972, *Stress and Coping: An Anthology*, New York: Columbia University Press.

Murphy, L.R., 1988, Workplace intervention for stress reduction and prevention. In C.L. Cooper and R. Payne (eds.), *Causes, Coping and Consequences of Stress at Work*, Chichester: Willey.

Newman, J.E. and Beehr, T.A., 1979, Personal and organizational strategies for handling job stress: A review of research and opinion, *Personnel Psychology*, Vol. 32: 1-43.

Pareek, U., 1982, *Executive glow up and burn out: Summary of Larsen and Toubro Lecture*, IIM, Ahmedabad, 20th February.

———, 1983a, Preventing and resolving conflict, In L.D. Goodstein and J.W. Pfeiffer (eds.), *The 1983 Manual for Facilitators, Trainers and Consultants*, pp. 143-45, San Diego, California: University Associates.

———, 1983b, Role stress scale, *ORS scale Booklet, Answer sheet and Manual*, Ahmedabad: Navin Publications.

Pestonjee, D.M., 1984a, Stress a major killer, M. Neri, (ed.), Reining in the Stress Killer, *Business world*, December 3-16.

———, 1984b, Stressors or Loads: A diagrammatic presentation of the stress phenomenon, Teaching note for programme on Management of Executive Stress, IIM, Ahmedabad.

———, 1989, *Stress and Coping*, New Delhi: Indira Gandhi National Open University.

Pestonjee, D.M. and Singh, U.B., 1982, Job satisfaction as a moderator of role stress-satisfaction relationship, Paper presented at XXth International Congress of Applied Psychology, Edinburgh, July 25-31.

Renne, K.S., 1974, Measurement of social health in general population survey, *Social Science Research*, Vol. 3, pp. 25-44.

Sen, P.C., 1981, A study of personnel and Organizational correlates of role stress and coping strategies in some public sector banks, Ph.D. Thesis, Gujarat University, Ahmedabad.

Sharma, S. and Sharma, U., 1984, Relationship or organizational role efficacy with anxiety and job satisfaction at two job levels, *Indian Journal of Clinical Psychology*, Vol. 10: 319-23.

SEVEN

Gender Differences in Stress, Job Outcomes and Some Personality Variables in Different Sex-Typed Jobs

PATIRAJ KUMARI *and* ASHOK P. SINGH

Stress has a negative impact on the individual worker's well-being as well as on the employing organization's economic health. The research on sex differences in work stress has become a topic of importance for both individuals and organizations due to potentially deleterious consequences of stress and the greater number of women at the workplace. It is generally assumed that excessive and persistent stress is harmful resulting in deterioration in employee's adequate and satisfactory adjustment with various dimensions of his professional life and personal life. Although there is disagreement over several conceptual and definitional issues in stress research, there seems to be consensus on the importance of individual differences. Many individual characteristics might be correlates of stress but we select here Type A behaviour pattern, locus of control and personal efficacy.

The importance of research into stress processes has been made clear by increasing evidence about the negative effects of psychological and social stresses on physical and mental health (Dohrenwend and Dohrenwend, 1974; Goldberger and Breznitz, 1982; Krantz, Glass, Contrada, and Miller, 1981). Progress in understanding these effects has been limited, however, by a focus on males and by the neglect of gender as a variable. The failure to "build women in" has impaired the accuracy and comprehensiveness of conceptual models and empirical findings in several areas. In organizational and industrial psychology, as in other social sciences men are over represented as subjects of study and that in fact, women are often ignored in Indian settings. The present study focuses on the issues, many of which were not studied by industrial or organizational psychologists in the past.

In some respects working women are different from working men, and there are a number of characteristics about organizations which will have different effects on both of them. Mednick (1982) reports a series of studies in which she found differences due to career orientation, sex-role identity, and perceived support from others. Working women are likely to experience stress from demands and challenges associated with work and non-work responsibilities. But because of problems stemming from sex-role stereotypes and occupational sex-discrimination, there is reason to expect an even greater likelihood of stress for women who are employed in non-traditional jobs and careers (Brief, Schuler, and Van Sell, 1981).

At present time whatever research has been conducted comparing men with women on personality variables, such as Type A behaviour, locus of control and personal efficacy suggests that in the general population, men are more likely than women to be Type A. Type A is more pronounced in women who work than in women who do not work (Chesney and Rosenman, 1980). Compared with men, there is a tendency for women to be more external (Johnson and Black, 1981). There seems to be a sense that things happen to them about which they have little or no control (Makosky, 1980). Women attribute events to luck more frequently than do men (Mednick, 1982). Few researches on personal efficacy and stress have been conducted in field settings with employed men and women. Kaufman and Felters (1980) found no difference between men and women on behaviour performance expectancies.

It is generally found that women have lower expectancies about their potential to bring about change and that women internalize failure and externalize success (Deaux, 1976; Mednick, 1982; O'Leary and Hansen, 1982).

Women might experience greater life stress than men. This could spillover to the job situation with negative effects (Bhagat, 1983). To the extent that women experience considerable stress at work, the job is unable to mediate life stress and might even exacerbate life stress. Although a good job can contribute to overall quality of life through increased income and more satisfying experiences than those available to a traditional housewife (Hoffman and Nye, 1974; Holahan and Gilbert, 1979; Warr and Parry, 1982), women who work outside the home are required to make many social readjustments that can contribute to stress. Motowidlo and Packard (1986) suggest that subjective stress generates anxiety, hostility and depression which, in turn, affect components of job performance.

Although much has been written about working women, stress and personality variables, there are large gaps between what we know and what we do not know about the gender differences in stress, job outcomes, and personality variables such as Type A behaviour, locus of control and personal efficacy. Hence, this study was planned to assess the level of stress (job and life), Type A behaviour, locus of control and personal efficacy of women and men across the two job categories, namely, masculine sex-typed blue-collar job and feminine sex-typed job. The effect of stress and sex on job outcomes (job satisfaction and performance) was also assessed.

Hypotheses

The following hypotheses have been formulated and tested:

1. Women are likely to have high negative job stress, negative personal life stress and total negative life stress mean score as compared to men across two job categories, namely, masculine sex-typed blue-collar job and feminine sex-typed job.
2. Women are likely to have high positive job stress, positive personal life stress and total positive life stress mean score as compared to men across the two job categories.

3. Women are likely to have low Type A behaviour and personal efficacy mean score as compared to men across the two job categories.
4. Women are likely to have high external locus of control mean score as compared to men across the two job categories.
5. Women are likely to have low job satisfaction and performance mean score as compared to men across the two job categories.
6. High stress group (negative and positive job stress, negative and positive personal life stress, total positive and negative life stress) is likely to have low job satisfaction and performance mean score as compared to low stress group.

Method

Sample

The present study was conducted on 150 subjects (Male-75, Female-75) belonging to two job categories, masculine sex-typed blue-collar job and feminine sex-typed job. "Proportional Stratified Random Sampling" technique was used for the selection of the subjects to ensure that all the sections/departments of the organization were represented. Only those respondents were selected who had put in at least five years job exposure in the present service. The subjects were matched with regard to their demographic data.

Seventy-five subjects were selected from masculine sex-typed blue-collar job (Factory workers — Local high technology organisation, Varanasi). Out of 75 subjects, 35 were female. Level of education ranged from vocational training to postgraduate. The mean age was 35 years.

Seventy-five subjects were selected from feminine sex-typed job (Nurses — Sir Sunderlal Hospital, Banaras Hindu University, Varanasi). Out of 75 subjects, 35 were female. Level of education ranged from vocational training to postgraduate. The mean age was 35 years.

Procedure

The six psychometric devices were simultaneously administered to the selected subjects personally and they were asked to read carefully the instructions given in the questionnaire. In some cases subjects were verbally explained the instructions by the investigator. The subjects were allowed to take their own time to complete the questionnaire.

Scoring for all the questionnaires was done accordingly as instructed in their manuals.

Measures

1. *Life Changes Experience Survey:* Total life stress was measured by using an eighty-three items checklist developed by Dohrenwend, Krasnoff, Askenasy and Dohrenwend (1978). This scale measures the degree of positive or negative impact on a person of 78 different events that may have occurred during the person's life (the remaining five items are blank spaces for the person to list unique events that may not have been included in the checklist). The subjects were instructed to check an event only if it occurred during the 3 years prior to testing and to rate the impact on a 7-point scale from –3 to +3 (extremely negative to positive) that the event had on their lives. Events that occurred more than 3 years ago were acceptable if they continued to impact on the subjects' lives.

Internal consistency reliabilities (Cronbach's Alpha) were found to be 0.53 for negative job stress, 0.70 for negative personal life stress, 0.74 for total negative life stress, 0.58 for positive job stress, 0.73 for positive personal life stress, and 0.77 for total positive life stress.

2. *Jenkins Activity Survey:* For the assessment of Type A behaviour Jenkins Activity Survey (JAS) (Form C — 1979) was used. The JAS (Form C) is a self-report multiple-choice questionnaire of 52 items designed to measure the Type A behaviour pattern found to be strongly associated with the risk of coronary heart disease.

The estimated internal consistency reliability was 0.83 using Kendall's taub one-year test-retest coefficients. However, the reliability coefficient was found to be 0.85 in terms of squared multiple correlation which is an another technique of estimating the internal consistency of the JAS.

The validity of the JAS has been established in several ways. Initially, the instrument was developed by writing questions that would distinguish persons classified as Type A or Type B on the basis of the structured interview. Thus, the first evidence of the test's validity is the agreement between scores on the JAS and interviewer ratings.

3. *Social Reaction Inventory:* Locus of control was assessed by using Social Reaction Inventory (Rotter, 1966). The Inventory consists of 23 question pairs using a forced choice format plus six filler questions. Internal statements are paired with external statements.

An internal consistency coefficient (Kuder Richardson) of 0.70 was obtained from a sample of 400 college students (Rotter, 1966). For discriminant validity Rotter has reported that correlations with the Marlow-Crowne social desirability scale range from –0.70 to –0.35.

4. *Personal Efficacy Scale:* Personal efficacy was assessed with the help of Personal Efficacy Scale (Kumari and Singh, 1990). This scale consists of 24 items. Each item has five response alternatives, namely, strongly disagree, disagree, undecided, agree, strongly agree.

The split-half reliability of the scale was determined by Spearman-Brown formula and it was found to be 0.72. The scores on Social Reaction Inventory and Rosenberg Self-Esteem Questionnaire were used as the validation criteria for this scale. The coefficient of correlation between the scores of Social Reaction Inventory and Personal Efficacy Scale was found to be +0.72 on a representative sample of 300 subjects. The coefficient of correlation between the scores of Rosenberg Self-Esteem and Personal Efficacy Scale was found to be 0.81.

5. *S-D Employee's Inventory:* The Satisfaction-Dissatisfaction (S-D) Employee's Inventory was used to measure the level of job satisfaction of workers. This inventory was developed and standardized by Pestonjee (1973). This inventory comprises of 80 items which covers four areas, namely, job, management, social relations and personal adjustment. Respondents are required to give their responses either in 'Yes' or 'No'.

The areawise split half reliability was found to be 0.99 for job, 0.99 for management, 0.98 for personal adjustment, and 0.98 for social relations. The validity was assessed by the 'known group' technique and the 'item test correlation' technique (Pestonjee, 1973).

6. *Performance Rating Scale:* Performance Rating Scale (Pestonjee and Singh, 1978) was used to measure the performance of the subjects. The reliability of the Performance Rating Scale was determined by computing the Cronbach's (1951) alpha coefficient which was also obtained by split half method and it was found to be 0.92 indicating satisfactory level of reliability.

The index of homogeneity and the internal validity of the items were tested by computing the point-biserial correlation (rph). The actual performance was taken as one of the validation criteria for the Performance Rating Scale. The coefficient of correlation between the actual performance and the scores of Performance Rating Scale was found to be +0.84 on a representative sample of 200 blue-collar industrial workers (Pestonjee and Singh, 1978).

Results

The statistics applied in this study were the coefficient of correlation, mean, standard deviation and the test of the significance of difference (CR). The coefficient of correlations among stress, Type A behaviour, locus of control, personal efficacy, job satisfaction and performance for the sample of blue-collar workers and nurses were computed and recorded in Tables 1 and 2 respectively. From the results presented in Table 1 it was clear that stress was significantly correlated with Type A behaviour in a positive direction ($P < 0.05, 0.01$); however, it had significant negative relationship with job satisfaction ($P<0.05$) Type A behaviour was positively correlated with job performance ($P<0.05$) and negatively associated with job satisfaction ($P<0.05$; <0.01). External locus of control had significant negative correlation with job satisfaction ($P<0.05$) and Personal efficacy had significant positive correlation with job satisfaction ($P<0.05$).

Results recorded in Table 2 revealed that stress had significant positive correlation with Type A behaviour (job involvement, $P<0.05$), and it had significant negative correlation with

TABLE 1

INTERCORRELATION MATRIX FOR STRESS, LOCUS OF CONTROL, PERSONAL EFFICACY, TYPE A BEHAVIOUR, JOB SATISFACTION, AND PERFORMANCE OF BLUE-COLLAR EMPLOYEES (MASCULINE SEX-TYPED BLUE-COLLAR JOB)

Variable	1	2	3	4	5	6	7	8	9	10
1. Negative job stress	x	0.421*	0.836*	-0.389*	-0.030	-0.199	0.239+	-0.061	0.186	0.189
2. Negative personal life stress		x	0.849*	-0.189	-0.173	-0.219	-0.105	-0.118	0.145	0.363*
3. Total negative life stress			x	-0.346*	-0.122	-0.248+	-0.203	-0.106	0.196	0.329*
4. Positive job stress				x	0.274+	0.664*	-0.053	0.019	0.198	0.016
5. Positive personal life stress					x	0.901*	0.052	0.083	0.098	0.099
6. Total positive life stress						x	0.016	0.073	0.155	0.070
7. Locus of control							x	-0.170	0.067	0.340*
8. Personal efficacy								x	-0.035	-0.105
9. Type A (Type A behaviour)									x	0.362*
10. Factor S (Speed and impatience)										x
11. Factor J (Job involvement)										
12. Factor H (Hard-driving and competitive)										
13. Job										
14. Management										
15. On-the-job (J+M)										
16. Social relation										
17. Personal adjustment										
18. Off-the-job (SR+PA)										
19. Overall job satisfaction										
20. Performance										

	11	12	13	14	15	16	17	18	19	20
1. Negative job stress	0.060	0.139	-0.278+	0.062	0.171	0.164	0.182	0.190	0.198	0.115
2. Negative personal life stress	0.018	0.035	0.068	0.044	0.060	0.064	0.031	0.052	0.061	0.188
3. Total negative life stress	0.046	0.132	0.203	0.063	0.136	0.134	0.125	0.142	0.152	0.180
4. Positive job stress	0.355*	0.342*	-0.124	-0.134	-0.145	-0.139	-0.101	-0.131	-0.151	-0.002
5. Positive personal life stress	0.223	0.125	-0.118	-0.045	0.084	-0.084	-0.141	-0.124	-0.114	0.074
6. Total positive life stress	0.334*	0.251+	-0.148	-0.095	-0.131	-0.128	-0.155	-0.155	-0.157	0.067
7. Locus of control	-0.093	-0.010	-0.152	-0.069	-0.116	-0.097	-0.245+	-0.189	-0.167	-0.188
8. Personal efficacy	0.094	0.199	0.299+	0.183	0.259+	0.175	0.241*	0.229	0.267+	0.094
9. Type A (Type A behaviour)	0.088	0.447*	-0.166	-0.118	-0.154	-0.041	-0.109	-0.083	-0.130	0.251+
10. Factor S (Speed and impatience)	-0.050	-0.157	-0.316*	-0.217	-0.288+	-0.273+	-0.263+	-0.293+	-0.318*	-0.068
11. Factor J (Job involvement)	x	0.265+	0.193	0.206	0.223	0.178	0.115	0.159	0.209	-0.002
12. Factor H (Hard-driving and competitive)		x	0.093	-0.043	-0.072	-0.020	-0.048	-0.037	-0.060	0.015
13. Job			x	0.603*	0.858*	0.593*	0.667*	0.690*	0.489*	0.069
14. Management				x	0.927*	0.516	0.459*	0.532*	0.800*	0.025
15. On-the-job (J+M)					x	0.611*	0.609*	0.667*	-0.914*	0.049
16. Social relation						x	0.671*	0.909*	0.831*	0.190
17. Personal adjustment							x	0.919*	0.836*	0.080
18. Off-the-job (SR+PA)								x	0.912*	0.150
19. Overall job satisfaction									x	0.109
20. Performance										x

Level of Significance 0.302 < 0.01 0.232 < 0.05 df = 73 *P < 0.01

TABLE 2

INTERCORRELATION MATRIX FOR STRESS, LOCUS OF CONTROL, PERSONAL EFFICACY, TYPE A BEHAVIOUR, JOB SATISFACTION, AND PERFORMANCE OF NURSES (FEMININE SEX-TYPED JOB)

Variable	*1*	*2*	*3*	*4*	*5*	*6*	*7*	*8*	*9*	*10*
1. Negative job stress	x	0.289+	0.773*	-0.004	0.022	-0.013	-0.156+	0.181	0.059	0.088
2. Negative personal life stress		x	0.830*	-0.154	-0.115	-0.019	-0.006	0.111	0.218	0.114
3. Total negative life stress			x	-0.128	-0.089	-0.020	-0.094	0.179	0.179	0.127
4. Positive job stress				x	0.204	0.758*	-0.164	0.049	0.025	0.184
5. Positive personal life stress					x	0.793*	0.033	0.146	0.087	0.056
6. Total positive life stress						x	0.080	0.128	0.074	0.152
7. Locus of control							x	-0.230	-0.112	0.184
8. Personal efficacy								x	-0.064	-0.121
9. Type A (Type A behaviour)									x	0.419*
10. Factor S (Speed and impatience)										x
11. Factor J (Job involvement)										
12. Factor H (Hard-driving and competitive)										
13. Job										
14. Management										
15. On-the-job (J+M)										
16. Social relation										
17. Personal adjustment										
18. Off-the-job (SR+PA)										
19. Overall job satisfaction										
20. Performance										

Level of Significance 0.302 < 0.01 0.232 < 0.05 df = 73 *P < 0.01 +P < 0.05

	11	12	13	14	15	16	17	18	19	20
1. Negative job stress	0.271+	0.010	0.221	0.130	0.188	-0.304*	-0.232+	-0.290+	-0.303*	-0.260+
2. Negative personal life stress	0.166	0.081	-0.296+	0.176	-0.263+	-0.335*	0.135	-0.250+	-0.315*	-0.023
3. Total negative life stress	0.267+	0.059	-0.325*	-0.193	-0.276+	-0.398*	0.224	-0.335*	-0.385*	0.136
4. Positive job stress	0.034	0.014	0.152	-0.363*	-0.304*	-0.098	0.078	-0.006	0.174	0.103
5. Positive personal life stress	0.035	0.096	0.001	0.131	0.084	-0.008	0.016	0.014	0.058	0.135
6. Total positive life stress	0.002	0.073	0.095	-0.313*	-0.245+	-0.056	0.059	0.005	0.147	0.154
7. Locus of control	-0.023	-0.230	-0.189	-0.338*	-0.305*	-0.110	-0.273+	-0.214	-0.321*	-0.100
8. Personal efficacy	0.057	0.327*	0.175	0.297+	0.273+	0.222	0.307*	0.291+	0.354*	0.144
9. Type A (Type A behaviour)	0.129	0.696*	0.029	0.057	0.050	-0.063	-0.114	-0.098	-0.036	0.202
10. Factor S (Speed and impatience)	0.124	0.104	-0.146	-0.111	-0.140	-0.094	-0.317*	-0.230	-0.236+	0.111
11. Factor J (Job involvement)	x	0.178	0.140	0.059	0.104	-0.243+	0.092	0.178	0.180	0.059
12. Factor H (Hard-driving and competitive)		x	0.187	0.161	0.191	0.125	-0.232+	0.198	-0.244+	0.317*
13. Job			x	0.608*	0.861*	0.314*	0.240+	0.300+	0.704*	0.255+
14. Management				x	0.927*	0.202	0.177	0.206	0.680*	0.197
15. On-the-job (J+M)					x	0.278+	0.226	0.274+	0.767*	0.246+
16. Social relation						x	0.677*	0.906*	0.767*	0.213
17. Personal adjustment							x	0.925*	0.749*	0.133
18. Off-the-job (SR+PA)								x	0.827*	0.187
19. Overall job satisfaction									x	0.268+
20. Performance										x

Level of Significance 0.302 < 0.01 0.232 < 0.05 df = 73 *P < 0.01 +P < 0.05

TABLE 3

SIGNIFICANCE OF DIFFERENCE BETWEEN MEAN SCORES OF STRESS, LOCUS OF CONTROL, PERSONAL EFFICACY, TYPE A BEHAVIOUR, JOB SATISFACTION, AND PERFORMANCE OF MEN AND WOMEN (BLUE-COLLAR WORKERS)

		Men			*Women*			*CR*	*P*
	Variable	*N*	*Mean*	*SD*	*N*	*Mean*	*SD*		
1.	Negative job stress	40	-1.4750	1.4848	35	-3.0571	2.2088	-3.6801	0.01
2.	Negative personal life stress	40	-3.3000	1.9638	35	-3.6571	2.2353	-0.7367	N.S.
3.	Total negative life stress	40	-4.7750	2.7688	35	-6.7143	3.8849	-2.5120	0.05
4.	Positive job stress	40	5.0750	1.8030	35	5.3429	3.0864	0.4658	N.S.
5.	Positive personal life stress	40	5.8250	3.3884	35	6.7143	5.0850	0.9012	N.S.
6.	Total positive life stress	40	10.9000	4.1683	35	12.0571	6.6816	0.9116	N.S.
7.	Locus of control	40	8.7750	2.9741	35	10.6571	4.2074	2.2579	0.05
8.	Personal efficacy	40	80.8000	7.3492	35	76.9714	10.4895	-1.8482	N.S.
9.	Type (Type A behaviour)	40	-0.5900	7.0367	35	1.7029	7.0566	1.4060	N.S.
10.	Factor S (Speed and impatience)	40	-4.7475	6.9691	35	1.7486	9.1558	3.4817	0.01
11.	Factor J (Job involvement)	40	-3.6200	6.8397	35	-3.0600	6.0654	0.3728	N.S.
12.	Factor H (Hard driving and competitive)	40	-1.2500	8.9889	35	-1.0286	11.2680	0.0946	N.S.
13.	Overall job satisfaction	40	55.0500	11.8017	35	49.6571	9.8367	2.1316	0.05
14.	Performance	40	47.0500	8.3634	35	47.7714	7.4719	0.3915	N.S.

Note: NS = Not Significant; CR = Critical Ratio

TABLE 4

SIGNIFICANCE OF DIFFERENCE BETWEEN MEAN SCORES OF STRESS, LOCUS OF CONTROL, PERSONAL EFFICACY, TYPE A BEHAVIOUR, JOB SATISFACTION, AND PERFORMANCE OF MEN AND WOMEN (NURSES FEMININE SEX-TYPED JOB)

Variable	Men			Women			CR	P
	N	Mean	SD	N	Mean	SD		
1. Negative job stress	40	-2.2000	2.1862	35	-4.2286	2.8085	-3.5122	0.01
2. Negative personal life stress	40	-3.5750	2.8813	35	-3.9714	3.2583	-0.5592	N.S.
3. Total negative life stress	40	-5.7750	3.8861	35	-8.2000	5.0573	-2.3439	0.05
4. Positive job stress	40	6.5250	3.8630	35	8.3143	3.4537	2.1019	0.05
5. Positive personal life stress	40	6.7250	3.3588	35	8.4571	4.5461	1.8916	N.S.
6. Total positive life stress	40	13.2500	5.6330	35	16.7714	6.0249	2.6164	0.01
7. Locus of control	40	9.9000	2.8537	35	11.0571	3.2534	1.6411	N.S.
8. Personal efficacy	40	79.4500	15.8873	35	73.1714	12.9490	-1.8589	N.S
9. Type (Type A behaviour)	40	2.5750	6.8748	35	2.2371	6.8935	-0.2121	N.S.
10. Factor S (Speed and impatience)	40	-5.9975	7.7693	35	-4.7029	8.0300	0.7088	N.S.
11. Factor J (Job involvement)	40	-5.5675	5.2828	35	-7.8543	7.9264	-1.4866	N.S.
12. Factor H (Hard driving and competitive)	40	7.7750	12.8911	35	3.2914	10.4437	-1.6369	N.S
13. Overall job satisfaction	40	45.4750	10.9193	35	39.0000	9.7558	2.6916	0.01
14. Performance	40	48.7250	7.6594	35	46.6571	6.9195	1.2198	N.S

Note: NS = Not Significant; CR = Critical Ratio

(performance, P<0.05) and job satisfaction (P<0.05; 0.01). External locus of control had significant negative relationship with job satisfaction (P<0.05; 0.01). Personal efficacy was significantly related with job satisfaction (P<0.05; 0.01) in positive direction. Type A behaviour had significant positive correlation with performance (P<0.01) and negative correlation with job satisfaction (P<0.05; 0.01).

The mean scores of stress, Type A behaviour, locus of control, and personal efficacy were compared between male and female across two job categories, masculine sex-typed blue-collar job and feminine sex-typed job.

In Table 3 the scores of stress, Type A behaviour, locus of control and personal efficacy of men and women (masculine sex-typed blue-collar job) in terms of men and standard deviation were recorded. Critical-ratio had been computed to test the significance of difference. Results indicated that mean negative job stress score, mean total negative life stress score, and mean locus of control (external) score of the women in blue-collar masculine sex-typed job were comparatively higher than that of the men in the same job. The critical-ratios were found to be statistically significant beyond the 0.01 and 0.05 levels. The mean score of speed and impatience (Type A behaviour) of women was comparatively higher than that of the men. The critical-ratio was found to be statistically significant beyond the 0.01 level. Hypothesis 1 and 4 were supported. Hypothesis 3 was not supported.

Table 4 recorded the scores of stress, Type A behaviour, locus of control and personal efficacy of men and women (nurses-feminine sex-typed job). The means and standard deviation had been calculated separately for men and women. To test the significance of difference the critical-ratio had been computed. It was obvious from the Table 4 that mean negative job stress score, mean total negative life stress score, mean positive job stress score, mean total positive life stress score of women in feminine sex-typed job were significantly higher in comparison to that of the men. The obtained critical-ratios were found to be statistically significant beyond the 0.05 and 0.01 levels. Hypotheses first and second were supported.

To explore the impact of negative and positive job stress, negative and positive personal life stress and total negative and positive life stress on job outcomes (job satisfaction and performance) of blue-collar workers, the entire sample had been divided into high and low stress groups based on Q3 and Q1 scores. Separate means and standard deviations were computed for high and low negative and positive job stress groups, high and low negative and positive personal life stress groups, and high and low total negative and positive life stress groups. To test the significance of difference, the critical-ratios were computed.

It was found that the mean overall job satisfaction score of high negative job stress group was lower in comparison to that of the low negative job stress group. The critical-ratios were found to be statistically significant ($P<0.05$). There was no significant difference between the high negative personal life stress and low negative personal life stress groups. The mean performance score of high total negative life stress group was lower than that of the low total negative life stress group. The critical-ratios were found to be significant beyond the 0.05 level. There was no significant difference between high and low positive job stress groups, high and low positive personal life stress groups, and high and low total positive life stress groups.

In order to test the impact of negative and positive job stress, negative and positive personal life stress, and total negative and positive life stress on job outcomes (job satisfaction and performance) of nurses (FSTJ), the entire sample was divided into two groups, namely, high and low negative job stress and personal life stress groups, high and low positive job stress and personal life stress groups, and high and low total negative and total positive life stress groups.

The mean social relation (JS) score, off-the-job (JS) score, overall job satisfaction score, and performance score of high negative job stress group were lower in comparison to that of low negative job stress group. The critical-ratios were found to be statistically significant. Comparing the scores of high negative personal life stress group and low negative personal life stress group, we found that the mean job score (JS), social relations score, off-the-job score, and overall job satisfaction score of high negative personal life stress group were lower in comparison to the scores of low negative personal life stress group. The critical-ratios were found to be statistically significant beyond the 0.05 and 0.01 levels.

From the results, it was also obvious that the mean social relations score, personal adjustment score, off-the-job score, and overall job satisfaction score of high total negative life stress group were lower than low total negative life stress group. The mean management score, and on-the-job score of high positive job stress group were lower than that of the low positive job stress group. The critical-ratios were found to be significant beyond the 0.01 levels. The results indicated no significant difference between high and low positive personal life stress groups and between high and low total positive life stress groups. Hypothesis six was supported.

To assess the effects of sex on job satisfaction and performance the mean and standard deviation of the job satisfaction scores and performance scores of male and female were calculated separately. To test the significance of difference, the critical-ratios had been computed.

It was found that mean job (JS) score, personal adjustment score, off-the-job score and overall job satisfaction score of male blue-collar workers were higher in comparison to that of the female blue-collar workers. The critical-ratios were found to be statistically significant beyond the 0.05 and 0.01 levels. The mean job score, social relation score, personal adjustment score, off-the-job score, and overall job satisfaction score of female nurses were inferior to that of the male nurses. The critical-ratios were found to be statistically significant beyond the 0.05 and 0.01 levels. Thus, our fifth hypothesis was supported.

Discussion

Claims are often made about the stressful nature of particular occupations, but there are few comparative data on the stress of various occupations in which women experience more stress than men. We have administered stress tests to men and women in two occupations. Sex differences appear on negative job stress, total negative life stress, Type A behaviour and locus of control in masculine sex-typed blue-collar job. Women in masculine sex-typed blue-collar job, experience more job stress and total negative life stress, have high external locus of control and they are found to be more impatient in comparison to their male counterparts. In feminine sex-typed job, sex-differences appear on negative job stress, total negative life stress, positive job stress and total positive life stress. In comparison to men, women report more negative and positive job stress, more total negative and positive life stress.

Very few painstaking research studies are available on women in blue-collar masculine sex-typed job. However, considerable agreement is found on certain issues. In spite of technological advancements reducing the need for physical strength and stamina, women in some blue-collar jobs report minor problems associated with physical demands inherent in the work (Deaux and Ullman, 1982). Physical demands of work can be a problem, but it does not affect all women. A second problem area capable of producing stress is related to technical and mechanical skills. A third stressor for women in masculine sex typed blue-collar jobs stems from the fact that work settings are designed in such a way which do not include women.

Like other studies (Johnson and Black, 1981) we find there is a tendency for women to be more external than men. Probably women think that things happen to them about which they have little or no control (Makosky, 1980). Women attribute events to luck more frequently than men. We find that in masculine sex-typed blue-collar jobs women are more likely to be Type A. However, researches suggest that in general population, men are more likely than women to be Type A. As with men, the Type A behaviour pattern is related to career success and marital failure for women (Waldron, 1978).

Our findings support the idea that in feminine sex-typed job women (nurses) experience more stress than their male counterparts. The results of the present study may be justified in view of the fact that feminine sex-typed jobs have been associated with high stress (Colligan, Smith, and Hurrell, 1977; Albrecht, 1979), and women who work outside the home in feminine sex-typed jobs are susceptible to stress intrinsic to the nature of these occupations. In addition, these women are likely to hold traditional sex role attitudes and be primarily responsible for maintaining the home.

To assess the effect of stress on job satisfaction and performance, the sample has been classified into high and low stress groups. The results provide evidence that negative stress from both an employee's job and personal life would have a greater effect on job outcomes. Negative and positive stress affect job satisfaction and performance. This finding lends support to the notion that job stress is an important predictor of job outcomes (Gupta and Beehr, 1979). Results also indicate that personal life stress has an impact on job outcomes.

The relationship between personal life stress and the job outcomes indicates that people do not separate their personal lives from their job lives, that is, there is a spillover of the effects of non-work stress on organizational outcomes. Spillover effects between work and non-work are often supported (Burke and Bradshaw, 1981; Near, Rice, and Hunt, 1980; Staines, 1980).

The findings of significant relationships between job stress and job satisfaction are consistent with large numbers of empirical studies (Jamal, 1984; Kahn, Wolfe, Quinn, Snoek, and Rosenthal, 1964; Landeweerd and Boumans, 1988; Spector, Dwyer and Jex, 1988). Our results also corroborate the finding of Kaur and Chaddha (1988) who have stated that job stress is the predictor of job satisfaction and leads to dissatisfaction.

Our findings lend further support to the notion that stress generally interferes with performance (Torrance, 1965). While small amounts of stress might lead to increase in performance, large amounts disrupt and impair performance (Schoonmaker, 1969). Hockey (1983) indicates that degradation in the performance of job tasks can be the result of stress.

The results of the present investigation also suggest that gender and job outcomes are related. We have found that men and women differ in respect of their job satisfaction. On the basis of our findings we may conclude that women have lower job satisfaction than men have. Previous research has devoted a great deal of attention to gender related difference in work satisfaction. The findings in this area are not entirely consistent. Some studies, like our findings, have found men to be more satisfied than women (Hulin and Smith, 1965; Smith, Kendall and Hulin, 1969; Weaver, 1974; Shapiro and Stern, 1975; Forgionne and Peeters, 1982). One common explanation for this result is that men and women have different expectations and work satisfaction is a function of what is expected and what is received.

The results show no significant difference between men and women in job performance. The present data indicate that men and women in two job categories, i.e. masculine sex-typed blue-collar job and feminine sex-typed job have very similar perceptions of work rewards and possess very similar work values.

Concluding Remarks

In the light of findings of the present investigation we may conclude that in masculine sex-typed blue-collar job and in feminine sex-typed job, female workers, differ from their male counterparts on stress, Type A behaviour, locus of control and job satisfaction.

On the basis of results we may also conclude that a high degree of stress exerts a deteriorating effect on job outcomes. The findings of the present study also enable us to conclude that male workers are more satisfied with their jobs in comparison to their female counterparts.

Suggestions

On the basis of the results of this investigation we may suggest that professional counselling programmes are necessary in order to help the employees to cope more successfully with both work and non-work stress, so that they may feel satisfied with their organizations and maintain their higher performance capacity. Efforts must be made to improve job satisfaction of women who are found to be comparatively low on this measure in comparison to their male counterparts.

Organizational researchers should focus attention on personal life stresses as possible sources of variance in the prediction of attitudinal and behavioural outcomes within organizational contexts.

REFERENCES

Albrecht, K., 1979, *Stress and the Manager*. Englewood Cliffs, NJ: Prentice-Hall.

Bhagat, R.S., 1983, Effects of stressful life events on individual performance effectiveness and work adjustment processes with organizational settings: A research model, *Academy of Management Review*, 8: 660-71.

Brief, A.P., Schuler, R.S., and Van Sell, M., 1981, *Managing Job Stress*. Boston: Little, Brown.

Burke, R.J., and Bradshaw, P., 1981, Occupational and life stress and the family, *Small Group Behaviour*, 12: 329-75.

Chesney, M.A., and Rosenman, R.H., 1980, Type A behavior in the work setting, In C.L. Cooper and R. Payne (eds.), *Current Concerns in Occupational Stress*. New York: Wiley.

Colligan, M.J., Smith, M., and Hurrell, J., 1977, Occupational incidence rates of mental health disorders, *Journal of Human Stress*, 3: 34-39.

Deaux, K., 1976, *The Behavior of Women and Men*, Monterey, Calif.: Brooks/ Cole.

Deaux, K., and Ullman, J.C., 1982, Hard-hitted women: Reflections on blue-collar employment, In J. Sgro & H.J. Bernardin (eds.), *Women in the Work Force*. New York: Praeger.

Dohrenwend, B.S., and Dohrenwend, B.P. (eds.), 1974, *Stressful Life Events: Their Nature and Effect*. New York: Wiley.

Dohrenwend, B.S., Krasnoff, L., Askenasy, A.R., & Dohrenwend, B.P. 1978. Exemplification of a method for scaling life events. The PERI life events scale, *Journal of Health and Social Behavior*, 19: 205-29.

Forgionne, G.A., and Peeters, V.E., 1982, Differences in job motivation and satisfaction among female and male managers, *Human Relations*, 35: 101-18.

Gupta, N., and Beehr, T.A., 1979, Job stress and employee behaviors, *Organizational Behavior and Human Performance*, 23: 373-87.

Hockey, R., (ed.), 1983, *Stress and Fatigue in Human Performance*. New York: Wiley.

Hoffman, L.W., & Nye, R.I., 1974, *Working Mothers*, San Francisco: Jossey-Bass.

Holahan, C.K., and Gilbert, L.A., 1979, Interrole conflict for working women: Career vs. jobs, *Journal of Applied Psychology*, 64: 86-90.

Hulin, C., and Smith, P., 1965, Sex difference in job satisfaction, *Journal of Applied Psychology*, 49: 209-16.

Jamal, M., 1984, Job stress and job performance controversy: An empirical assessment, *Organizational Behavior and Human Performances*, 33: 1-21.

Jenkins, C.D., 1979, *Jenkins Activity Survey*, New York: The Psychological Corporation.

Johnson, S.J., and Black, N., 1981, The relationship between sex-role identity and beliefs in personal control, *Sex Roles*, 8: 425-31.

Kahn, R.L., Wolfe, D.M., Quinn, R.P., Snoek, J.R., and Rosenthal, R.A., 1964, *Organizational Stress: Studies in Role Conflict and Ambiguity*, New York: Wiley.

Kaufman, D., and Felters, M.L., 1980, Work motivation and job values among professional men and women: A new accounting. *Journal of Vocational Behavior*, 17: 251-61.

Kaur, R., and Chaddha, N.K., 1988, Study of job stress with job involvement and job satisfaction. *Indian Journal of Behaviour*, 12: 34-40.

Krantz, D.S., Glass, D.C., Contrada, R., and Miller, N., 1981, *Behavior and Health*, New York: Social Science Research Council.

Kumari, P., and Singh, A.P., 1990, Personal Efficacy Scale, An unpublished standardized measure of personal efficacy. Department of Psychology, Banaras Hindu University.

Landeweerd, J.A. and Boumans, N.P.G., 1988, Work satisfaction, health and stress: A study of Dutch nurses, *Work and Stress*, 2: 17-26.

Makosky, V.P., 1980, Stress and the mental health of women: A discussion of research and issues. In M. Guttentag, S. Salasin, and D. Belle (eds.), *The Mental Health of Women*. New York: Academic Press.

Mednick, M.T., 1982, Women and the psychology of achievement: Implication for personal and social change. In J. Sgro and H.J. Bernardin (eds.), *Women in the Work Force*, New York: Praeger.

Motowidlo, S.J., and Packard, J.S., 1986, Occupational stress: Its causes and consequences for job performance, *Journal of Applied Psychology*, 71: 618-29.

Near, J.P., Rice, R.W. and Hunt, R.G., 1980, The relationship between work and non-work domains: A review of empirical research, *Academy of Management Review*, 5: 415-29.

O'Leary, V.E., and Hansen, R.D., 1982, Trying hurts women, helps men: The meaning of effort, In J. Sgro and H.J. Bernardin (eds.), *Women in the Work Force*. New York: Praeger.

Pestonjee, D.M., 1973, *Organizational Structures and Job Attitudes*. Calcutta: Minerva Associates.

Pestonjee, D.M., and Singh, A.P., 1978, *Performance Rating Scale*. Varanasi: Abhishek Publications.

Rice, R.W., Near, J.P. and Hunt, R.G., 1980, The job satisfaction/life satisfaction relationship: A review of empirical research, *Basic and Applied Social Psychology*, 1: 37-64.

Rotter, J.B., 1966, Generalized expectancies for internal vs. external control of reinforcement, *Psychological Monographs*, 20: 609.

Schoonmaker, A.N., 1969, *Anxiety and the Executive*. New York: The American Management Association.

Shapiro, J. and Stern, L., 1975, Job satisfaction: Male and female professional and non-professional workers, *Personnel Psychology*, 54: 388-89.

Spector, P.B., Dwyer, D.J., and Jex, S.M., (1988), Relation of job stressors to affective, health and performance outcomes: A comparison of multiple data sources. *Journal of Applied Psychology*, 73: 11-19.

Staines, G.L., 1980, Spillover versus compensation: A review of the literature on the relationship between work and non-work, *Human Relations*, 33: 111-29.

Torrance, E.P., 1965, *Mental Health and Constructive Behavior*, Belmont, Calif: Wadsworth.

Waldron, I., 1978, the coronary-prone behavior pattern, blood pressure, employment and socio-economic status in women, *Journal of Psychosomatic Research*, 22: 79-87.

Warr, P., and Parry, G., 1982, Paid employment and women's psychological well-being, *Psychological Bulletin*, 91: 498-516.

Weaver, C., 1974, Correlates of job satisfaction : Some evidence from the national surveys, *Academy of Management Journal*. 17: 373-75.

EIGHT

Stress and Burnout as Related to Social Support in Medical Professionals

NEELIMA MISRA

Stress as a source of emotional disturbance and psychological distress has attracted the attention of psychologists for quite a long time and is continuing to do so. Stress may be experienced due to stressors in the work setting which is termed as Work Stress, Job Stress or Organizational Role Stress. Stresses due to sources in non-work settings are described as family stress, life stress, non-work stress, or non-work role stress and life stress. Life stress may arise due to major changes in life events.

As noted by Thoits (1983), life events in themselves are no doubt stressful; they produce additional stress. For example, loss of spouse, which is a tragic life event, may force a widow to cope with a variety of daily hassles, e.g., reallocation of financial resources, single parenting, doing many household works which are outside the boundary of the house such as paying electricity or telephone bills or drawing money from bank. All these contribute to her life stress.

Stresses from work settings may influence the impact of non-work stressors on the individual and vice versa. Job performance and job satisfaction are to a great extent affected by experiences in non-work roles (Campbell et al., 1976). Similarly, role behaviour and satisfaction with regard to non-work roles is affected by experiences in work roles. For example, it is not uncommon to find that work stress of an executive has an adverse effect on his family life. We also observe that many non-work related factors can buffer work stressors. Piotrikowski and Katz (1983) reported that there exists a moderate positive correlation between positive moods at home and on the job.

Social support can influence stress experience and its consequences. Caplan (1976) has suggested that support systems may aid members to mobilize their psychological resources, master strain, share tasks and obtain necessary supplies such as information and skills. Cohen and Mokay (1984) stated that perceived support may serve as a stress buffer by influencing the individual's interpretation of stressors and knowledge of coping strategies.

Several reviews have shown the benefits of social support for psychological and physical health in the face of general life stress (Cobb, 1976; Dean and Lin, 1977; Kaplan, Casseik and Gore, 1977) and for occupational stress in particular (La-Rocce, House and French, 1980).

Gender difference in the effects of perceived social support have been reported by Etzion (1984), the relationship between work stress and burnout being moderated by support in life for women and support in work by men. Same evidence is extended by Clary and Kassler, (1982); Thoits, (1982); Holaban and Moss, (1985).

Burnout is one of the many dysfunctional consequences of stress. It is a natural consequence of stress in doctors as they are required to spend considerable time with troubled people and the exchanges commonly becoming charged with feelings of anger, embarrassment, frustration and fear of despair (Maslach and Jackson, 1981). The resulting chronic tension could be emotionally draining and this causes the professionals to feel "empty" and "burned out". High social support can reduce burn out directly by adding positive need fulfilling elements into one's life (Kaner, Kefry and Pines, 1978) or can buffer against stress and strain which becoming chronic may result in burnout.

With this background in this present study an attempt is made to see the relationship among stress, social support, and burnout in medical professionals.

Method

Sample

The observations made in this study are based on the partial data of three studies. Study 1 was conducted on 200 male allopathic doctors working in King George Medical College, Lucknow. Study 2 was conducted on another sample of male doctors from same Medical College and Study 3 was done on a sample of 50 doctor couples working in Government hospitals and maternity homes.

Tools

1. Organizational Role Stress (Udai Pareek, 1976).
2. Life Stress Questionnaire (Misra, 1991; modified by Pradhan, 1994).
3. Social Support Questionnaire (Sarason and Sarason, 1981).
4. Maslach Burnout Inventory (Maslach and Jackson, 1981).

Results and Discussions

Stress: The findings revealed that though the level of experienced organizational role stress does not exceed moderate level; role erosion, role stagnation, self role distance and inter-role distance were experienced to a much higher level than role ambiguity and role overload. Surti (1982) also found inter-role distance to be the most severe role stress in doctors as compared to other professional groups; probably because the doctor's role is a very specialized one and while playing multiple roles, the doctor experiences stress due to various expectations from different role senders which he might find difficult to fulfil. Long and uncertain working hours, rare vacations and poor working conditions in government hospitals hamper with meeting the demands of their multiple roles. However, stress measured in another sample of doctors was above average; stress experienced with regard to relationships to be somewhat more than stress due to factors related with personal growth and organizational policies and other structural variables.

One study focusing on gender differences showed that female

doctors experienced more stress in general as well as more work stress than their spouse who were in the same profession. These findings are explainable in terms of the spillover effect of non-work stress to work area for female doctors. Since the non-work roles are no less salient for them, stress experienced in those roles influences their experiences in work roles and work settings.

Apte (1984) observed that poor self-perceptions as a person as well as a spouse led to stress in both males and females.

Crouter (1984) contends that the extent to which an employee's family life influences his or her work life is in part determined by the individual's role as a family member. Moreover, the family to work influences are closely linked to family life cycle stages and the changing nature of the maternal role in the case of women. Women with young children find more difficulty in meeting work role demands than women with older children. Women with young children are at risk for perceiving the impact of family upon work as generally negative, primarily because their family responsibilities at times result in their being absent, tardy, inattentive, inefficient or unable to accept new responsibilities. This pattern seems to diminish for women with older children. In case of female doctors with young children, the possibility of being emotionally exhausted out due to chronic stress is much more than for those with older children.

Burnout: The feeling of being burnt out is generally low in male doctors. Lack of personal accomplishment was found to be experienced to a greater extent than the other two components of burnout, namely emotional exhaustion and depersonalization. Comparing these two, it was observed that depersonalization is felt in a lesser degree than emotional exhaustion.

Studies done in the west have provided evidence for high level of burnout in medical professionals. Thus, it seems that cultural variables play an important role in the development of the feelings of burnout.

Further, the study done on doctor couples examined gender differences in the experience of burnout. The findings revealed that female doctors experience moderate level of burnout, which is much higher in comparison to the burnout level obtained in male doctors. Further, some variation with regard to the level of the three components of burnout was also observed in the two sub-groups; females experienced both emotional exhaustion and lack of personal accomplishment to a greater extent than depersonalization while males experienced lack of personal accomplishment more than either emotional exhaustion or depersonalization. These findings suggest that role definitions for both male and female doctors differentially determine the outcomes of stress in medical professionals.

Maslach (1980) also reported that women tend to experience more emotional exhaustion and to experience it more intensely than men. She attributes this difference to the difference in sex roles. Women are more likely to become emotionally involved with people, so they run a greater risk of emotional exhaustion. Considerable anecdotal information exists suggesting that women are more compassionate than men. This explains males exhibiting more depersonalization as a consequence of chronic stress. Scott (1985) stated that female physicians communicated at higher level of empathy and respect with their patients than their male counterparts.

Stress and Burnout: Stress and burnout were found to have low positive but to be significant correlation and there was no gender difference in the relationship between the two variables. These findings are supportive of many previous studies done on different samples in the west. But it is worth mentioning that in male doctors both work stress and family stress were found to be related to burnout, while in female doctors only work stress was found to be related to it. This finding suggests that female doctors do not carry over their home stresses to work areas. Bolger et al (1989) also reported that home to work spillover is more evident in males as compared to females.

A worth mentioning finding is that though the difference was not statistically significant, higher magnitude of correlation coefficient was obtained between work stress and depersonalization in females than in males. It needs attention because it looks incongruent to the feminine image to become depersonalized in response to stress. A clue for explaining this was found when some female doctors were interviewed. They reported that in spite of their repeated attempts, patients were careless towards themselves. This might have developed feelings of depersonalization towards the clients. Maslach (1982) suggests that when clients do not provide for the fulfilment of the needs of the caregivers, the caregiver may become frustrated and this frustration is likely to be expressed in hostility towards the clients and may be accompanied by depression as well.

Two other studies on male allopathic doctors also bring out that stress results in the feelings of burnout. Additionally, various components of job stress or organizational role stress have different relationship with each of the three components of burnout. One study showed that role overload is related to all components, but other components or role stress relate differently with burnout.

Social Support, Stress and Burnout: In male doctors, in spite of small number of social support agents, the satisfaction with social support was found to be high. In both studies conducted on male doctors, number of social support agents was below average, but satisfaction with social support was much above average. Both the variables, number of agents and satisfaction with social support, were found to be negatively related with burnout and no gender difference was observed in the relationship.

The evidence regarding social support-stress relationship is equivocal. In one study, only satisfaction with social support was found to have a significant negative relationship with organizational role stress in the other study, no relationship was found between work stress and either the satisfaction level or number of social agents or satisfaction with social support. A probable reason for these findings may be that the measure of social support used in these studies was global; it did not measure obtained social support and satisfaction with it with regard to different kinds of stresses e.g. work stress or family stress. It may be added that some previous studies have also not found any relationship between stress and social support (House and Well, 1977).

However, in another study, spouse support satisfaction was found to be negatively related to life stress in male doctors, but not in female doctors. Thus, we can say that spouse support is more beneficial in reducing the stress experienced by men. Lee (1988) also found that among older married persons, men were more likely than women to name their spouses as confident and women perceive less emotional support in marriage than men. It is also possible that like black women (Brown and Gary, 1985), Indian women generally do not go to their husbands for support unless they face very serious problems.

Thus the findings suggest that social support satisfaction has different implications for stress experience and its outcomes. While it influences the stress experience on males and females differently, its effect on burnout, a consequence of chronic interpersonal stress in the work setting, is almost the same.

REFERENCES

Bolger, N. De Longis, A. Kessler, R.C., and Wethington, E., 1989, The contagion of stress across multiple roles, *Journal of Marriage and the Family*, 51: 175-83.

Brown, Diane R. and Lawrence E. Gary, 1985, Social Support network differentials among married and non-married black females, *Psychology of Women Quarterly*, 9: 229-41.

Campbell, A., Converse, P.E., and Prodgers, W.L., 1976, *The Quality of American Life; Perceptions, Evaluations, and Satisfactions*. New York: Russell Sage Foundation.

Campbell, A., Converse, P.E. and Rodgers, W.L., 1976, *The Quality of American life*. New York: Russell Sage Foundation.

Cobb, S., 1976, Social support as a mediator of life stress, *Psychosomatic Medicine*, 38: 300-14.

Cohen, S. and Mckay, G., 1984, Social Support, Stress and the Buffering Hypothesis, A theoretical analysis: In A. Baum J.E. Singer, S.E Taylor, Hillsdale, (eds.), *Handbook of Psychology and Health*. N.J.: Erlbaum.

Cleary, P.D. and Kessler, R.C., 1982, The estimation and interpretation of modified effect, *Journal of Health and Social Behaviour*, 23: 159-69.

Dean, A., Lin. N., 1977, The stress buffering and social support, *Journal of Nervous and Mental Diseases*, 165: 403-13.

Etzion, D., 1984, Moderating effect of social support on the stress-burnout relationship, *Journal of Applied Psychology*, Vol. 69, No. 4: 615-22.

Holahan, C.J., and Moos, R.H., 1985, (Sep.), Life stress and health personality, Coping and Family Support in Stress Resistance, *Journal of Personality and Social Psychology*, Vol. 49, No. 3.

Kanner, A., Kafry, D., and Pines, A., 1978, Conspicuous in its absence: The lack of positive conditions as a source of Stress. *Journal of Human Stress*, 4: 33-39.

Kaplan. B.H., Cassel, J.C., & Gore, S., 1977, Social support and health, *Medical Care*, 25 (S. Supplement): 47-88.

LaRacco, J.M., House, J.S. and French, J.R.P., Jr., 1980, Social Support, Occupational Stress, and Health, *Journal of Health and Social Behaviour*, 21: 202-18.

Lee, Gary R., 1938, Marital intimacy among older persons, The spouse is confident, *Journal of Family Issues*, 9: 273-84..

Maslach, C., and Jackson, S.E., 1981b, Maslach Burnout Inventory, Research Edition Manual, Palo Alto, California: Counseling Psychologist Press.

———, 1981a, The measurement of experienced burnout, *Journal of Occupational Behaviour*, 2: 99-113.

Maslach, C., 1982b, *Burnout: The cost of caring*. Englewood Cliffs, NJ: Prentice Hall.

Sarason, I.G., Levine, H.N., Basham, R.B. and Sarason, B.R., 1983, Assessing Social Support. The Social Support Questionnaire, *Journal of Personality and Social Psychology*, 44: 127-39.

Scott, D.E., 1985, Pediatricians interpersonal skills and parents satisfaction with the Medical Interview, Unpublished Dissertation, California School of Professional Psychology, Berkely.

Thoits, P.A., 1982, Conceptual Methodological and theoretical problems in studying social support as a buffer against life stress, *Journal of Health and Social Behaviour*, 23: 145-59.

NINE

Self-Management of Occupational Stress: Cognitive-Behavioural Approach

A.K. SRIVASTAVA

The concept of stress and research on stress have reached an all time peak in popularity during the past few years. The study of man's reactions to intense psychosocial stresses has became a major concern of psychological investigations in the present day world. It is evident from available literature and researches that frequency and severity of stress and its ill consequences are consistently increasing in every walk of life in modern societies. Consistent deterioration in psychological well-being of majority of people, increased rate of psychosomatic and mental diseases, and the general feeling of dissatisfaction in urban population reflects the adverse consequences of high stress being experienced by people.

People's working life where they actively spend about one-third of their daily routine seems to be a major source of satisfaction of their various social and psychological needs as well as stress and frustrations. It has also been empirically established that consistent and high job stress put significant impairing effect on employees' job behaviour, job attitudes, and physical as well as mental health corresponding serious cost to the organizations in human and monetary terms. Psychologists, psychiatrists and medical scientists are going on investigating and analysing the psychological and physiological ill consequences of high stress all over the world. But the alarming issue is — "how to effectively deal with this ever enlarging problem of 'high stress' "? Though stress has become an inevitable part of our social functioning, it may not be considered as totally uncontrollable and unmanageable. It can be prevented, dealt with, and effectively managed, to a considerable extent, through planned efforts. It has become a big responsibility on the part of organizational and clinical psychologists in collaboration of management scientists to evolve effective strategies for management of stress in organizational settings. It is a legitimate field of endeavour and is taking shape in response to the widely perceived need of urban societies. In view of its deleterious effects psychologists have systematically investigated the efficacy of numerous stress-reduction techniques. Though some techniques have been in practice for reducing or coping with adversities and challenges of life since long back, the field of stress-management has progressed substantially after Woolfolk and Lehrer (1984) published *Principles and Practice of Stress Management*, Stress researchers in India have also initiated working in this direction. However, 'yoga' and 'meditation' are being used as effective methods of stress-relief in our country since ancient times.

Stresses of working life can be conveniently managed, to a large extent, at different stages of its operation through various individual (cognitive-behavioural) and organizational interventions. These interventions may be made in the following order:

1. Prevention of stress through organizational interventions at management level, such as selection of suitable personnel, proper job designing, and training, adequate work conditions, effective supervision and incentive system, effective communication system participative management, etc.
2. Prevention or alleviation of job stresses through cognitive and behavioural interventions at individual employee level, such as proper, rational and optimistic cognitive appraisal and constellation of job-constituents and conditions as well as of personal (capability) and organizational resources, cognitive coping; systematic and unrashed performance of job activities, etc.

3. Minimizing the frequency and intensity of stressful situations integral to the job at organizational level.
4. Moderating the intensity of integral job stressors and their consequent strains through the effect of other variables of positive value, such as high or extra wages, non-financial incentives, social support, generating team-feeling, participative decision making, etc.
5. Active dealing with confronting stressing situations through effective coping strategies.
6. Adjusting with consequent strains and minimizing its long term ill-effects through cognitive i.e. rationalization, intellectualization, substitutions, diversion, reversal of effect, etc. and behavioural interventions.

Stressful circumstances do not take their toll from a passive individual, but from an individual who is imbuing stressful situations with personal meaning and struggling to control and master these circumstances. Stressors initially emerge in environment, and most of the time the focal person does not have any direct control over them. Yet, since the experience of stress is an outcome of the transaction between adverse environmental (social or physical) situations and the focal person, the individual, to a considerable extent, can prevent, mitigate or moderate the severity of the stress as well as its adverse effects through his cognitive restructuring of the stressors, cognitive coping and behavioural interventions at his own level. It would be the best and most convenient part of stress-management if the focal person himself could prevent or moderate his stresses and consequent strains by adopting certain specific cognitive and behavioural strategies without depending on others.

Cognitive Intervention

Since experience of stress is determined by the mediating psychological processes, at first stage, the individual can avoid the situations of stress at his cognitive level. It is because the actual stress experienced by the person is largely determined by his cognitive appraisal of the stressful situation. By developing specific patterns of perception and cognitive appraisal and restructuring of the stressful situations, employee can avoid or moderate the experience of job stress. Of course, for developing such stress-resistant cognitive patterns, the employee is initially required to develop some specific beliefs, values, attitudes and orientations as well as high self-control.

Integral to the employee's perception of job stress and reactions to it are his evaluation of the stress-situations, i.e. how he perceives the threat; and to what sources he attributes his feelings of being threatened. The intensity of stress is determined mainly by the appraisal of how much appears to be at stake in the transaction (in terms of values, motives or commitments) and the relative power of the environmental demand to do harm, compared with the power of the person to prevent or manage such harms. The threatening quality of the stressors can be manipulated by cognitive means. The focal employee restructures the stress-situations at work and its consequences after appraising them in the framework of his values, motivation, abilities and environmental resources. That is why same event or situation is perceived and reacted in different manner by different people, or even by the same person on different occasions. This basic principle of cognitive model of stress reactions can be elaborated as follows:

> One's cognitive structure of a situation is an active and continuing process that includes successive appraisal of the external situation, and the risks, costs, and gains of a particular response. When the individual's vital interests appear to be at stake, the cognitive process provides a highly selective conceptualization.

Depending upon the content of the cognitive constellation, the behavioural inclination may be a desire to flee, attack, approach or avoid.

In conceptualizing a particular event, the cognitive set influences the 'picture' obtained by an individual. Whether the mental image of the stress-situation is broad, skewed, or narrow, clear or blurred, acute or distorted, depends upon the characteristics of the existing cognitive set. These cognitive sets determine which aspects are to be magnified, minimized and excluded. The focal individual appraises the characteristics of the stress-situations and the nature of threat at this level of cognitive appraisal. At the same time that the nature of threat is being evaluated, the individual assesses his or her behavioural and environmental resources for dealing with it. This assessment aims to provide concrete information regarding the individual's coping mechanism and ability to absorb the impact of any assault. The final structure of the stress-situation is based on an equation that takes into account the amount and the probabilities of damage inherent in the threat as opposed to the individual's capacity to deal with it. The employee may be suggested to develop/ adopt, by self-behaviour modification, stress-resistant cognitive strategies, in order to avoid or moderate the severity of the stresses of their working life at their own level.

The employee can develop, through self-learning or training, the stress-resistant cognitive strategies to prevent, mitigate or effectively cope with the situations of job stress. Though it is a difficult task, yet not totally beyond the capability of the individual. Lazarus and his associates (1965) have suggested 'intellectualization'; 'rationalization'; 'isolation' and 'denial' as effective cognitive-coping strategies. Though 'denial' and 'isolation' may not be considered as very healthy coping strategies wherein the individual denies the stressfullness of the situation and adopts a detached attitude towards the situation of stress and threat, this cognitive strategy may be quite appropriate when the situation of stress is totally beyond the control and coping capacity of the focal person. The employees can adopt the following cognitive restructuring and cognitive-coping strategies to avoid or moderate the experience of job stress. Many of these coping strategies are the speciality of our Indian culture.

1. Consider difficult, adverse, or demanding job situations as inevitable parts of working life.
2. Perceive stressful job situation as a temporary phase of the job.
3. Try to rationalize the situation of stress and its consequences.
4. Try to see demanding situation as an opportunity to learn, develop new skills, and to enhance self-confidence.
5. Take the excessive job demands as a challenge.
6. Assess the severity of job stresses with reference to the others who are facing similar or more severe stresses in their jobs.
7. Think that time itself takes care of such situations. Positive attitude in life always helps to tackle the problems in critical situations.

8. Accept the situations of stress thinking that there is nothing you can do to change them.
9. Simultaneously think about the positive outcomes of successful dealing with the situation of stress.
10. Believe that every problem ultimately has some remedy.
11. Think that no one is totally free from stresses, though of different nature and severity.
12. Accept the situations of stress as realities of life.
13. Try to react with optimistic and positive affect to the hardships of job life.
14. Remind yourself that work is not everything. Try to give time to your family and friends. Social gathering should be an essential part of life.
15. Believe in *Geeta's* philosophy that "Your right is to do your job only, not to the fruit thereof." If you will not think about the fruit of your work, stress and tension cannot disturb you.
16. Accept the situations of stress as desire of God.
17. Have faith in God and His kindness.

Behaviour (Action) Intervention

Besides the cognitive-coping strategies the employee can develop certain temperamental qualities and adopt specific behaviour patterns or habit which could help in preventing, mitigating or effectively coping with the situations of job stress. Following is an inventory of some temperamental qualities, skills and behaviour patterns and habits, which can help employees, to a considerable extent, in preventing, minimizing, moderating and effectively coping with the stresses of job life at their own level. Though practice of some of these behavioural pattern is difficult, the employee can develop them through self-imposed behaviour modification method.

1. Increase self-esteem and the level of tolerance and patience.
2. Do not be rigid in your ways of functioning attitudes and decisions.
3. Recognize the potential sources of stress in your job.
4. Do things at work in planned and systematic manner.
5. Try to separate, and maintain coordination between your job and other roles.
6. Avoid doing many things simultaneously.

7. Set your priorities for job activities.
8. Do efficiently but avoid competitions.
9. Work on changing or modifying the style, methodology and policies which caused the situation or experience of stress.
10. Devote more time and energy to your job.
11. Discuss the problems with supervisor or/and other competent colleagues or superiors.
12. Try to maintain good relationship with your superiors, colleagues and subordinates, and have a few dependable friends.
13. Throw yourself into your job and work harder and sincerely.
14. Avoid time pressures and role overloading being regular and making proper distribution of the time for your job activities.
15. Avoid taking responsibilities or committing beyond your capability and resources.
16. Do not try to reach the perfection level in all routine job activities.
17. Do sincerely, but do not be over enthusiastic all the time in discharging your duties.
18. Frankly tell your limitations and inabilities.
19. Try to find out complete or durable solutions to the job related problems.
20. Try to nip the problems in the bud.
21. Be a realist. Aspire within the framework of your capabilities and resources.
22. Do not poke your nose in others' or irrelevant affairs.
23. Try to overlook rather than to react to the irritating situations or behaviour of people at work.
24. Before doing something, consider its all possible consequences.
25. If there is no way out, do your best to get out of the situation gracefully.

Besides the above cognitive-coping and behavioural intervention at work, the employee can use some off-the-job techniques to get relief from his job stresses, such as relaxation, yoga, meditation, biofeedback training, seeking company of good friends, attending sporting, cultural, religious events, listening music, watching favourite TV programmes, reading newspaper, magazines or books of your interest, avoid thinking, diversion of mind, etc.

Currently most of the writers on stress management refer to one of the three forms of stress management practice:

1. *Employees Assistance Programmes:* It has provisions for employees counselling services by an organization (Murphy, 1988).
2. *Stress Management Training:* The SMT includes training courses designed to provide employees with improved coping with their job stresses, skills, including training in techniques such as meditation, biofeedback, muscle relaxation and stress induction (Newton, 1992).
3. *Stress Reduction Interventions:* It includes interventions designed to change the level or form of job stressors experienced by employees, usually through job redesigning or work reform.

Among the variety of stress management techniques being practiced, the stress-resistant cognitive-behavioural strategies seem to be more convenient because the focal employee can adopt most of these strategies at his own level without seeking help or assistance from others. Since the stress is a very personal psychological experience, this psychological approach would prove to be more effective in avoiding, moderating or coping with the stresses of working life. Cognitive and behavioural strategies help each other in cyclic pattern (i.e. Cognitive restructuring - Behavioural intervention - Cognitive restructuring ......) in preventing and moderating the job stressors as well as experience and undesirable consequences of stresses.

REFERENCES

Lazarus, R.S., 1966, *Psychological Stress and the Coping Process*. New York: McGraw-Hill.

Murphy, L.R., 1988, Workplace interventions for stress reduction and prevention. In C.L. Cooper and R. Payne (eds.), *Causes, Coping and Consequences of Stress at Work*. Chichester: Wiley.

Newtan, T.J., 1992, Stress management in caring services. In C. Duncan (ed.), *The Evolution of Public Management: Concepts and Techniques for the 1990s*. Basingstoke: Macmillan.

Woolfolk, R.L. and Lahrer, P.M., 1984, *Principle and Practice of Stress Management*. New York: Guilford Press.

TEN

Exposure to Organic Solvents: Memory and Stress Reactions

BHAVANA GULATI *and* MUKTA RANI RASTOGI

The health status of an individual, a community or a nation is determined by the interplay and integration of two ecological universes: the internal environment of man himself and the external environment which surrounds him. When the environment around holds too much of toxic agents and the individual is in constant contact with them, it leads to disturb the delicate balance between man and his environment and it is injurious to human health and growth. Subsequently man's physical and psychological health is adversely affected by this imbalance, resulting in the performance also. Behavioural scientists, more specifically psychologists have taken cognizance of these adverse effects of toxic agents, and Behavioural Toxicology has emerged as a new discipline.

For the convenience, we have divided the present study into the following three sections.

Section I deals with Behavioural Toxicology, its historical perspective, the routes of administration of toxic agents, their post absorptive behaviours, their actions and the causes modifying their actions. It also deals with the classification of the toxins.

Section II illustrates the Organic Solvents, more specifically those used in dye-stuffs including their health effects, the chronic symptoms related to solvent exposure and their neurological and psychological evaluations.

Section III reports a study conducted on the workers exposed to dyes.

SECTION I

Behavioural Toxicology

During the past few years an increasing number of studies have been reported in which impairment of the nervous system's functional capacity during exposure to neurotoxic substances was assessed by means of behavioural performance tests while no overt signs of toxicity were present. As a result of these studies, a new field of occupational health research, known as Behavioural Toxicology, is rapidly developing (Gamberale, 1975).

A behaviour toxicity study aims to evaluate the neurotoxicity of a certain exposure agent, or to evaluate neurotoxic risks in certain working or living conditions with multiple exposures. Some of these studies may focus on more specific questions, such as the thresholds for the deleterious effects, the prognosis, or the neuropsychological description of the effects.

Interest in Behavioural Toxicology in the United States began in the part of the 1950's (Elkins, 1961; Smyth 1962), when the first volume of *Annual Reviews of Pharmacology* was published in 1960, it had a long report by Dews and Morse on Behavioural Pharmacology.

Behavioural Toxicological studies were initiated in the United States by Bernard Weiss and Laties in the late 1950's, while Helena Hanninen (1978) became the initiator in Europe. This domain of occupational health research took birth by the name of 'Toxicopsychology', which was later modified by the term 'Behavioural Toxicology' (Weiss, 1975).

Since its growth, it concerned itself with the consequences of "neurobehavioural toxicity" such as the functional disturbances of the nervous system ranging from neurometer and sensory deficits to the malfunction of the higher Central Nervous System (CNS) activities such as memory, learning, and emotional control and also the changes in the Autonomic Nervous System (ANS) and the failure of special senses. The term 'neurobehavioural toxicity' encompasses within its purview toxicity occurring due to chemical agents like pesticides, organophosphate insecticides, solvents, drug and alcohol, heavy metals, exhaust gases, and irritant vapours, and physical agents like noise vibration and heat.

Routes of Administration of Toxic Agents

According to Harte et al. (1991) toxins may enter into the body by various external and internal routes. The toxic agents, by and large act in three ways — Local Action, Inhalation and Ingestion. The ill-effects produced depends upon the duration of exposure, the quantum of exposure and individual susceptibility.

Local Action

The blood supply to the skin is one of the richest in the body. If a toxic substance can penetrate the outer skin layers, it will be rapidly transported throughout the body.

Some toxins cause dermatitis, eczema, ulcers and even cancer by primary irritant action; some cause dermatitis by allergic action. They can also cause acne type lesions, hair loss, lumps and bumps and pigmentation changes.

Inhalation

Inhalation normally regarded as the prime routes of uptake depends on several factors : concentration of toxins in the inhaled air, blood/air partition coefficient, alveolar ventilation rate, blood perfusion of the lungs, and duration of exposure. Toxins can be inhaled in the form of either dusts, or gases, or liquid aerosols. In many cases, the liver or the kidney is the target organ.

Particles smaller than three microns that are directly inhaled into the lungs and retained there are called respirable dust. The soluble dusts dissolve slowly enter the systemic circulation and are eventually eliminated by body metabolism. The insoluble dusts remain more or less permanently in the lungs.

Gases are sometimes classified as Simple Gases (e.g. Oxygen, Hydrogen), Asphyxiating Gases (e.g. Carbon Monoxide, Cyanide Gas, Sulphur Dioxide, Chlorine), and Anesthetic Gases (e.g. Chloroform, Ether, Trichlorethylene).

Ingestion

Ingestion of chemical substances such as lead, mercury, arsenic, zinc, chromium, cadmium, phosphorus, etc., may lead to toxic effects. Usually, these substances are swallowed in minute amounts through contaminated hands, food or cigarettes. Swallowed chemicals can be quickly or slowly absorbed, depending on the chemical and the state of the gastrointestinal tract (which depends on the time since the last meal). Toxic substances that damage liver are most dangerous when swallowed because they directly head to liver.

Post Absorptive Behaviour of Toxic Agents

Toxins once absorbed can be held within the body for variable periods of time. They may be held as much or after chemical or biochemical modifications. The latter called, Biotransformations, can result in detoxication of a toxin as likely as they can liberate toxic moities from an innocuous substance. Three processes limit the amount of potentially damaging chemical hitting the target organs at once. They are:

(i) Altering toxic chemicals into safe ones via metabolism;
(ii) Binding toxic materials to blood proteins so that they cannot cause immediate harm; and
(iii) Removing them from circulation by storing them in other body tissue.

Action of Toxic Agent

According to Modi (1988), the action of toxins may be local, remote, local and remote combined and general.

Local Action

The local action results from the direct action of toxin on the part and may cause corrosion as in case of strong mineral acids; irritation and inflammation, as in the case of cantharides and tartar emetic or certain nervous effects; for example, dilation of pupil by atropine.

Remote Action

The remote action results from the absorption of the toxin into the system. After absorption it may produce either specific or non-specific action. The specific action depends on the effects of the toxin on certain organs with which it has special affinity. As, for example, opium and its alkaloid act entirely on the cerebral cortex. Remote action may be seen localized to a definite area such as liver during the process of detoxication, for example, carbon tetrachloride; or kidney during excretion, for example, turpentine.

Certain toxins such as corrosives are capable of producing a remote non-specific action, such as shock, similar to that which often results from severe mechanical injury.

Combined Local and Remote Action

There are certain toxins which produce both local and remote actions. In such cases, while there is a destructive action on the local tissues, there is also a toxic effect after absorption. An example of this type of toxin is Oxalic Acid.

General Action

General action results when the absorption of the toxin evokes response from a wide variety of tissue beyond the limits of one or two systems, as, for example, arsenic, mercury, DDT, etc.

Causes Modifying the Action of Toxins

Apart from the different kinds of actions that the toxins produce in the body, there can be several causes that modify the action of these toxins. These may include the quantity, form and the mode of administration of the toxin and also the condition of the body of the individual.

The action of a toxin varies with the quantity of its dose. For instance, Oxalic Acid, when administered in a large dose produces a local corrosive action and may result in instantaneous death from shock, but a smaller quantity may prove, fatal by acting on the heart, while in still smaller quantity, it acts on the spinal nervous system and the brain.

Besides, toxins in the form of gases or vapours act at once and energetically. Toxins in the form of solids act very slowly because they are difficult to be absorbed. The action of toxin also depends upon the combination. Certain toxins which are almost insoluble in water may become dissolved in the acid secretion of the stomach, and then readily absorbed into blood.

A toxin acts more rapidly when inhaled in a gaseous or vaporous form or by introduction into the blood current or by application to an open wound. Next in rapidity is the action of a toxin which is applied to a serious surface, next when introduced into a cellular tissue and next when applied to a mucous membrane. The least rapid is the action of a poison applied to the unbroken skin case, a toxin dissolved in oil acts more rapidly than a water solution.

The conditions of the body such as age, allergy or hypersensitivity, genetic factors and idiosyncrasy, habit, tolerance and drug-dependence, drug-interactions, state of health, sleep and intoxication and other factors which may modify the action of toxins for instance. Poisons have greater effect at the two extremes of age because of slow inactivation and excretion of the poisons.

Classification of Toxins

No classification of toxins is entirely satisfactory, as many of them fall into more than one group. However, the classification given below according to the mode of action of poisons is the most commonly used (Modi, 1988) by the prominent psychologists and writers.

Systemic

Systemic poisons are those which have a deteriorating effect on the systems of body. This group consists of toxins as neurotics, cardiacs and asphyxiants.

Neurotics

Neurotic poisons are those which effect the nervous system of the individual. This sub-group includes cerebral, spinal and peripheral toxins:

Cerebral

Cerebral toxins are those which effect the brain or the cerebral cortex. These can be classified into the following three types:

Somniferous: It includes opium and its alkaloids and also barbiturate.

Inebriant: It includes alcohol, ether and chloroform.

Delirient: It includes Dhatura, Belladona, Hyoscyamus and Canabis Indica.

Spinal

Spinal toxins have deteriorating effect on the spinal cord of the individual. They include nuxvomica, and Gelsemium.

Peripheral

Peripheral toxins are those which effect the peripheral nerves. Such toxins are curare, conium, etc.

Cardiac and Vascular Poisons

Those poisons which have a bad effect on the heart and the blood vessels are the cardiac and vascular poisons respectively. These include Aconite, Digitalis, Oleander, Tobbaco, Hydrocyanic acid, etc.

Asphyxiants

Those poisons which effect the lungs are known as asphyxiants. These can be poisonous irrespirable gases, e.g. Carbon Dioxide, Carbon Monoxide, Coal gas, etc.

Corrosives

A corrosive toxin is simply a highly active irritant and not only produces inflammation but also actual ulceration of the tissues. This group consists of strong acids and alkalies they include the mineral acids such as sulphuric acid, nitric acid, hydrochloric acid; and organic acids such as oxalic acid, carbolic acid and acetic acid, salidyic acid; and vegetable acids as, for example Hydrocyanic acid; and concentrated alkalies, such as caustic soda, caustic potash, and carbonates of ammonium, sodium and potassium.

Irritants

Irritant toxins produce symptoms of pain in the abdomen, vomiting and purging. This group consists of mechanical, inorganic, and organic substances. Corrosives in dilute solutions act as irritants.

Mechanical

The mechanical sub-group includes powdered glass, chopped hair, dried sponge and diamond dust, etc.

Inorganic

The inorganic sub-group consists of non-metallic and metallic toxins. The non-metallic toxins include phosphorus, chlorine, bromine, iodine and boron. The metallic toxins include arsenic, antimony, mercury, copper, lead, zinc, silver, thallium, manganese, barium and other radioactive substances.

Organic

The organic sub-group consists of vegetable and animal poisons. The vegetable toxins include castor oil seeds, croton oil, *abrus precatorius*, colocynth, ergot, capsicum, marking nut, *madar, aloes, chitra, lal-chitra*, etc. The animal toxins include cantharides, snakes, scorpions, spiders, and other poisonous insects bites.

SECTION II

According to a Report on a Joint WHO/Nordic Council of Ministers Working Group (1985) Solvents are a group of chemicals that have many varied uses in industry and the home. The term Organic Solvents is a generic name for a group of chemical compounds or mixtures which are liquid in the temperature range of approximately 0 - 250 °C. They are volatile, and relatively chemically inert. Solvents are used industrially to extract, dissolve or suspend materials not soluble in water (e.g. fats, lipids, resins and polymers). Solvents are thus, hydrocarbons that are used to dissolve other hydrocarbons. Because solvents quickly evaporate and leave almost no residue, they are used to wash dust from precision electronic and machined parts. Solvents are also used to thin paints and glues, dryclean fabrics, and extract oils and waxes from impure materials. They are also used in many household products, dyes and drugs. Harte et al, (1991) are of the view that the most common solvents fall into five general categories. These are:

The Alcohols (such as methanol and isopropyl alcohol);

The Ketones (such as methyl, ethyl ketone and acetone);

The Aliphatic ("chain");

The Hydrocarbons (such as hexane), the aromatic ("ring") hydrocarbons (such as benzene, toluene, xylene), and finally the halogenated hydrocarbons (such as trichlorethylene, methylene chloride and CFCs).

Glycol Ethers and Acetates: Most solvents are hazardous; some are flammable, others explode easily, some are corrosive, and most are toxic. In general, the solvents that contain halogens (chlorine, flourine, bromine, and iodine) are less apt to catch fire, explode or corrode than non-halogenated organic solvents. Unfortunately, chlorinated solvents, like most other halogenated solvents, are toxic.

Chronic Symptoms Associated with Solvent Exposure

The symptoms reported in chronic toxic encephalopathy reflect a basic change in personality, developing gradually and affecting energy, intellect, emotion and motivation. The chronic symptoms reportedly associated with solvent exposure can be divided into characteristic or core symptoms and other commonly associated symptoms. In a previously healthy individual, personality change will be succeeded by the core symptoms and a variable number of other symptoms. If the individual has any pre-existing psychoneurotic traits, all the core symptoms may then assume more importance, especially if the social effect is comparable to those in an individual in whom all the core symptoms are present.

The core symptoms according to a Report on a Joint WHO/ Nordic Council of Ministers Working Group (1985) are fatigability, bad memory, difficulties in concentration, and loss of initiative. Among the other symptoms, the most frequent are depression, dysphoria, emotional liability, headache, irritability, paresthesia, sleep disturbances, and vertigo.

Morphological Changes in Human Beings

Well defined morphological changes are known to occur in only three solvent intoxications, namely hexacarbons, carbon disulfide and tetrachloroethylene. In a fourth, toluene, there is presumptive clinical evidence for structural damage at least to the cerebellum (Joint WHO/Nordic Council of Ministers Working Group 1985).

Out of these solvents, only toluene is the one used in dye stuffs. Long term intoxication of toluene in high doses has been associated with development of ataxia which, in several instances did not disappear even many months after cessation of exposure to toluene. Radiological evidence of cerebellar atrophy has been found, but pathological material is not available to confirm the occurrence of structural damage.

Experimental neurotoxicology has helped to clarify the mechanism of pathogenesis in occupational neuropathies due to carbon disulfide, hexacarbon ketones and hexane. However, many neurotoxins are relatively insensitive. This problem is due partly to the fact that the complexity and heterogeneity of the CNS cannot be denied as readily as that of other organs. Growing experimental evidence suggests that during long term exposure, organic solvents interact by modifying membrane and protein metabolism in ways that vary with different organic solvents.

Studies conducted in the Nordic Countries reveal that long term exposure to many different organic solvents result in irreversible changes in the nervous system, which are based on structural breakdown and cellular alterations. The biotropic interactions between different cell types of the nervous system are not fully understood especially with regard to chemical agents which interfere with normal function.

However, experimental evidence indicates that certain solvents could induce irreversible astrogliotic alterations, a sign of damage in some brain areas known to be sensitive, for instance, to chronic ethanol intake. Such cellular alterations could also be observed in human brain in senile dementia of different etiology.

Different solvents exhibit characteristic patterns or irreversible effects in different brain areas with various functions. Thus, experimental data show that several different brain functions associated with a district brain area could be affected upon exposure to organic solvent mixtures, irrespective of the way in which the various solvents interact.

Clinical Signs and Symptoms

According to a Report on a Joint WHO/Nordic Council of Ministers Working Group (1985), the most common symptoms associated with long-term exposure to organic solvents are increased fatigability, bad memory, concentration difficulties and personality changes (emotional liability, irritability, depression). However, other diffuse and non-specific symptoms may be at hand such as headache, dizziness and paresthesia. In the clinical examination, the neurological results are quite normal although tremor, disturbances of gait and station, and cerebellar and pyramidal signs may be seen. Psychometric tests empirically proven to be sensitive to diffuse organic brain damage, are used in clinical practice.

The expected clinical picture comprises signs of diffuse brain damage, with impairments particularly in perception, memory and psychomotor functions. Nerve conduction velocity has, in many cases, indicated an increased frequency at polyneuropathy.

Symptoms associated with solvent exposure may cover the entire range from mild to severe and should be considered as a part of a continuum. Most cases are mild and there is no agreement as to the extent to which the symptoms may remit once the patient is removed from exposure, but some improvement can occur. It is also not well-known whether or not the early symptoms of solvent intoxication are reliable predictors of chronic effects. Few data are available on exposure response relationships. In general, the probability of chronic symptoms developing is thought to relate to the length and extent of exposure although some individual variations in susceptibility occur. Since workers are usually exposed to several solvents simultaneously, few data are available on the toxicity of individual solvents. It is possible that any solvent can induce the symptoms.

Possible Progression of the Disease

When exposure is extended over a long period of time, the disease may progress in more susceptible subjects. Clinical experiences from the Nordic Countries (Report on a Joint WHO/ Nordic Council of Ministers Working Group 1985) indicate that symptoms and signs are more likely to be irreversible at this later stage. These signs will include some of the following:

- Impairment of higher nervous function such as memory, cognition, and emotion.
- Cerebellar signs (tremor, gait, station and coordination disturbances)
- Neuropathy (hypoflexia, sensory motor and automatic disturbances)

Predicting the course of the clinical picture on the basis of presence of acute intoxication is not yet possible. The longer the symptoms and signs persist after cessation of exposure, the less likely they are to be ultimately reversible.

Any symptom or sign that can impair daily life, personal well being or working capacity and that with a reasonable certainty, could be associated with solvent exposure, must be regarded as an adverse effect of the solvents.

Neurological Evaluation

The basic physiological mechanisms of solvent neurotoxicity are not fully understood but changing in neuronal metabolism, membrane properties, axoplasmic transport or transmitter functions are probable. However, each mechanism may differ for various solvents.

The earliest symptoms and signs may point to involvement of the CNS or PNS, but more commonly, both levels are involved and this association would strengthen the probability of the diagnosis. Therefore, the neurological examination should include tests of both CNS and PNS functions. The total clinical picture in terms of the diagnostic procedures would thus, emerge as shown in Figure 1.

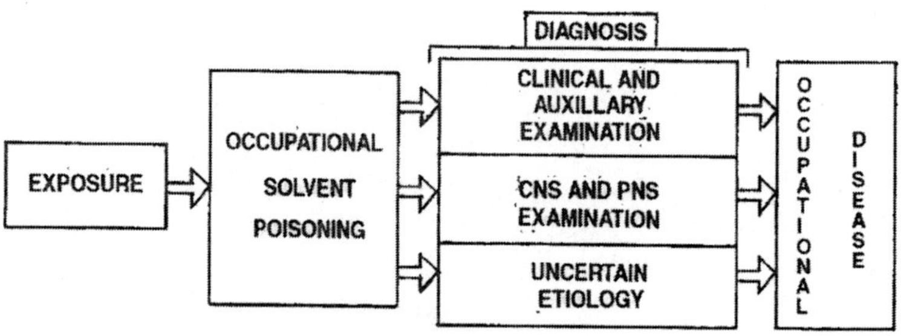

Fig. 1: CLINICAL PICTURE

While making an assessment of the deleterious effects of exposure to organic solvents at three levels, as depicted in Figure 1, it is important to take into consideration the evidence of exposure, the epidemiological data, the toxicological date, and the reliability of date obtained. The four factors are found to moderate the relationship between occupational solvent poisoning and occupational disease.

Other factors that should be considered on examination are alcohol (drinking habits); drugs (psychotropic, potentially neurotoxic and analgesics), food (nutritional deficiencies), chemicals (lead, mercury and other metals or chemicals in hobbies and work), diseases (differential diagnosis, present or earlier), trauma (head injuries), constitutional factors (hereditary or acquired), aging and socio-economic factors (nutrition, etc.).

In the present study, effects of organic solvents in the form of dye-stuffs have been investigated. Dye-stuffs are substances used to impart colour to textiles, leather, paper, etc. They are generally organic compounds containing conjugated double bonds. The group producing the colour is the Chromophore.

Chromophores are generally groups of atoms having delocalized electrons. The other non-coloured groups that insify the colour are called Auxochromes. Auxochromes are groups such as —OH and —NH_2; containing lone pairs of electrons that can be delocalized only with delocalized electrons of the chromophore (Backett, 1986).

Dyes can be classified according to the chemical structure of dye molecules. All these are given in Figure 2.

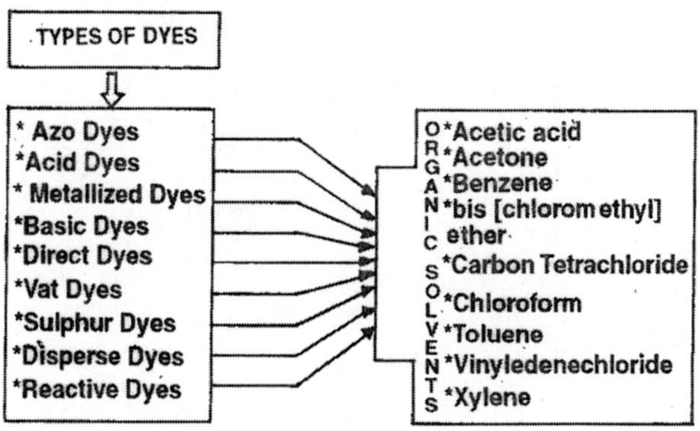

Fig. 2: Classification of dyes with organic solvents contained in them.

COMMON EFFECTS

* Severe irritation to eyes, skin, mucous membrane, throat and respiratory tract.
* Skin ulcers and cancers
* Dermatitis
* Depression of CNS [dizziness headache, weakness, nausea, cunvulsions, drowsiness, fatigue, loss of consciousness, vomiting, mental dulness, slowed respiration, confusion, insomnia, tremors, slowed reaction time, restlessness]
* Kidney damage
* liver damage

SPECIFIC EFFECTS

ACETIC ACID	ACETONE	BENZENE	BIS [CHROLO METHYL] ETHER	CARBON TETRA-CHLORIDE	CHLORO-FORM	TOLUENE	VINYLEDEN-ECHLORIDE	XYLENE
* Blackened skin * Bronchitis * Chronic sore throat * Tooth damage	* Drying and splitting of finger nails	* Pulmonary edema and haemorrhage * Aplastic anemia * Changes in production of WBC and RBC in bone marrow * Chromosomal aberrations * Leukemia	* Cancers of mucous membrane, skin, lungs * Edema * Pulmonary congestion * Eye damage * Reduced lung function * Cough * Difficulty in breathing * Coughing up of blood	* Loss of coordination * Abdominal pain and diarrhoea heart arrhythmias * Convulsions * Coma * Harmful changes in blood * Reduced visual field * Abnormal accumulation of fat in liver	* Dilation of pupils * Paralysis * Fatigue * Anorexia * Anemia * Blurred vision * Weakness * Memory Loss * Tremors * Enlarged liver * Jaundice * Kidney damage	* Confusion * Euphoria * Dilated pupils * Insomnia * Extreme light sensitivity * Skin irritation and malfunctions of the nerves that control movement * Irregular heart rate	* Liver and kidney damage * Cancer	* Coughing * Hoarseness * Pulmonary edema * Symptoms resembling drunkenness * Death caused by respiratory arrest * Sometimes stopping of heartbeat

SPECIFIC EFFECTS

FIG. III: COMMON AND SPECIFIC EFFECTS OF ORGANIC SOLVENTS USED IN DYES.

The organic solvents contained in dyes may have both common and specific effects of various types on human being. Figure 3 shows these effects of organic solvents used in dyes.

Some of these organic solvents have such intense effects that the International Agency for Research on Cancer classifies them as carcinogens. It is, however, always to be remembered that the severity of the solvents depends upon the amount and duration of exposure.

SECTION III

From the above discussion, it is evident that exposure to organic solvents is deleterious for the human beings in multiple ways. To investigate some of these deleterious effects, a study was conducted in the Dyeing and Printing Departments of the workshop of Gandhi Ashram, Barabanki (U.P.).

Purpose

The main objective of the study was to see the effect of exposure and its duration along with the prior exposure of the workers to organic solvents available in dyes on stress reactions of the workers and short term memory. Here, short term memory includes both auditory and visual memory. Since the reaction to any exposure depends upon the sensitivity of the individual, the environmental sensitivity was taken as a moderator variable.

Since organic solvents have a detrimental effect on both Peripheral and Central Nervous Systems, it was hypothesized that the exposed workers would show poor short term memory as compared to non-exposed workers.

Secondly, it was also assumed that exposed workers would show more stress reactions than non-exposed workers.

Finally, workers with longer duration of exposure and also with prior exposure would be more vulnerable to stress reactions and impaired memory.

Sample

The sample was divided into exposed and non-exposed groups to make a comparative study. The exposed group consisted of 19 workers from the dyeing department and 11 from the printing department,while the 30 workers of the non-exposed group were from the storekeeping department. The samples were matched on the basis of age, the mean age of the exposed group being 36.36 and that of non-exposed group being 36.53.

Variables

The following were the independent variables in the present study:

Exposure and its Duration

The exposed group in the present study was divided into four sub-groups in terms of duration of exposure. These include exposure from 0-5 years, 6-10 years, 11-15 years and 16-20 years.

Prior Exposure

This includes the engagement of the exposed group of workers in similar tasks of dyeing and printing prior to working in this particular workshop.

The Dependent Variables in the study were:

Stress Reactions

The stress reactions were studied in five aspects of the workers lives which include the physical, emotional, spiritual, mental and relational reactions.

Auditory Memory

Here memory refers to the short-term memory of the workers. This is the memory for the auditory information that has received minimal processing or interpretation.

Visual Memory

This is the memory for the visual information that has received minimal processing or interpretation.

The moderator variable in the present study was Environmental Sensitivity.

Tools

These include:

(i) Sensitivity Questionnaire developed by Rastogi and Tripathi (1995).

(ii) Stress Symptom Inventory by Ross and Altamaier (1944).

(iii) Digit Span Test and Visual Reproduction Test from Wechsters Memory Scale (1944).

RESULTS

Memory

First of all the effect of exposure to organic solvents on memory was examined for which mean memory scores (auditory and visual memory separately) were obtained for Exposed and Non-Exposed Groups, and the difference was tested by applying T-Test (Table I).

TABLE 1
DIFFERENCE IN AUDITORY AND VISUAL MEMORY BETWEEN EXPOSED AND NON-EXPOSED WORKERS

Memory	*Groups*	*Mean*	*S.D.*	*Mean Difference*	*t-value*	*p*
Visual Memory	Exposed groups	4.46	1.52			
	Non-exposed Group	4.83	1.47			
Auditory Memory	Exposed Group	2.6	1.47			
	Non-exposed Group	3.26	1.77			

As is evident from the table, the mean memory scores are more or less similar and the results do not yield any significant difference in memory between the exposed and non-exposed workers.

The study deals with the duration of exposure also. As reported earlier the exposed group was initially divided into four groups on the basis of duration of exposure, i.e., 0-5 years, 6-10 years, 11-20 years of duration. Due to presence of only two workers in the category of 0-5 years, the first two categories were merged to form one group of 0-10 years. For examining the effect of Duration of Exposure of Memory, analysis of variance was applied. The means are provided in Table 2.

TABLE 2
MEAN AUDITORY AND VISUAL MEMORY SCORES ACCORDING TO DURATION OF EXPOSURE

Duration of Exposure	*Mean Visual Memory*	*F-value*	*Mean Auditory Memory*	*F-Value*
0-10 years	4.08		2.91	
11-15 years	5.00	1.82*	2.18	0.69*
16-20 years	3.57		2.71	

*Statistically insignificant.

An analysis of the means of the three groups in terms of Visual Memory shows that the Mean Visual Memory of the third group of exposed workers whose duration of exposure is 16-20 is the lowest. Thus, although the ANOVA reveals no significant effect of duration of exposure on the visual memory, yet the trend of the means show that after a longer duration of exposure, the visual memory tends to be affected by the organic solvents.

In case of auditory memory on the other hand, neither the ANOVA nor the means show a significant effect of duration of exposure on auditory memory. Although several researchers have experimentally proved that the more the duration of exposure to organic solvents, the greater it impairs the short term memory of the workers (Johnson and Xintaras, 1985).

Besides seeing the effect of exposure and its duration, the effect of prior exposure was also examined on visual and auditory memory. For this, the exposed group was further sub-divided into two sub-groups, the previously exposed group and the previously non-exposed group. The mean memory scores (auditory and visual) for these two groups were obtained which are depicted in Table 3. The difference in mean scores between the two groups was tested through t-test.

A perusal of Table 3 reveals that prior exposure has cast a significant detrimental effect on both Visual Memory as well as Auditory Memory. Empirical Researches have already shown that the exposure and its duration does have a deleterious effect on the short term memory. As a result of the prior exposure, the duration of exposure to the toxins obviously increased. Hence, the hypothesis that the workers with an additional prior exposure along with the present duration of exposure will have a marked negative influence on their short term memories is confirmed.

TABLE 3
DIFFERENCE IN VISUAL AND AUDITORY MEMORY BETWEEN PREVIOUSLY EXPOSED AND PREVIOUSLY NON-EXPOSED GROUPS.

Memory	*Groups*	*Mean*	*S.D.*	*Mean Difference*	*t-value*	*p*
Visual Memory	Previously Exposed Group	3.82	1.34	1.02	3.67	<0.01
	Previously Non-exposed Group	4.84	1.49			
Auditory Memory	Previously Exposed Group	1.54	1.36	1.62	3.14	<0.01
	Previously Non-exposed Group	3.16	1.18			

It can be said that up to a certain period, the impairing effects remain at the subclinical level. The effects may begin to appear after some time because as a result of the prior exposure, the individual worker reaches to the extent that the exposure starts marginalizing the cognitive effects as such. Such effects should not be ignored as when they begin to appear, they may vehemently harm the worker.

Environmental sensitivity as a moderator variable is here, likely to moderate the effect of exposure to solvents as memory. Sensitivity always lowers down the threshold to respond. It was therefore, hypothesized that those workers who have a higher environmental sensitivity are more likely to be adversely affected by this exposure.

On the basis of an obtained median, the workers of the exposed group were divided into two groups namely, high sensitivity and low sensitivity. In order to test whether these groups significantly differed in terms of their Visual and Auditory Memories, t-tests were carried out (Table 4).

TABLE 4
MEAN AUDITORY AND VISUAL MEMORY SCORES ACCORDING TO ENVIRONMENTAL SENSITIVITY

Memory	*Groups*	*Mean*	*S.D.*	*Mean Diffe-rence*	*t-value*	*p*
Visual Memory	Low Sensitivity Group	4.86	1.31	0.8	1.503	>0.05
	High Sensitivity Group	4.06	1.61			
Auditory Memory	Low Sensitivity Group	3.0	1.36	0.8	1.547	>0.05
	High Sensitivity Group	2.2	1.47			

Looking at Table 4, it may be said that environmental sensitivity is bringing down the level of memory in terms of the mean visual and auditory memory scores. But, when tested statistically, the differences have not emerged significant.

Thus, summarizing the results pertaining to memory, it may be concluded that the duration of exposure, either in terms of length of exposure in the workshop or in the form of prior exposure added to the current exposure of the workers had proved to be highly detrimental to auditory and visual memory of the exposed workers.

Stress Reactions

The effects of exposure to organic solvents were studied on the stress reactions of the workers. Stress reactions include five areas, namely, physical, emotional, spiritual, mental and relational reactions. These areas were obtained for the exposed and non-exposed groups. To find out whether these groups significantly differed with regard to all the stress reactions manifested in their behaviour and personality, t-test was applied (Table 5).

TABLE 5
DIFFERENCE BETWEEN EXPOSED AND NON-EXPOSED GROUPS OF WORKERS REGARDING THIS STRESS REACTIONS

Memory	*Groups*	*Mean*	*S.D.*	*Mean Difference*	*t-value*	*p*
Visual Memory	Exposed Group	7.17	1.6			
	Non-exposed Group	4.66	1.5			
Emotional Reactions	Exposed Group	2.36	1.62			
	Non-exposed Group	1.16	1.1			
Spiritual Reactions	Exposed Group	1.13	1.12			
	Non-exposed Group	1.2	0.94			
Mental Reactions	Exposed Group	2.8	1.69			
	Non-exposed Group	2.4	1.68			
Relational Reactions	Exposed Group	1.36	1.25			
	Non-exposed Group	0.97	0.96			

As hypothesized, a marked difference was found to be prevalent in the physical and emotional reactions of the workers of the exposed and non-exposed groups. The exposed group showed far more strong and intense physical and emotional reactions than did the non-exposed group of workers.

As regards physical reactions, Brugnone et al. (1982) demonstrated the blood concentration of solvents in industrial exposure, and their physical manifestations. Over the last few years, samples were simultaneously collected of environmental air at breathing zone level, alveolar air and venous blood samples from industrial workers, both during the work shift and before they leave the work place. While measuring the concentration of industrial solvents in these samples, it was found in particular that both alveolar and blood concentrations correlated with the environmental concentration and with each other (Poerbellini and Brugnone, 1984).

Regarding emotional reactions a significant difference between the exposed and non-exposed workers is not unexpected. It is so because emotional reactions are always associated with the physical stress reactions. A big amount of literature in abnormal and clinical psychology has arrived to the conclusion that pathological behaviour is the resultant of physical stress, and emotional pathology results in physical pathology (Coleman, 1988).

Unlike the physical and emotional reactions, the two groups did not significantly differ regarding the spiritual, mental and relational reactions. In other words, the physical and emotional lives of the individual workers are more prominently influenced by the exposure to organic solvents than their spiritual, mental or relational lives. The reason for this could be that the physical and emotional reactions are much more prominent, manifest and salient aspects of ones life and therefore, the problems in these areas are perceived much more quickly as compared to the areas of mental, spiritual, and relational reactions. Also, data linking pollution and environmental stressors to physical and psychiatric health problems show that people tend to adapt to these stressors psychologically.

Also, the effect of duration of exposure on the stress reactions was analyzed. The scores of the workers lying in the three groups of 0-10 years, 11-15 years and 16-20 years regarding all the five areas of stress reactions were first obtained. Their respective means were then calculated and the data was subjected to analysis of variance. The results are provided in Table 6.

Thus, evaluating the effect of duration of exposure on stress reactions, it is seen that a significant effect is not evident on any of the reactions, although the means for each of them show an increasing trend along with an increase in the duration of exposure.

Several studies have, however, led to demonstrate that long term exposure does have a detrimental influence at least on the physical, emotional and mental aspect of the worker's life.

TABLE 6
MEAN STRESS REACTION SCORES ACCORDING TO DURATION OF EXPOSURE

Stress Reactions	*Duration of Exposure*	*Mean Scores*	*F-Value*
Physical Reactions	0-10 years	6.58	
	11-15 years	7.45	1.39*
	16-20 years	7.71	
Emotional Reactions	0-10 years	2.00	
	11-15 years	2.27	1.09*
	16-20 years	3.14	
Spiritual Reactions	0-10 years	0.92	
	11-15 years	1.27	0.344*
	16-20 years	1.28	
Mental Reactions	0-10 years	3.08	
	11-15 years	1.90	3.044*
	16-20 years	3.71	
Relational Reactions	0-10 years	1.41	
	11-15 years	1.81	0.107*
	16-20 years	1.42	

*Statistically insignificant.

Undoubtedly, duration of exposure effects on the reactions of stress and the effect of prior exposure of the worker (which obviously increases) on the stress reactions was also examined. For this, the mean scores of the two sub-groups of prior exposure for all the five types of stress reactions were calculated. The data was subjected to t-test to find out whether the two groups differed significantly with regard to stress reactions (Table 7).

Thus, the effect of prior exposure has not been found to be significant with regard to any of the stress reactions. Although studies have revealed that long term exposure to organic solvents leads to the psycho-organic syndrome (Bleular, 1966; Lindstrom, 1984) also demonstrated the behavioural effects of long term exposure to organic solvents.

Since environmental sensitivity tends to vary from person to person, one person may be very sensitive to a mild stressor, while another may show minimal or no sensitivity at all in relation to the same or even a more intense stressor.

TABLE 7
DIFFERENCE BETWEEN PREVIOUSLY EXPOSED AND PREVIOUSLY NON-EXPOSED GROUPS REGARDING THE STRESS REACTIONS

Memory	*Groups*	*Mean*	*S.D.*	*Mean Diffe-rence*	*t-value*	*p*
Physical Reactions	Previously Exposed Group	7.54	1.43	0.6	1.07	>0.05
	Previously Non-exposed Group	6.94	1.63			
Emotional Reactions	Previously Exposed Group	2.09	1.61	0.54	0.886	>0.05
	Previously Non-exposed Group	2.63	1.60			
Spiritual Reactions	Previously Exposed Group	1.18	1.05	0.13	0.33	>0.05
	Previously Non-exposed Group	1.05	1.09			
Mental Reactions	Previously Exposed Group	2.45	1.49	0.55	0.91	>0.05
	Previously Non-exposed Group	3.0	1.74			
Relational Reactions	Previously Exposed Group	1.27	1.404	0.15	0.597	>0.05
	Previously Non-exposed Group	1.42	1.17			

To see how environmental sensitivity moderates the effect of exposure to solvents on the stress reactions, the mean scores of the previously exposed and previously non-exposed group for all stress reactions were calculated and a t-test was applied to find out if they differed significantly in this regard (Table 8).

TABLE 8
MEAN STRESS REACTIONS OF THE LOW SENSITIVITY AND HIGH SENSITIVITY SUB-GROUPS (EXPOSED GROUP)

Memory	*Groups*	*Mean*	*S.D.*	*Mean Diffe-rence*	*t-value*	*p*
Physical Reactions	Low Sensitivity Group	7.13	1.58	0.07	0.13	>0.05
	High Sensitivity Group	7.2	1.51			
Emotional Reactions	Low Sensitivity Group	2.28	1.57	0.2	0.57	>0.05
	High Sensitivity Group	2.46	1.66			
Spiritual Reactions	Low Sensitivity Group	1.06	1.12	0.14	0.344	>0.05
	High Sensitivity Group	1.2	1.11			
Mental Reactions	Low Sensitivity Group	2.8	1.76	0	0	—
	High Sensitivity Group	2.8	1.6			
Relational Reactions	Low Sensitivity Group	3.05	1.79	0.49	0.74	>0.05
	High Sensitivity Group	3.54	1.69			

Thus, the two groups of high and low sensitivity (exposed group) in terms of the different stress reactions do not differ significantly. Taking the means in consideration, we see that the means of the high sensitivity group for each of the stress reactions, apart from that of mental reactions are greater than the means of low sensitivity group. In this relation, it can be said that a person who has a greater sensitivity towards the environmental stressors is obviously likely to express more of stress reactions than those who have lesser environmental sensitivity. There have been several studies which have dealt with high environmental sensitivity and its physical consequences, e.g., the environmental stressor of noise has been found to be associated with high blood pressure (Johnson and Hansson, 1977).

Thus, to summarize the results pertaining to stress reactions, it may be concluded that the exposed and non-exposed groups differ significantly only in terms of physical and emotional reactions. Also, duration of exposure, prior exposure and environmental sensitivity do not show any significant effect on the five stress reactions. Perhaps a longitudinal study in this direction would yield more reliable and significant results.

REFERENCES

Backet, A.H., 1986, *A Dictionary of Chemistry*, CBS Publishers and Distributors, pp. 100-101.

Bleular, E., 1966, *Lehrbuch de Psychiatrie Neẁdruch der 10 Aulfage*, Berlin: Springer Verlag.

Bnignone, F. et al., 1984, Blood concentration of solvents in industrial exposure. In *Toxicovigilance industrielle: Acteldu X Congres du Medichem*, Paris, pp. 165-68.

Elkins, H.B., 1961, Maximum Acceptable Concentration, *Arch. Environ. Health*, Vol. 2, pp. 25-49.

Gamberale, F., 1975, Behavioral Toxicology: A New Field of Job Health Research, *Ambio*, Vol. IV, No. 1, pp. 43-45.

Hanninen, H., Hernberg, S, Mantere P. et al., 1978, Psychological performance of subjects with low exposure to lead, *Journal of Occupational Medicine*, Vol. XX, pp. 240-55.

Harte, J., Holdren, C., Schneider, R., Shirley, C., 1991, *Toxics A to Z: A Guide to Everyday Pollution Hazards*.

Johnson, B. and Xintaras, C., 1985, *Prevention of neurotoxic disease in working populations*, Geneva: WHO.

Lindstrom, K. et al., 1984, Occupational solvent exposure and neuropsychiatric disorders, *Scandinavian Journal of Work, Environment and Health*, Vol. X, pp. 321-23.

Modi, J.P., 1988, *Medical Jurisprudence and Toxicology: Poisons and their Medico Legal Aspects*, N.M. Tripathi Pvt. Ltd.

Perbellini, L. and Brugnone, F., 1984, Occupational Exposure to n-hexane. Environmental and biological monitoring, International conference on organic solvent toxicity. Stockholm.

Rastogi, M.R. and Tripathi, J., 1995, *Sensitivity Questionnaire*, Department of Psychology, Lucknow University.

Ross, R.R. and Altmaier, E.M., 1994, *Intervention in Occupational Stress; Stress Symptom Inventory.*

Smyth, H.R., Jr. A., 1962, Toxicologists view of threshold limits, *Amer. Indust. Hyg. Assn. Jnl.* Vol. XXIII. pp. 41-44.

Wechsler, 1944, *Wechslers Memory Scale Digit Span Test, Visual Reproduction Test.*

Weiss, B., 1975, Behavioral Toxicology and environmental health science, *Amer. Psych.*, Vol. XXXVIII, pp. 1174-87.

WHO and Nordic Council of Ministers, 1985, Chronic effects of Organic Solvents on the Central Nervous System and Diagnostic Criteria.

Xintaras, C., Johnson, B.L., Groot, IDO, D., 1974, *Behavioral Toxicology: Early detection of occupational hazards*, National Technical Information Service, Springfield.

ELEVEN

Drug Abuse in Sports

AKBAR HUSAIN *and* JAOWAD ALI

Drug abuse in sports, of late, is beginning to assume alarming proportions. Often the declared winners are being stripped off their awards, bearing serious implications to sports in general, sportsperson's health in particular and above all the national honour of their respective countries. International Sports Organizations have provided statistics regarding the incidence and prevalence of drug abuse among athletes, with most of the data being derived from their respective urine drug screening programmes. Sports persons have been searching a path to get success, some legitimate ones, i.e., through the skill of sports and exercise physiology; and the others through the illegitimate use of performance enhancing drugs. Sports Sciences Research Foundation (1993) firmly believes that "drug abuse in sports threatens the safety, health and longevity of athletes while preventing the original intent of sports".

Death of Sportspersons

The first case of sports-related death due to the use of 'trimethyl' stimulant was reported in 1886. During the Olympic Games in St. Louis, Thomas Hicks, the winner of marathon, collapsed and died in 1904. He died as a consequence of using 'strychmine and brandy' which was feeded by his trainers (Todd,

1987). Danish cyclist Kurt Enemar Knud Jensen died after using a stimulant in 1960 in Rome Olympics. The cyclists Tommy Simpson and Yves Mottin died from 'amphetamines' in 1967 and 1968 respectively (Wadler & Hainline, 1989).

Soviet Union and other Soviet block countries were experiencing an excess premature deaths of their elite athletes (26 Olympic medalists) due to the use of 'anabolic steroids'. Harries (1985) and Rogol (1989) have opined that premature deaths may be a consequence of performance-enhancing drugs.

In 1987, an alarming number of deaths of the fittest and healthiest sportspersons of Belgium, Denmark, Holland, Sweden were reported. These deaths were limited to cycling and orienteering sports. Since 1987, 18 Dutch and Belgian amateur and professional cyclists have died unexpectedly (Escher & Maierhofer, 1992; Pena, 1991). Between 1989 and 1992, seven top Swedish orienteers suddenly died (Gnarpe et al., 1992; Marshall, 1992; Wesslen et al., 1992). In 1987, a 17 year old female orienteer died during competition (cf. Wadler, 1994). Between 1985 and 1987, three elite Norwegian males in their twenties died during practice sessions or competitions.

The evidence concerning the mortality among athletes suggests that drug abuse, and particularly blood doping or 'erythropoietin' (EPO) abuse, may have been a significant contributing factor.

Drugs of Abuse

Drugs of abuse have been categorized using various schemes such as the intent of the abuse, the legality of the abused drugs and the pharmacological properties of the drug. Wadler and Hainline (1989) classified abused drugs into three categories :

(i) Performance enhancing (ergogenic) drugs
(ii) Therapeutic drugs
(iii) Street/entertainment/pleasure drugs.

The present article discusses only the performance enhancing drugs which are widely abused by the athletes.

Motivation for Using Steroids

Sportspersons take anabolic androgenic steroids in order to :

(a) improve performance

(b) increase muscles and strength
(c) increase competitiveness
(d) develop stamina for longer duration
(e) promote the quality of training
(f) alleviate stress, tension, anxiety, etc.

Anabolic Androgenic Steroids (AAS) and its Side Effects

The AAS used by sportspersons are a group of powerful natural or synthetic compounds similar to male hormone (testosterone). Androgenic steroids promote the development of male characteristics while anabolic steroids stimulate the build up of muscle tissues and also enhance the development of secondary sexual characteristics in males. In the females, these drugs have masculinizing effects. The earliest reference dates back to the mid 1950's, when the Russian male and female world class athletes abused anabolic androgenic steroids (Wadler & Hainline, 1989). Anabolic androgenic steroids are mainly used in those sports which call for power and endurance, for example, in sprints, distance races, shot-put, javelin, discus, hammer throw, weightlifting, swimming, cycling, wrestling and in recent years in tennis, football, volleyball, basketball and so on.

Since 1994, the International Olympic Committee has banned the following AAS.

Anabolic Androgenic Steroids

Chemical Name	*Indian Trade Name*
(a) Bolasterone	-
(b) Boladenone	-
(c) Clostebol	-
(d) Dehydrochlomethyl Testosterone	-
(e) Fluoxymesterone	-
(f) Mesterone	Provironum*
(g) Methadienone	Hembol*
(h) Metenolone	-
(i) Methytestosterone	Mixogen**
(j) Nandrolone	Biodebol, Bionabolin, Deca-durabolin, Decaneurabol**,

		Docabolin, Durabolin*, Durapolon, Evabolin, Grothic**, Metabol**, Metadec**, Neurabol*.
(k)	Norenthandrolone	Orabolin*
(l)	Oxandrolone	-
(m)	Oxymesterone	-
(n)	Oxymetholone	Adroyd*
(o)	Stanzolol	Menabol, Neurabol Caps*, Stromoa*
(p)	Testosterone	Acquaviron**, Mixogen*, Nuvir*, Sustanon**, Testanon**, Testoviron**, Testoviron Depot**.

And related compounds.

Other Anabolic Agents

Beta-2 Agonists	Clenbuterol Salbutemol

* Available in tablet or capsule form.

** Available in injection form.

The most pervasive form of androgen abuse is by male athletes in the expectation that muscle development and athletic performance will be improved. Adequately controlled studies, however, suggest that androgens do not improve performance consistently.

The physician of US weightlifting team, Dr. John Zigler, recognized the strength-enhancing properties of testosterone in the mid 1950's. The Ciba Pharmaceutical Company in 1958 introduced 'methandrostenolone' and 'dianabol', to the US market in order to minimize the undesirable effects of anabolic androgenic steroids. There are, probably no synthetic steroids in which the androgenic properties have been completely dissociated from the anabolic properties (Council on Scientific Affairs, 1990). Some synthetic steroids, however, present a partial dissociation between the two properties, possibly as a result of differences in the metabolism of these drugs (Celotti & Negri, 1992).

Androgenic anabolic steroids abuse have become a part of the bodybuilder's and weightlifter's subculture in gymnastics throughout the United States. They are taken orally and through deep intramuscular injection. Those that are orally effective have had their 17-α hydroxyl group alkyloted to slow their removal by the liver. In contrast, those that are administered intramuscularly have had their 17-β hydroxyl group esterified so as to slow their release into the circulation.

Wadler (1994) posits that the adverse effects of AAS abuse can broadly be divided into four categories: (1) effects on secondary sex characteristics and related hormonal functions; (2) effects on somatic tissues, including thrombogenesis and tumour production; (3) effects related to drug adulteration, including infectious diseases, specifically hepatitis B and HIV infection; and (4) effects on behaviour and mental health, including the development of dependency.

Such drugs have harmful effects if taken for longer duration. Numerous studies have been published supporting both improvement in strength (Ariel, 1973; Berg and Keul, 1974; Harvey, et al., 1981; Stamford and Mofott, 1974; Ward, 1973) as well as nonsignificant improvement in strength of male athletes (Harvey, 1975; Johnson, et al., 1975; Loughton and Ruhline, 1977; Stromme, et al., 1974). A review published by the American College of Sports Medicine (1977) concluded that there is no scientific evidence that large doses of AAS either aid or hinder athletic performance.

With prolonged use of anabolic steroids, the sportspersons can develop liver cancer, kidney dysfunction, kidney tumours, blood filled cysts in liver, vomiting of blood, unexplained weight loss and purple or red coloured spots on the body. Its use also increases the risk of muscle ruptures, tears and number of stress fractures. These effects are made worse by 'stackin' (several types of anabolic steroids being taken simultaneously), 'cycling' (alternating the use of several types of androgenic anabolic steroids) and frequently using high doses, and prolonged duration of its use.

Some effects appear in males while the others in females. Males develop features like acne, hepatocellular carcinoma, increased aggressiveness and sexual apetite, testicular atrophy, infertility, premature baldness, enlargement of prostate glands, prostatitis soreness. Females develop features like males, menstrual irregularities, enlarged clitoris, baldness, shrinking of breasts, infertility, etc. (Mac Dougall, 1983; Overly, et al., 1984; Pande and Gupta, 1987).

For the sportspersons, the use of AAS can lead to decline in physical health and can possibly lead to premature death. The use of performance enhancing drugs, not only affect the user but every one around them — the family, the teammates, the trainers or coaches, and the sports doctors.

Human Growth Hormone (hGH) and its Side Effects

Human growth hormone samatotropin, is a naturally occurring polypetide hormone produced by the pituitary gland. It is an integral part of a complex system involving many organs, neurotransmitters (e.g. dopamine and serotonin), and hormones e.g., growth hormone — releasing hormone and samatotropin — release inhibiting hormone (Rogol, 1989). A major function of hGH is the maintenance of normal linear growth velocity from birth until the attainment of adult height, with its most apparent effects occurring during adolescence (Shulman, et al., 1999).

hGH is commonly used by body-builders and athletes (Cowart, 1990). According to the General Accounting Office, the quantities of hGH used in sports have been much less than that of AAS.

Wadler (1994) has suggested the following reasons for the popularity of bioengineered hGH.

1. Widespread drug testing for anabolic androgenic steroids, many athletes think that growth hormone used will give them the sought-after effects of steroids without being detected. Currently no reliable method is available to detect hGH by means of urine testing.
2. Some abusers believe that the desired effects attributed to AAS can be obtained without any of the adverse effects of steroid abuse.
3. Some adolescents believe that growth hormone can artificially increase their physical stature, specifically their height.

Growth hormone is both anabolic and liplytic. Well controlled studies have failed to demonstrate actual improvements in strength or endurance as a consequence of its use (Rogol, 1988; Smith and Perry, 1992; Yarasneski, et al., 1992). This is not surprising because the muscles of acromegolic patients are myopathic (Nagulesparen, et al., 1976).

Erythropoietin and its Side Effects

Laboratory studies have suggested that when an athlete's total haemoglobin is increased by 10 per cent to 20 per cent there is a concomitant improvement in maximal oxygen consumption and endurance performance. Athletes have used various ways to increase their total haemoglobin levels (Spriet, 1991), and to increase the number of oxygen carrying red blood cells in their blood circulations. They have utilized physiologic methods such as training at high altitudes to stimulate the production of red blood cells physiologically in response to lower ambient oxygen levels. Illegal and dangerous methods, such as blood doping and more recently genetically engineered EPO, have also been used.

Blood doping refers to the practice of intravenously infusing autologous blood into an individual to raise haemoglobin. Normally two units of blood are taken and frozen for the length of time it takes for the body to regenerate one's red blood cells to baseline levels, generally from 4 to 8 weeks. The red cells are isolated and stored in a frozen state. Meanwhile, the athlete continues to train at full aerobic capacity. Several days before a competition, the stored red cells are thawed and reinfused into the athlete, leaving the athlete with a supernormal quantity of oxygen-carrying red blood cells. Blood doping or EPO abuse may have contributed to the excess mortality. This is because there is no test for EPO abuse at postmortem examination.

Synthetic EPO (rEPO) has been widely used by the athletes as an alternative to blood doping despite a paucity of studies on the effect of rEPO on athletic performance (Cowart, 1990; Eichner, 1990; Wright and Cowart, 1990). Spence (1990) reported that the marathoners administered rEPO had a staggering 10 per cent increase in endurance during a 6-week test. Ekblom and Berglund's (1991) study was the first to assess the effect of rEPO on maximal aerobic power (Vo_2 max) in healthy males. When the results of these studies were compared with the effects that blood doping had on Vo_2 max of the same subjects, it was concluded that the effects of rEPO and blood doping were similar.

The abuse of rEPO by athletes poses a serious health hazard. Its abuse raises the hematocrit in a linear fashion and with it the viscosity of the blood. Self-induced erythrocythenia develops because of increase in viscosity. At hematocritic above 60 per cent the blood viscosity increases exponentially, thereby substantially increasing the risk of coronary or cerebral artery occlusions. The abuse of rEPO carries with it the risk of hepatitis, HIV infection, and other infections associated with the use of unsterile needles and shared injectible drugs (Wadler, 1994).

Clenbuterol and its Side Effects

Stimulants were first used by Gladiators as early as 600 BC to overcome fatigue (Wadler & Hainline, 1989). In sports, stimulants include a variety of drugs: psychomotor stimulants and the central nervous system stimulants (e.g. amphetamines, cocaine, caffeine, and nicotine) and the sympathomimetic amines (e.g., ephedrine, pseudoehedrine, phenylephrine, and phenylpropanolamine).

Presently athletes use stimulants to reduce fatigue, increase reaction time, increase alertness and wakefulness, increase concentration, decrease sensitivity to pain, improve endurance, increase competitiveness, and prevent or treat asthma.

In 1992 Barcelona Olympics Clenbuterol, a β_2 — agonist was being used by athletes to promote muscle growth. Clenbuterol has the ability to increase markedly the amount of lean mass and decrease the amount of fat produced per pound of feed. It is a nutrient partitioning agent. Clenbuterol has the ability to stimulate protein deposition in satiated muscle by as much as 20 per cent while simultaneously, through its thermogenic properties, reducing muscle glycogen and body fat deposition by 20 per cent (Lancet, 1992). Its lipolytic effect is not uniform throughout the body's fat depots.

Clenbuterol is almost completely absorbed when taken orally and has a half-life of approximately 27 hours, clearing the system almost completely in less than five days (Couet, et al., 1989). Salbutamol, a β_2 - agonist has a half-life of only 3 to 6 hours (Palmer, et al., 1992). The International Olympic Committee (IOC) continues to ban the oral use of these β_2 - agonist drugs.

Beckett (1992) has cautioned that the abuse of β_2 - agonists is rapidly increasing. "Action should be taken, but only after careful thought and definition of rules clearly stating what is banned and what is not and due consideration of the medical implications of the ban".

Guidelines for Sportspersons, Professional Workers and Sports Bodies

Considering the importance of drug abuse in sports it is necessary to develop awareness among sports persons about the performance enhancing drugs and their physical and psychological effects. The dope control experts, i.e., physicians, physical instructors, or educationists, physiotherapists, sports psychologists should have a list of anabolic steroids prohibited by the International Olympic Committee 1994.

Sports persons should not take any medicine without consulting his/her team doctor or physician. If the physician is not aware of the list of banned drugs, no drug should be prescribed unless it has been approved by some competent authority.

All bodies of sports should determine the normative values for haemoglobin and hematocrit levels in endurance athletes and the concept of blood doping would have to be accepted in those sports that are at risk for blood doping or rEPO abuse.

Dope control experts should develop awareness among sports persons about the legal sanctions imposed by the IOC for steroids: (1) Two-year ban for the first offence; (2) Life ban for second offence. Over a 6-1 ratio of testosterone to epitestosterone is considered illegal under doping guidelines set by IOC. Awareness about these legal sanctions will not only refrain the sportspersons from using the steroids, rather it will also help the doctors in prescribing the banned anabolic steroids.

It has been brought to light that sports persons are often advised by trainers and coaches to use the drugs. There is a need for strong sanctions or penalties against coaches, trainers and team doctors who assist sportspersons to take performance-enhancing drugs.

The professional experts, i.e., sports scientists, psychologists and physician have to play a vital role in minimizing drug abuse among sports persons. They have to teach the athletes that banned drugs adversely affect the physical and mental health of the individual and consequently cannot enhance performance. Thus they should make the athletes realize that the physical energy is inherent in their bodies and they should develop the 'will power' to avoid drug abuse. Sports scientists should prepare a broad based curriculum including preparation of nutritious diet for the athletes, physical disorders among them and a strategy to rehabilitate drug abusers. Milkha Singh, the flying Sikh says, "My record has stood since 1960. Despite the use of drugs, present athletes have not come anywhere near my record. I improved due to sheer hard work and dedication, on an ordinary diet. Drug taking will prove ruinous to our athletes."

Sports persons should devote at least one hour a day to perform yoga exercises. These exercises can improve one's performance and psychological well-being for the remaining 23 hours of a day. Focussing on sports or exercise activity may help one to cope with the stress that may have been generated in one's life.

Another innovative strategy would be to develop awareness among the masses against the drug abuse. Students in schools and colleges may be made aware about the bad influences of drug abuse. National and international sports association should be associated in this regard. Poster campaign should be launched and interesting posters should be displayed at public places and in the educational institutions. Also on the occasion of organizing sport's days an oath should be administered to the young to resist the use of banned drugs.

The Sports Authority of India should organize orientation courses for the coaches, trainers and managers of teams to avoid drug abuse. Such programmes should be organized in different parts of the country and intensive training should be imparted to the target group.

Conclusion

It is advisable for the sports persons that a gold medal should be achieved through physical fitness with locus of effort and dedication to perform well and not to take the help of illicit drugs. Winning a gold medal or any prize in sports is a matter of honour to the country, community as well as the individual. Honour has to be achieved through honourable means and not through dubious means such as drug abuse.

REFERENCES

American College of Sports Medicine, 1977, Position statement of the use and abuse of androgenic steroids in sports, *Medicine and Science of Sports*, 9, XI-XIII.

Ariel, G., 1973, The effect of anabolic steroid upon skeletal muscle contractile force, *Journal of Sports Medicine and Physical Fitness*, 13: 187-90.

Beckett, A.H., 1992, Clenbuterol and sport (Letter), *Lancet*, 340: 1165.

Berg, A. and Keul, J., 1974, Der Einfluss von anabolen substanzen auf das verhalten der freien serumaminosauren von normal person and scwerathteten in rule and bei korperarbeit, *Oester Z Sports Medicine*, 4: 11-18.

Celloti, F. and Negri, C.P., 1992, Anabolic steroids: A review of their effects on the muscles, of their possible mechanisms of action and their use in athletics, *Journal of Steroid Biochemical Molecular Biology*, 43: 469.

Couet, W., Girault, J., Reigner, B.G. et al., 1989, Steady-state bio-availability and pharmacokinetics of ambroxol and clenbuterol administered alone and combined in a new oral formulation, *International Journal of Clinical Pharmacology Ther Tox*, 27: 467.

Council on Scientific Affairs, 1990, Medical and nonmedical uses of anabolic-androgenic steroids, *JAMA*, 264: 2923.

Cowart, V.S., 1980, Blunting "steroid epidemic" requires alternatives, innovative education, JAMA, 264: 1641.

Eichner, E.R., 1990, Sports hematology, Presented at the Annual Meeting of the American College of Sports Medicine, Salt Lake City.

Ekblom, B. and Berglund, B., 1991, Effect of erythropoietin administration on maximal aerobic power, *Scandinavian Journal of Medical Science Sports*, 1: 88-93.

Escher, S. and Maierhofer, W.J., 1992, Erythropoietin and endurance: A recipe for disaster, *Your Patient and Fitness*, 6: 15.

Gnarpe, H., Gnarpe, J., Sundelof, B., et al., 1992, Prevalence of specific antibodies to Chalmydia Pneumoniae (TWAR) in Swedish orienteers *Lancet*, 340: 1047.

Harries, M., 1985, Death of athletes, *BMJ*, 290: 656.

Hervey, G.R., 1975, Are athletes wrong about anabolic steroids? *British Journal of Sports Medicine*: 74-77.

Hervey, G.R., Kribbs, A.V., Burkinshaw, L., et al., 1981, Effects of methandienone on the performance and body composition of men undergoing athletic training, *Clinical Science*, 60: 457-61.

Johnson, L.D., Roundy, E.S., Allsen, P.E., et al., 1975, Effects of anabolic steroid treatment on endurance, *Medicine Science Sports*, 7: 287-89.

Loughton, B.V. and Ruhline, R.D., 1977, Human strength and endurance responses to anabolic steroids and training, *Journal of Sports Medicine and Physical Fitness*, 17: 285-96.

MacDougall, D., 1983, Anabolic steroids, *Physical Sports Medicine*, 11: 95-99.

Marshall, A. (1982), Mystery death of orienteers, *The Independent*, Nov. 15, (Copyright: Newspaper Publishing PLC).

Muscling in on clenbutrol, (Editorial), *Lancet*, 340: 403, 1992.

Nagulesparen, M., Trickey, R., Davies, M.J., et al., 1976, Muscle changes in acromegaly, *BMJ*, 2: 914.

Overly, W.L., Dankoff, J.A. Wang, B.K., et al., 1984, Androgens and hepatocellular carcinoma in an athlete, *Annual Internal Medicine*, 100: 158.

Palmer, J.B.D., Shepherd, G.L., Cifelli, A.T., 1992, Muscling in on Salbutamol (Letter), *Lancet*, 340: 1407.

Pande, P.K. and Gupta L.C., 1987, *Outline of Sports Medicine*, New Delhi: Jaypee Brothers.

Pena, N., 1991, Lethal injection, *Bicycling*, 32: 80-81.

Rogol, A., 1989, Growth hormone: Physiology, therapeutic use, and potential for abuse, *Excerpts of Sports Science Review*, 17: 353.

Shulman, L., Miller, J.L. and Rose, L.I., 1990, Growth hormone therapy, *Am Fam Pract*, 41: 1541.

Smith, D.A. and Perry, P.J., 1992, The efficiency of ergogenic agents in athletic competition, Part I: Anabolic-androgenic steroids, *Ann. Pharmacother*, 26: 520.

Spence, M., 1990, Doctors concerned about side effects of chemical erythropoietin, *The Olympian*, p. 61.

Sports Science Research Foundation, 1993, New Delhi.

Spriet, L.L., 1991, Blood doping and oxygen transport, In D.H. Lamb., and M.H. Williams (eds.), *Perspectives in Sports Medicine*, Vol. 4, Ergogenics - Enhancement of performance in exercise and sport, Indianapolis: Brown & Benchmark, p. 213.

Stamford, B.A. and Moffatt, R., 1974, Anabolic steroid effectiveness as an energetic aid to experienced weight trainers, *Journal of Sports Medicine and Physical Fitness*, 14: 191-97.

Stromme, S.B., Meen, H.D. and Aakvaag. A., 1974, Effects of an androgenicanabolic steroid on strength development and plasma testosterone levels in normal males, *Medicine Science Sports*, 6: 203-208.

Todd, T., 1987, Anabolic steroids: The gremlins of sport, *Journal of Sport History*, 14: 87.

Wadler, G.I., 1994, Drug use update, *Sports Medicine*, 78: 439-55.

Wadler, G. and Hainline, B., 1989, Drug testing, In *Drugs and the Athlete*, p. 195, Philadelphia: FA Davis.

———, Introduction, In *Drugs and the Athlete*, p. 3, Philadelphia: FA Davis.

Ward, P., 1973, The effect of an anabolic steroid on lean body mass, *Medicine Science Sports*. 5: 227-82.

Wesslen, L., Pahlson, C., Friman, G., et al., 1992, Myocarditis caused by Chlamydia pneumoniae (TWAR) and sudden unexpected death in a Swedish orienteer, *Lancet*, 340: 427.

Wright, J.F. and Cowart, V.S., 1990, Performance enhancement, In *Anabolic Steroids: Altered States*, p. 159, Carmel: Benchmark Press.

Yarasneski, K.E., Campbell, J.A., Smith, K., et al., 1992, Effect of growth hormone and resistance exercise on muscle growth in young men, *American Journal of Physiology*, 262: E261.

TWELVE

Elderly as Target Group for Human Resource Development

AKBAR HUSAIN

After independence, India has rapidly progressed in all the sectors, i.e. agriculture, science, technology, economic, industry, atomic energy, etc. The population has also been recording a very rapid growth. As per 1991 census, India has a population of 846.3 million. A large chunk of this population is of elderly people whose number is swelling with the availability of better medical care. The development of any country or society is mainly based on the people's capabilities, skills, facilities and quality of life. The basic necessity of a society or group is to have the improvements in education, housing, health care facilities, employment and technology for the well-being of its members.

Human resource development (HRD) has been a topic of speculation and investigation in recent years. Human resource, which includes men, women and children, is one of the real wealths of a country. Rao (1996) has pointed out that the world is facing two major developmental challenges: "To ensure the fruits of development should reach the most needy through equitable distribution of resources, opportunities" and "to develop human capabilities and address the challenges of development — political, economic and social." Few centuries have reached the level of success in achieving these challenges and "have demonstrated the importance of investing in developing people and improving their quality of life through the adoption of human resource development strategies" (Rao, 1996).

A few years back the Government of India recognized the significance of HRD and renamed the Ministry of Education as the Ministry of 'Human Resource Development' (HRD). This has led to the establishment of HRD divisions in almost every governmental and non-governmental organizations. The indicators and dimensions of HRD for a particular organization may vary, but the focus is uniform.

Life span expectancy has increased, the infant mortality has been greatly reduced due to the proper health care programmes and awareness about health among the masses. The increasing number of elderly people in the population is placing a growing burden upon the health care and social services in institutionalized homes. Various solutions have been proposed and an emphasis is being placed upon providing services or care to the elderly.

The present study is an attempt to provide insights into the role of elderly in HRD priorities for improving the quality of life of people through education, health care, rural development and voluntary services.

Theoretical Approaches to Retirement

Psychological theories which may be relevant to the effective utilization of the potential of elderly are those which are concerned with the mutual interaction of the individual and environment. Such theories may be found in the area of life-span developmental psychology.

Activity Theory

Havighurst (1964) advocated that it is important for old people to remain involved in society if they want to have a happy and healthy old age. He believed that social roles are important in determining someone's feelings of self-worth. Retirement usually involves a decline in the 'role count', and this in turn produces a decline in personal feelings of self-worth. The person, as a result is less likely to put as much effort into taking care of himself and is, therefore, likely to decline with age. Since the process of retirement means that people lose a significant number of social roles — all those connected with their working careers — Havighurst regarded it as important for old people to keep up their 'role count' by replacing the social roles that they have lost through retirement with new ones. They should be motivated to assume new responsibilities, perhaps by involvement within the family and community. An increased role count would mean that the person would have higher level of self-esteem, more inclined to look after himself and would have a productive and happy environment. The activity theory of aging has been the model for a number of organizations concerned with providing opportunities for older people. It takes a positive view of aging, seeing the old person as an active agent in his or her own life and is able to make his own decisions.

Utility Theory

It emphasizes the need of all people, including the aged, to feel that there is some reason, some purpose, or some use of what they do. If people can define goals or purposes and move towards these goals, definitely they will be happier, healthier, and more effective (Hamlin, 1967). Beginning around the age of 60, people are designated as 'old' or 'roleless' and are forced to withdraw from the mainstream of life, regardless of their mental capabilities, motivations or health. Elderly do not necessarily become markedly impaired in all spheres beginning at the age of sixty.

Social Exchange Theory

Dowd (1975) looked at retirement as a social exchange, the two sides of the social contact are: the old person implicitly agrees to participate less in society's activities, thus vacating places in the work force for the younger people, while society agrees to grant that person an honourable discharge from the work ethic. They gain social approval for their years of leisure and the right to enjoy them as they feel inclined.

For some old people, this social exchange results in disengagement, as they feel themselves to be no longer fully part of the society, while for others the social exchange means that they seek alternative activities in other fields. Dyson (1980) suggested that the social exchange of retirement actually places the old person in a 'double-bind', in which they are trapped by their situations. As members of society, old people acknowledge the 'fairness' of the unspoken agreement. As individuals, however, often with many healthy and active years ahead, the contract is often seen as inappropriate for them personally. This makes it difficult for old people to challenge the way that society marginalizes them, because an attempt to do so is seen as demanding special and unfair treatment.

This has the effect of reducing the possibility for social cohesion among other people. Since they implicitly accept the 'fairness' of the social contract, they conclude if they don't fit the accepted view of the older person, there must be something wrong with themselves — that they are not 'typical'. The exchange theory states that older person's disengagement is not mutually satisfying for the individual and society as claimed by the proponents of the disengagement theory.

Continuity Theory

Covey (1982) and Ryff (1982) have replaced earlier theories of activity or disengagement as the optimal outcome of successful aging. The continuity of experience, skills and preferences throughout the life-span are emphasized, and the complex nature of the interrelationships among biological, psychological, and social influences that lead to stability or change in each individual are elucidated. It follows from this approach that it is important to pay close attention to each person's life course to replace the lost roles.

How should the elderly serve as a resource for the development of society and others? This is a problem worth studying both in its theoretical and its practical implications. With the advent of HRD ministry, the children, youth, women and labour all are the target groups of development process. We hold the belief that the old are useless when they do no work and cannot produce. Elderly is one of the target groups which is considered only as a problem rather than a resource for the well-being of the family, rural development, education, health care and other services. Development of the elderly becomes a critical step for building the future of any nation in multifarious fields.

Majority of India's labour force is engaged in unorganized sectors, like agriculture, small scale industries, transportation, business and in various professions such as those of lawyers, doctors, engineers, architects, contractors, chartered accountants, and so on. Engagement or opting for these vocations as the part of their employment indicates absence of the concept of retirement. Whereas, those serving in the organized sector have to retire at a specific age (58 or 60 years) irrespective of their health status and capacity to continue working. Retirement leads to various social-psychological changes. Generally elderly retired are engaged in household tasks and responsibilities and look after their grandchildren.

Elderly possess vast reservoir of experience and skills and as long as their health (physical and mental) does not deteriorate, their services should be utilized for the human resource development programmes. The retired elderly in the age group of 58-70 years may be treated as target group whose skills, experience and time could be utilized for the well-being of the entire community or society.

Prior to starting any new HRD programme, existing organizations of the elderly such as Association of Senior Citizens, Citizenship Development Society and Helpage India need to coordinate their activities for better human resource development. The following steps could be taken towards the utilization of resources of the elderlies: First, identification of active elderly, their qualifications, their specialized skills and their experience in the government or non-government organizations. Second, to assess their willingness to participate in the developmental programmes at the locality, city, district, region, state and national levels in accordance with their interests and aptitudes. Third, the elderly could be motivated towards the development of the nation by highlighting their needs, problems and potentials.

There are some areas where the elderly could meaningfully contribute towards the human resource development.

Education

Education is an important component of HRD. The National Literacy Mission has set its goal of achieving functional literacy for all sections of the population particularly for the age group of 15-35 years by 2000 AD. Kerala is the first state which has already achieved dramatic results in this field.

The elderly, as individuals, or in groups, or their organizations could serve as a resource of learning for imparting basic education, adult education, higher education, non-formal education and distance education, technical and vocational education. The "World Conference on Education for All" emphasized the spectrum of basic education for all with the following considerations in mind: Universalizing access and promoting equity, focus on learning, broadening the means and scope of basic education, enhancing the environment for learning, and strengthening partnerships. If the goal of universalization of education is to be achieved, elderlies resources have to be utilized for providing basic education to all children, the youth and adults. There is need for a greater participation to adduce the literacy campaigns. With the vast reservoir of knowledge, skill and experience, the elderly could convey the message of literacy by preparing the programmes and schemes keeping in view the requirement of the targeted group in mind. They could also nurture better citizens through transmitting the message of literacy in their native regional languages.

On the eve of the International Literacy Day, the then President of India Dr Shankar Dayal Sharma said "our people must demand literacy and treat it as a necessity of life". Literacy improves quality of life in terms of children's health, family welfare and status of people.

Peace Education

The International Peace Research Association (IPRA), views peace education as a fundamental aspect of the educational process. In the educational institutions (i.e. formal education), the elderly as a target group could do something for the new generation in terms of the development of moral values. Peace education shows concern for the role values play in shaping of our lives and our physical world. Peace education can introduce the process of moral reasoning in the classroom.

The role and orientation of the retired teachers should be considered important to peace education. They could freely discuss the problems of students and teachers and encourage them to resolve areas of disagreement. Peace education as part of the HRD programmes can be made more successful by the school administration if they seek support and cooperation of elderly people, particularly the retired teachers.

Informal peace education can also be started by the elderly with two major purposes as Gupta (1990) points; (a) "to provide accurate and unbiased information about the state of affairs with which the people of the world are faced and must deal, including problems of environment, population, resources, energy and violence". (b) "to encourage individuals who are learning these facts to have opinions, to question, to search and a as result to develop their individual judgement and their sense of responsibility for their neighbourhoods, society, and the world. In short, peace education is value oriented study of human problems from a global and futuristic perspective". Peace can be achieved only through social action of the senior citizens of the country.

Several psychological approaches to peace making have been advanced by social psychologists. Peace making methods are the methods employed for improving interpersonal relationships or harmony. The following methods are used for this purpose:

(i) Developing effective communication and discussion;
(ii) Improving self-esteem;
(iii) Providing good models;
(iv) Problem solving: and
(v) Enhancing empathy.

All these methods can easily be exercised if the educated elderly play a more dominant role in the society. Elderly as educators could promote the self-development through individualized instruction, and increased opportunities for educational innovation.

Environmental Education

Environmental education may be considered as an action process, which aims at providing an environmentally-oriented education system. It is assumed that the elderly may help in resolving the environmental crisis by creating awareness among the masses towards improving the environment.

In recent years environmental degradation in terms of some undesirable effects of industrialization and technology has become a matter of concern in our country. The development of public awareness and sensitivity towards the environment should be reinforced. Besides the formal and non-formal education, elderly can be immensely effective in creating awareness, motivating people to participate in the task of environmental assessment, and environmental management. They could also be helpful in conducting attitude surveys towards pollution control and specific environmental problems.

The important components of environmental education are as follows:

(a) Knowledge and understanding of the environment and its related problems.
(b) Attitudes and social values of the people toward the environment.
(c) Desire to improve health or environmental quality of life.
(d) Ability to manage and solve environmental problems.
(e) Ability to evaluate environmental measures and educational intervention programmes in terms of ecological, socio-cultural, political, economic and other factors.
(f) Identification of major pollutants and their control.
(g) Preparing the syllabi or structure of educational content, educational strategies and methods of learning for schools.

Retired elderly teachers could chalk out teacher-training programmes to achieve an integrated environmental approach. They may initiate researches in identifying the needs of the different groups and developing suitable materials for effective teaching-learning process.

Need for Adult Education and Extension Services

Retired teachers and professional people from many walks of life have much to contribute to the Adult Education programmes by imparting — vocational skills, general education, and information referral services. Elderly people can provide counselling for employment and job placement to individuals. The elderly people seeking gainful employment can be motivated to opt for part-time jobs and to entrepreneurship. Elderly persons, probably in better health and with better skill and abilities, will be involved in human resource development.

Extension service may legitimize the activity and involvement, whether at work or leisure, and may lead to personal growth. Behavioural and social scientists should become concerned with the differential impact of the possibility of increasing the flexibility of work - non-work schedules of the elderly on their developments.

Importance of National Open School in Education

Current trends in National Policy on Education, 1986 include efforts to improve the "universalization of education", "achievement of social equity and justice", and "creation of a learning society" through the National Open School (NOS). There is growing recognition of the effort of NOS to enable the youth to continue education, the youth who are either out of school or who had missed an educational opportunity. At a more pragmatic level, it has been observed that the formal education significantly affects educational achievements of girls, children and youngsters from scheduled castes, scheduled tribes and minorities especially from the rural areas. These school drop-outs, due to poor economic condition or social taboos take to unskilled wage employment or they become engaged in household work.

Elderly as a resource, could create awareness among the school drop-outs and the neo-literates to offer NOS courses or programmes like: (a) open basic education, (b) open secondary and senior secondary education, (c) open vocational education, and (d) open continuing and life enrichment programme. Retired teachers as educators could promote the self-development of each individual learner, and improve the learning skills of the students. The elderly could also utilize their expertises in developing or preparing the instructional material, managing and utilizing information technology in planning, monitoring and evaluation. The training should be imparted to the teachers, coordinators and administrative personnel of the study centres.

Health Care

The problem of providing health care to all must be viewed in the context of an alarming growth of population. Voluntary Health

Association of India (VHAI) opines that the health status of people varies from state to state, and group to group. States like Kerala, Maharashtra, Punjab and Tamil Nadu are doing fairly well; but the picture in states like Bihar, Madhya Pradesh, Orissa, Rajasthan and Uttar Pradesh is quite depressing. The status of the poor, especially the socially disadvantaged groups is a matter of grave concern. Medical services are inadequate to the socially disadvantaged. For example, rural people suffer disproportionately from cutbacks in medicare. Doctors and para-medical workers are understaffed in rural areas. There can be little doubt, however, that many of our health problems are aggravated by the kind of medical care made available to them. The availability and use of medical care are directly related to socio-economic status and locale. Low income affects the health of the poor from birth. People in the low socio-economic status tend to have higher rates of untreated illness and disability and higher mortality rates for most diseases than people in the middle and high socio-economic strata. Other factors besides availability of health care professionals can also affect the health of the poor. Thus, environmental pollution and drug addiction contribute to the high incidence of health problems. Mr. Alok Mukhopadhyay, President of the Voluntary Health Association of India, has proposed that rural health care services can be strengthened through: (1) allocation of more resources for primary health care services, (2) decentralized planning and people's participation, (3) ensuring the availability of medicines and other essential facilities in primary health centres, and (4) ensuring medical personnel stationed at work places and made accountable to local committees and organizations in districts and panchayats.

Elderly can be helpful in running health and nutrition education programmes particularly for the children and women. The intervention programmes may include the immunization of children and expectant mothers, nutrition and balanced diet, lack of parental care, etc. The elderly could contribute with their fruitful experiences in improving people's knowledge, attitude and practices relating to health care, self-care behaviour and in implementation of health care programmes for the well-being of others and to the self (i.e. elderly). The elderly, as individuals or in groups could also prove to be good samaritans in various services such as taking patients to hospitals, old age homes, etc They could play a prominent role in supervising the health care services, hospitals, nursing homes, clinics — as they could also open pharmaceutical stores in rural areas.

The elderly could form the Health Care Organizations (HCO) to prevent illnesses and other conditions that require hospitalization and surgery. HCO should revitalize the country's healthcare system to shift the emphasis from treatment to prevention. HCO should provide medical services to subscribers in a specific region or city or locality who pay a monthly fee.

The services of the elderly could be utilized to promote health care behaviour or the concept of 'wellness' among people. It involves teaching a person, how to do behavioural self-control, or self-regulation or self-monitoring in the direction of well-being. The techniques of meditation and relaxation are potentially important for developing awareness. The treatment of illnesses in hospitals, nursing homes and clinics relies more on repair strategies of short lived cure rather than maintaining health and promoting quality of health.

Rural Development

HRD in rural sector is important, but at the same time one should not forget the importance of the elderly for the well-being of rural folk. While compared to the urbanites the people living in rural areas tend to face more social and physical problems, more functional limitations and a greater number of hazards of daily life. In some respects such problems as transportation, non-availability and poor quality of health services, poor nutrition, unhealthy living and environmental conditions (poor sanitation, polluted drinking water, absence of proper drainage system) make rural life full of distress and miseries. Such conditions often force people to migrate from rural areas to urban areas in search of better amenities of life. Thus the availability, accessibility and affordability of resources tend to force migration which in its wake is a burden to the urban areas.

Migration has also contributed to some of the social problems such as unemployment and underemployment, urban poverty, exploitation of scheduled caste, crime, homelessness, and the stresses and costs of education, etc. The old are better placed to understand why migration has sometimes led to severe social problems and how they could promote opportunities to the children, youth and women for getting basic education and employment in their homeland and consequently to meet their needs.

The retired elderly with technical knowledge and skills can undertake or participate in various activities such as installation of pumps, construction of low cost housing, roads and sanitary latrines, etc., in rural areas. The Council for Advancement of People Action and Rural Technology helps the Non-Government Organisations (NGOs) in the field of rural development. In rural areas, the old could play a crucial role in providing social support systems and in improving quality of life of rural people by generating and creating quality consciousness, innovative thinking, inculcating scientific temper and the hopes of a better tomorrow.

They may help the rural people in achieving the basic HRD needs such as health, education, unpolluted water, better sanitation, food, environment and employment. In the field of agriculture, the main role of the elderly should be the development of manpower, using scientific method of farming and marketing facilities. The elderly could evolve technical skill development programmes in the unorganized sectors. As a result the cost of personnel recruitment and training may be saved.

Throughout India mostly people living in rural areas want to migrate in the suburban or urban areas. Usually they do not wish to entirely uproot themselves but hope to be working at the better-paying jobs that are said to be available in urban areas. If they can save and send money to their families in rural areas, definitely they may return to their native places where they can live better life.

Volunteer Services

Thousands of elderly people are still active and they can be useful to their families, communities, and themselves by volunteering for common services like payment of electricity, water and telephone bills, shopping, civic amenities, alleviating social problems such as dowry, poverty, etc. They could also maintain liaison with the various bodies of district administration and social welfare agencies for the uplift of the community and consequently to meet their needs.

Conclusion

In sum, the elderly could chalk out strategies directed towards developing the kind of environment which would provide growth and learning as well as development of the personality in the people. HRD should operate continually. The vast reservoir of experience of the retired elderly people should be utilized for HRD into the areas of education, health care programme, rural development and voluntary services. Poor HRD at present has resulted in poor socio-economic development of the country.

HRD of elderlies today would be HRD of the nation tomorrow.

REFERENCES

Covey, H., 1982, A reconceptualization of continuity theory: Some preliminary thoughts, *The Gerontologist*, 21: 628-33.

Dowd, J.H., 1975, Aging as exchange: A preface to theory, *Journal of Gerontology*, 30: 584-94.

Dyson, J., 1980, Sociopolitical influences on retirement research, *Bulletin of the British Psychological Society*, 33: 128-30.

Gupta, P., 1990, Science of peace in society, Presidential address at the 77th Science Congress in the Section of Psychology and Educational Sciences, Cochin.

Hamlin, R.M., 1967, A utility theory of old age, *The Gerontologist*, 7: 37-45.

Havighurst, R.J., 1964, Flexibility and the social roles of the retired, *American Journal of Sociology*, 59: 309-11.

Rao, T.V., 1996, *Human Resources Development: Experiences, Interventions, Strategies*. New Delhi: Sage Publications.

Ryff, C., 1982, Successful aging: A developmental approach, *The Gerontologist*, 21: 209-14.

THIRTEEN

Dynamics and Coping Strategies of Eve Teasing

VIDHU MOHAN *and* SHABNAM PRIYADARSHINI

Crimes against women have reached serious dimensions. Enactment of new laws and amendment of the Indian Penal Code, the Criminal Procedure Code and the Indian Evidence Act have been made to protect women in every walk of life. Nevertheless, violence is visible even in the safety of four walls of the home. Women find no security in streets and the workplace, where they are vulnerable and fall prey to the anti-socials, men colleagues and bosses. The recent example being the famous Rupan Deol Bajaj case where a senior IAS lady officer was slapped on her bottom by a senior IPS male officer in a social gathering. A light of hope of getting justice has come after seven long years of this shameful incident. If a senior IAS lady officer gets justice in seven years, what is the hope for a lay woman? This makes one go back to the times of the *Mahabharata,* where again the modesty of Draupadi who was wife to the five Pandava princes was outraged in public through *Chir Haran* and no one sitting in that Rajya Sabha came forward to her rescue.

Eve teasing has been a serious menace in our society. No village, city or town is free from it. Incidence of molestation of women and girls and eve teasing has assumed serious proportions and they are ever on the increase. Mohan (1994) mentions about eve teasing as a way of sexual harassment specially in the northern states of India. Eve teasing in the northern belt of India seems to be on the increase. In the state of Punjab in the year 1994, a woman was raped every 89 minutes; 31 women were molested everyday; and there is an eve teasing incident every 19 minutes (*The Times of India*, 30th May, 1995). Of course, many incidents go unreported most of the times because by reporting a woman is twice bitten — once by the act itself and second time at the hands of the justice giving agencies — the police and the law court. Women and girls are subjected to various forms of eve teasing in streets and public places, places of entertainment, campuses of educational institutions, crowded places like markets, railway platforms, bus stands, running buses and trains and workplace. Even places of worship are not spared by perpetrators of this crime (Mohan & Shabnam Priyadarshini, 1995a). Festivals and fairs provide a free hand to eve teasers. They pinch and touch women on the sly, pass lewd remarks, sing obscene and double meaning songs to embarrass girls, make anonymous phone calls and utter obscene and suggestive words.

Eve teasing is not only confined to students and unemployed youth. Boys from educated, cultured and affluent families also take part in eve teasing. In crowded buses and trains, the eve teasers stand or sit next to girls and unleash perverseness (Mohan & Shabnam Priyadarshini, 1995a). The general belief is that the eve teasers are young boys but it was found that middle and old aged men were also indulging in subtle ways of outraging modesty. They use their age factor as a very convenient camouflage to their lecherous intent.

A number of studies have been conducted in the area of violence against women but a review of literature on criminology, victimology and violence against women draws almost a blank on the issue of eve teasing, which has become the most common form of harassment faced by young girls and women in the Indian society. The previous two studies on eve teasing by the authors were the first attempt towards the understanding of this misbehaviour (Mohan & Shabnam Priyadarshini, 1995a; Mohan & Shabnam Priyadarshini, 1995b). These two studies revealed 36 different types of eve teasing and compared the perception of eve

III. Poor Socialization			
1. Narrow minded, closed and conservative society which puts a lot of constraints on the mixing up of boys and girls	23.5	31.9	1.27
2. Lack of healthy relationship and communication between boys and girls	17.4	32.7	4.67*
3. Parents keep double standards for their sons and daughters	12.2	0.0	12.20*
4. Parents consider it a taboo and do not talk about sex related matters with their children	0.0	9.7	9.70*
IV. Lack of Proper Training and Counselling			
1. Lack of sex education in schools	2.6	23.0	16.26*
2. No healthy seminars and open discussions among boys and girls in schools/colleges	1.7	17.7	13.20*
V. Educational System			
Co-educational institutions have a better atmosphere for a healthy understanding and better interaction between boys and girls	1.7	8.0	4.09*
VI. Media's Role			
1. Influence of cinema, TV and cable network programmes	16.5	23.9	1.36
2. Influence of pornographic literature	0.0	13.3	13.30*

TABLE 2
COPING STRATEGIES OF GIRLS

	Girls (in %)
I. Ignore the Teasing	
1. Ignore it totally	53.9
(a) Because of helplessness	
(b) Got used to it and think there is no point in banging their heads against the wall	
(c) If alone	
2. Ignore when the teasing is mild but confront when out of control	25.2
II. Confrontation	18.3
By embarrassing the offender or by fighting back	
III. Report to the Police	2.6

DISCUSSIONS OF RESULTS

I. Reasons of Eve Teasing

As presented in Table I, the various reasons of eve teasing could be categorized into 6 broad headings which are discussed as follows:

Blaming the Girls

While most of the boys held the girls responsible for this behaviour, a few girls also felt the same. According to these subjects, by wearing revealing and figure-hugging dresses, the girls provoked the boys to tease them. While 70.8 per cent of the boys attributed this reason for eve teasing, only 32.2 per cent of the girls gave the same reason, thus giving a significant X^2 value of 14.47. It seems that the boys have tried to rationalize their behaviour by blaming the girls. In a study by Valentine-French and Radtke (1989), male subjects attributed less responsibility to the perpetrator than the female subjects in sexual harassment.

Some subjects also reported that the girls enjoy being teased and encourage to tease them. Here also, the boys reported significantly higher than the girls. In a male dominated society, the female is often held responsible for provoking this behaviour towards herself. The fact that she is scared or helpless to retaliate is taken as a sign of encouragement to this behaviour. There is a tendency to blame innocent victims for their undeserved fate as a means of maintaining one's belief that the world is fair and just (Berner and Simmons, 1966; Lerner and Matthews, 1967).

Blaming the Boys

In this category, boys were blamed for this behaviour. Here also, the X^2 value was significant as more girls than boys held this reason responsible for eve teasing. In 1982, Jensen and Gutek discussed sex differences in attribution and assignment of responsibility for sexual harassment and concluded that male respondents would assign more responsibility to the women and women would assign less responsibility to the women and more to men. While 79.1 per cent of the girls attributed frustration in boys as the cause of eve teasing, only 34.5 per cent of the boys recorded this as one of the causes of eve teasing.

Some of the girls also felt that the boys indulge in this behaviour to show their superiority over girls. Adler (1925) stressed the importance of the struggle for power and the effort to overcome inferiority as a motivational force in human personality. Veroff (1958) defines need for power (nPow) as the concern of a person to control the means of influencing others which is expressed through a desire about wanting to win a point, showing dominance, gaining control, convincing someone of something and wanting to avoid weakness. Sometimes the means to achieve these goals are negative as in eve teasing. In her study, Gill (1982) found criminals to be higher on nPow as compared to non-criminals. She also found a trend for body offenders to be higher on nPow than the offenders against property. Boys indulging in physical eve teasing like touching and pinching girls can be put in the category of body offenders.

Another reason included in this category was that the law is not enforced and as a result the offenders are all the more encouraged because they know that they would get away with it. This is true because most of the girls ignore their being teased by boys and do not report. In spite of Section 509 of the Indian Penal Code available, girls do not seek legal action either because they are ignorant about it or they are afraid to do so. Most cases even if reported are hushed up.

Poor Socialization

This category of reasons of eve teasing held lack of proper upbringing of children responsible for this behaviour. Both boys and girls felt that the closed and conservative society in which the children are brought up are responsible for eve teasing. Instead of developing healthy heterosexual relationship, boys resort to such behaviour with girls because they do not get a chance to mix with them. Some of the subjects also felt that parents kept double standards for their sons and daughters. Hoffman (1972) found that girls as compared to boys have less encouragement for independence, more parental protectiveness, less pressure to establish an identity separate from the mother, they engage in less independent exploration of their environments. As a result they develop neither adequate skills nor confidence but continue to be dependent upon others. Children pick up the subtle attitudes of their parents or other caretakers. If the parents discriminate between sons and daughters, their children also learn similar attitudes and behave accordingly even outside home. Parents not talking about matters relating to sex was another reason which the subjects felt was responsible for eve teasing.

Lack of Counselling

This category of reasons held lack of proper training and counselling responsible for eve teasing. The boys reported this reason significantly higher than the girls. The subjects felt that lack of sex education in schools and open seminars involving boys and girls led the boys to indulge in this behaviour. Because our society is still reluctant to address these issues, institutional barriers continue to obstruct the provision of effective programmes that could help the youth to realize their sexuality in a positive and responsible manner. For instance, the furore in Dhanbad over Procter and Gamble's attempts to distribute booklets on menstruation along with sanitary napkins backfired when a local newspaper splashed headlines that the company was contributing indecent literature and a local unit of a political party took up the issue and accused the multinational of subverting Indian culture (*The Times of India*, 29th July, 1995). A recent survey found that a majority of teachers and students felt a strong need for sex education in schools. While 57 per cent students agreed that there should be such a curriculum, 53 per cent principals expressed a similar opinion (*The Times of India*, 29th July 1995). The pioneering family life and sex education programme of the Family Planning Association of India meets this need of the adolescents and young adults which provide specialized services and training in family life, marriage and sex counselling.

Faulty Educational System

Some subjects also felt that the coeducational institutions have a better atmosphere for developing healthy interaction amongst boys and girls which helps them to have a better understanding and respect towards each other. Moreton (1946) in a comparative study of coeducational and single sex schools found that 72 per cent of the subjects who were educated in coeducational schools said it had helped in their relations with the opposite sex. In a study by Schneider and Coutts (1982), it was found that as compared to the single sex schools, coeducational schools were perceived by their students as more gregarious, group centered and friendly, more entertaining and enjoyable, more tolerant of non-compliance, spontaneity and impetuosity, as more conducive to the development of feelings of self-confidence and self-respect, and as reflecting less prejudiced and traditional thinking.

Media's Role

The last category of reasons held external sources like media (both print and electronic) i.e., movies, cable TV programmes and pornographic literature responsible for eve teasing. These sources have played a great part in encouraging boys to indulge in eve teasing by giving them a false belief that by doing so they can impress and win hearts of the girls as shown in the movies and TV serials. Both boys and girls blamed cable TV and movies for eve teasing. 13.3 per cent of the boys also reported pornographic literature as the cause of eve teasing while none of the girls reported this. Children are exposed to three key conditions that influence their behaviour: their family, their peers, and the broader socio-cultural environment. In recent years, the focus has shifted from the influence of family and peer group models to the role of the broader socio-cultural environment, particularly the mass media in the development of aggressive behaviour (Coleman, 1976). The exposure of youth to violence in the media tends to sensitize them to violence in the world around them, and to foster the acceptance of violence as a means of resolving conflicts (Eron et al, 1974; Murray, 1973; Shaw, 1974).

II. Coping Strategies

As shown in Table II, the various types of coping strategies employed by girls to tackle eve teasing could be categorized into three headings.

Ignoring the Eve Teasing

The coping strategy most frequently used by girls was to ignore eve teasing. 53.9 per cent of the girls felt that it was the best way to deal with eve teasing. Out of these 13.9 per cent preferred ignoring because of helplessness, 1.7 per cent preferred it because they felt it was useless to take any drastic action against it, as whatever they do, it will not deter the eve teasers from indulging in this behaviour again, 1.7 per cent of the girls reported that they ignore it when they are alone but take some action when they are accompanied by other girls. In our culture, dependent behaviour is sex-related. The girls are permitted, and even encouraged to be far more dependent than the boys. This pattern of helplessness of girls since very early ages and their differentiation continues rather stably into adulthood. For example, young boys are usually taught that excessive dependency is 'unmasculine' and thus undesirable. Independence, autonomy and personal self-sufficiency are praised and rewarded as mature, desirable 'manly' attributes. Kagan and Moss (1960) in a study concluded that dependent behaviour is consistently more punished in boys than in girls. Maccoby (1963, 1966) has pointed out that girls are more conforming, suggestible, and dependent upon the opinion of others.

The percentage of girls who reported that they ignore eve teasing when it is mild but retaliate when it crosses the limit was 25.2.

Confrontation

Some girls reported that they confront the offender by embarrassing him verbally or by fighting back according to the degree of eve teasing experienced. The percentage of girls reported this strategy was 18.3.

Reporting to the Police

Only 2.6 per cent of the girls reported that they report the matter to the police. Thus, strengthening the results of a study reported in *The Times of India* (30th May, 1995) which revealed that 80 per cent of the crimes against women go unreported. According to the same study, the first case of eve teasing was registered in the state of Punjab in the year 1992, while no case was registered in 1993, only 3 cases were reported in 1994 whereas the unreported cases were as high as 27,530.

The survey revealed that the boys blame girls and vice versa for eve teasing. There is a need to develop a healthy and friendly atmosphere among the young boys and girls. This would help them to respect and understand each other and behave assertively. The solution lies in a willingness to change age old perceptions and move with the time and addressing the needs of the young generation. There is a need to introduce sex education in schools and counselling the youth to develop in them assertive behaviour and positive self-concept and self-esteem. There is also a need to make the girls aware of their legal rights so that they do not take eve teasing lightly and deal with it in an effective way.

REFERENCES

Adler, A., 1925, *The Practice and Theory of Individual Psychology*. New York: Harcourt, Brace and World.

Coleman, James C., 1976, *Abnormal Psychology and Modern Life*. New York: Scott. Foresman & Co.

Eron, L.D., Huesmann, L.R., Lefkowitz, M.M. and Walder, L.O., 1976, In Coleman, James C., (eds.), *Abnormal Psychology and Modern Life*. New York: Scott. Foresman & Co.

Gill, Surjeet Kaur, Study of Personality and Motives of criminals in relation to crime and duration of stay in open and closed jails, Ph.D thesis, 1982.

Hoffman, L.W., 1972, Early Childhood Experiences and Women's Achievement Motives, *Journal of Social Issues*, 28.

Jensen, I.W. and Gutek, B.A., 1982, Attribution and Assignment of responsibility in Sexual Harassment, *Journal of Social Issues*, 38: 121-36.

Kagan, J. and Moss, H.A., 1986, In McDavid, J.W. and Harari, H., *Social Psychology: Individuals, Groups, Societies*, Delhi: CBS Publishers and Distributors.

Lerner, M.J. and Matthews, G., 1967, Reactions to suffering of others under conditions of indirect responsibility, *Journal of Personality and Social Psychology*, 5: 319-25.

Lerner, M.J., and Simmons, C.H., 1966, Observer's reaction to the "innocent victim": Compassion or rejection? *Journal of Personality and Social Psychology*, 4: 203-14.

Maccoby, Eleanor, 1963, in Hoffman, L.W., Early Childhood Experiences and Women's Achievement Motives, *Journal of Social Issues*, 28, 1972.

McDavid,, J.W., and Harari, H., 1986, *Social Psychology: Individuals, Groups, Societies*, Delhi: CBS Publishers and Distributors.

Mohan, Vidhu, 1994, Exploitation of Women, in Dhoundial, V.R., Dhoundial, N.C., Shukla, Aradhana, (ed.), *The Indian Girls*, Almora: Shri Almora Book Depot.

Mohan, Vidhu, and Shabnam Priyadarshini, 1995a, A Survey on Eve Teasing as experienced by Girls, *The Indian Journal of Criminology & Criminalistics*, XVI, 1-7.

———, 1995b, A comparative Study of the Perception of boys and girls towards Eve Teasing, *The Indian Journal of Psychological Issues*, Vol. 3(2), 15-20.

Moreton, F.E., Attitudes of Teachers and Scholars towards Coeducation, 1946, *The British Journal of Educational Psychology*, XVI: 82-95.

Murray, J.P., 1976, in Coleman, James C., (ed.), *Abnormal Psychology and Modern Life*, New York: Scott. Foresman & Co.

Schneider, F.W., and Coutts, L.M., 1982, The High School Environment: A Comparison of Coeducational and Single Sex Schools, *Journal of Educational Psychology*, 74: 898-906.

Shaw, D., 1976, in Coleman, James C., (ed.), *Abnormal Psychology and Modern Life*, New York: Scott. Foreman & Co.

Tandon, M.P., and Tandon, R., 1989, *Indian Penal Code: With a Commentary, Critical and Explanatory, and latest Case Law*, (18th ed.), Allahabad: Allahabad Law Agency.

The Times of India, Most Crimes Against Women go Unreported in Punjab, New Delhi, May 30, 1995.

The Times of India, Who's afraid of Sex?, *Saturday Times*, New Delhi, July 29, 1995.

Valentine-French, Suzanne, and Radtke, H. Lorranine, 1989, Attributions of Responsibility for an Incident of Sexual Harassment in a University Setting, *Sex Roles*, 21: 545-55.

Veroff, J., A Scoring Manual for the Power Motive, 1958, in Atkinson, J.W., (ed.), *Motives in Fantasy, Action & Society*, New jersey: D. Van Nostrand, Princeton.

FOURTEEN

Strategies for Preparing Women and the Youth for Future Societies

MANI K. MADALA

Changing Scenario

We are living in a rapidly changing world which makes it difficult to live a happy and successful life with the values, habits and behaviour patterns acquired from our parents, they having prepared us to lead a life in a world viewed by them according to their own experiences and beliefs. Globally a lot of changes are occurring at every level which are described below.

Political Level

Centralised economies have collapsed; Most of the East European nations have given up communism; Berlin wall no longer exists; and China has opened up its doors to liberalization.

Economic Level

The USA which was a giant earlier, is now looking up to Japan. The East Asian economic miracle has thrown up many Asian tigers and dragons. Pacific rim countries are opening up; and many developing economies have collapsed due to the crisis of balance of payments and are hitching their wagons to the engine of IMF, World Bank package.

Technical Level

Technology is getting obsolete at a very rapid pace; Information technology and telecommunications have changed the face of the world.

Social Level

The support of extended family to the women and youth is rapidly decreasing; and patriarchal values are in transition.

At the Level of World of Work

It is rapidly changing. Its emphasis on improving productive efficiency cuts in expenditure on education, public infrastructure and increase of child labour with reduced hiring costs.

Many developing countries are in a state of transition. If the transition is not managed effectively, there are chances that some specific sections of the society particularly women and youth would be very badly damaged. If developmental needs of these sections are not adequately fulfilled, the society would suffer in the long run. All those societies which have opted for a short sighted economic development will pay a heavy price on the developmental front.

It is necessary to dwell at some length on the transition experiences of some Third World countries. World Bank Report clearly brings out how most of the Asian Tigers have risen economically by providing adequate resources for education and skills to the youth.

Transition Experiences of Some Developing Countries

In many countries, globalization, modernization and marketization involved the closure of a large number of industrial enterprises, leading to unemployment and social unrest. The big export drives reduced the domestic availability of goods pushing up their prices; decay of small units, reduction in social infrastructure, leading to a fall in levels of education, nutrition and health leading to rising social discontent and internal disorder, destroying the social fabric and particularly the lot of women and youth has been made deplorable.

Some Third World countries who have gone for a series of adjustment loans and followed IMF-World Bank package in letter and spirit have shown a great deterioration in their social welfare indices and we can learn an important lesson in this. More than sixty countries mainly from Africa, Latin America and Caribbean who hitched their wagons to the engine of the world trade, replaced inward looking development to export led growth and consequently collapsed. They underemphasized the basic human needs and paid heavy price (Levitt, Polanyi and Kavi, 1992). Both in Zambia and Venezuela, withdrawal of subsidies led to doubling of food prices leading to rioting and arson. Government finally had to reinstate the subsidies. When Zambia reduced the imports of drugs, it dramatically lowered the health status of her people with long term effects on economic growth.

In Brazil, export-oriented agriculture decreased the per capita production of basic goods. Poor workers had to put in, increasing number of working hours to buy the same basic items of food each month (263 hrs in 1983 as against 120 hrs in 1981). The IMF policy package in Egypt sought reallocation of resources to decrease domestic absorption, expand exports and fill the Balance of Payment (BoP) deficit which did not support the long term growth of the economy (Korayem, 1987).

Women and Youth in Transiting Societies

Most of the literature on stabilization and adjustment makes no reference to gender and women. However, reviewing the available literature, Elson (1991) reports consensus that the burdens borne by women, especially poor women, during the course of adjustment paved the way for a sustainable growth in the 1990's. Women's access to productive resources and services such as extension, credit and import subsidies that are diverted towards export production, limit women's productivity and this sabotages the goals of stable long term growth.

Prognosis for women and youth is not good. General recessionaries effect on employment will hit women more and the poor women much more, given the bias of the employers as well as the social constraints placed on them and their obligatory domestic responsibilities. Removal of subsidies and deregulation process, would mostly affect the women in the areas of food, housing, clothing, water transportation, etc. The problem would be compounded by the discrimination against women in the intra-household as well as intra-organisational distribution of resources and services.

In the erstwhile USSR, as well as East European countries which once enjoyed the distinction of the highest rates of female labour force participation, Women now face unemployment, marginalization from production process, loss of precious benefits and forms of social security. If social support for working women is insisted upon, it would mean loss of jobs for women and strengthening of patriarchal concepts about gender roles.

In the name of cost of production and efficiency, work burden actually shifted from paid male worker to unpaid female and young workers. Displaced by large-scale, sophisticated technology oriented multinationals, they shifted to unskilled areas in informal sector and often having to compete with, non-trainable old male workers and made to take up more strenuous work for lesser pay in sub-contract work, which is a process used by formal enterprises to reduce labour costs.

Women and youth who get trapped in this work outside government regulations do not enjoy the protection of employment and labour legislation. Even these demands in informal sector like domestic help, childcare, laundry, would shrink because of cutting back of public sector and also because of falls in real income with concomitant inflation.

The main burden of structural adjustment actually falls on those women: who have to provide their families; stand for hours in queue; often abandoned by men, to prostitution and other kinds of social misery.

Some of the crucial linkages between new Economic Policy components and the status of women and youth are :

1. High food prices—Low household food availability—Low nutrient Intake—Low nutritional status—High mortality.
2. Low income—Low food availability—Low food intake— Low nutrition—High mortality.
3. Low availability of health services—High personal illness — Low control of disease—High mortality.
4. High employment—Low income—Less food and low medical care availability for the mother—High mortality.

A country like India which already has a sex ratio adverse to women, can ill afford a scenario like the above.

Strategies to Protect Women and Youth

The gender dynamics of structural adjustment have been addressed in a number of studies (Commonwealth Secretariat, 1989; Standing, 1989; Benenia, 1991; Elson, 1991; Palmer, 1991; Vickers, 1991; Afshar and Dennis, 1992).

According to Mahbul Haq (1992) India's public policies have always been against the aged and the women. He feels that in the last 44 years not enough money has been spent to improve elementary education, rural economic opportunities as well as public health facilities.

All the economically successful countries including the Asian Tigers —South Korea, Malaysia, Singapore, Taiwan — achieved the economic miracles through plenty of state protection and building a sound social infrastructure like health and education.

It is important not to cut expenditure on health and education, when deprivation has been there for considerably long periods, growth will not take place even if resources are reallocated to basic health and education as can be seen from the experience of Ghana and Jamaica. But as can be seen from the experience of Botswana, Zimbabwe and South Korea where restoration of economic growth was only a medium term priority and resources allocation to basic health education and employment were quickly returned, growth of the economy quickly returned.

It, therefore, becomes necessary that the women's concerns need to be explicitly incorporated as integral elements of the objectives, content, monitoring of international support for structural adjustment.

India should make a significant increase in the expenditures on education, health and safe drinking water to alleviate the poverty, powerlessness, illiteracy, ignorance and lack of individual and collective autonomy.

The mix, sequencing and the speed of the Bank Funding Programme implementation should take into consideration the cultural, socio-legal impediments to women's economic role. Policies that discriminate against the women should not be encouraged.

It is necessary to clarify that long term economic growth and the growth of the women are not mutually exclusive. However, a goal of short term economic growth, with an eye on quick profits and cuts of social expenditure, would work against the growth of the women and consequently the growth of the economy on a long term basis.

The following strategies if implemented can significantly improve the adjustment of women to the economic crises. India should adopt a people-oriented approach, addressing various structural inequalities including gender inequality, as there is an important link between women's economic role and the success of adjustment programmes.

Special safety nets like the National Renewal Fund, should be created for women and special programmes drawn for the Retraining and Re-employment of women, taking into account the new areas of skills that could be needed in the context of new technologies and new processes.

At microlevel it is necessary to study the relationship among women, market and state as the programmes of stabilization and adjustment place great emphasis on market forces.

Flexibility in matters of hours, work and modes of operations should be encouraged to protect women's earning power.

Special training programmes for youth should be conducted which can impart the entrepreneurial skills that can help them to adopt emerging technologies.

Policy Perspective at Global Level to Enhance the Status of Women and Youth

- At a global level, all the developed countries should channelize their official development assistance fund, to programmes that would benefit especially women and youth.
- World Bank and IMF could provide a special fund to finance women and youth in development programmes to provide credit at lower interest rates for entrepreneurial activities.
- International trading policies should protect products like food so as to make it accessible to women and their families.

- International agencies like WHO should work towards improving access of women and youth to the markets of developed countries.

Macro Level Strategies for Survival and Growth of Women and Youth

- Overall policy stance to achieve equality for women.
- Identification of women friendly technologies.
- Identification of jobs, attitudes, skills that are needed in future.
- Strategies to build legal and administrative structure to facilitate the growth of women and youth.
- Strategies focussing on flexi career — flexi time to cater to women's special needs — just like child bearing, rearing, household management, etc.
- Strategies to build legal and administrative structure to facilitate the growth of women and youth.
- Strategies to allow youth to work and finance their developmental studies.
- Strategies involving paternity in child growth.
- Work for amendment in organizational procedures, policies which are now predominantly androgynous and anti-women and anti-youth.
- Environmental protection to safeguard the access of women to fuel wood, fodder and potable water. This will give the youth a greener society in future.
- Enhance the opportunities for women and youth to take up independent economic activity by ensuring access to credit and key services and implementing employment creation schemes specially favouring women's needs.
- Restore momentum for advancement through greater allocation of funds for education and health of women and youth.
- Full integration of women and youth into decision making process.
- Interests of women and youth should be represented at the various decision making centres.
- Establishing units in key economic ministries and

development agencies to ensure smooth structured adjustment for women and youth.

- Interests of women and youth should be adequately represented in the parliament and parliamentary committees to see that their interests are taken care of in the legislation.
- It is vital to involve people directly in developments rather than treat them as entities to be administered by a bureaucracy.
- Empowering the women at local level and improving the access to resources is necessary.
- Career Break Schemes — Introduce part time/flexible working and job sharing and working from home programmes to protect employment levels from further fall.
- Empowering — women and youth should be trained in result orientation, risk taking, originality, future orientation.
- Successful cases studies should be made popular models. In particular cases psychologically women suffer from fear of success. The barrier should be removed from their minds.
- Industry Associations like FICCI, CII, conscious of their social responsibilities, can be possible sources of organizing training for women and youth in the above areas.

Entrepreneurial Skills for Women and Youth

Policy framework should be made to make possible easy access to scarce capital, provide basic management skills, access to foreign exchange (reservation, allocation, etc.) improve infrastructure by providing small-scale decentralized power generation, access to water, roads to communities and villages as well as transport. It is important to provide state support in marketing, particularly international marketing. Skill development in these industries; agricultural raw material, forest products, medicinal plants, dairy and poultry products, construction materials based on domestic inputs. There will be scope in which specific parts and later assembled. Sericulture will be another important area.

Secondary sector will have a lot of scope for entrepreneurial work. Accounting, computer, software, financing, tailoring, laundry, beauty parlours, hostels/restaurants. In the aviation industry, pilots/navigators, space hostesses, space director; garment manufacture, marketing, advertising; Interior design, Geneting engineering, scientific instruments.

Unless the above strategies are emphasised and special care is taken to build up the building blocks of the society, namely, women and youth, the societies will come crashing down.

REFERENCES

Afshan, Haleh and Dennis, Carolyne (eds.), 1982, *Women and Adjustment Policies in the Third World*. London: MacMillan.

Common Welath Secretariat, 1989, Engendering, Adjustment for the 1990's. In Mary Chiney Hesse, et al., (eds.), London: Commonwealth Secretariat.

Elson Diane, 1991, Gender and Adjustment and the 1990's: An update and Evidence and Strategies; paper prepared for Inter Regional Meeting on Economic Distress, Structural Adjustment and Women; Commonwealth Secretariat, London, 13 April.

Haq. Mahbub-N1, 1992, *The Indian Express*, January 13, 1992.

Korayem, Karima, 1987, The impact of economic adjustment policies on the vulnerable families and children in Egypt, UNICEF.

Palmer Ingrid, 1977, *L. Internationalisation du capital*, Paris: Maspero.

Standing, Guy, 1989, Global Feminization through Flexible Labour, Working paper No. 31, Labour Market Analysis and Employment Planning WEP, ILO Geneva.

Vickers, Jeanne, 1991, *Women and World Economy*, London: Zed.

FIFTEEN

HRD of Youth through Vocational Education and Training

ASIYA AIJAZ

The number of school drop-outs, unemployed as well as underemployed youth are rising in proportion. They are facing difficulty either due to drop-out in school or could not reach university entrance standard. The number of skilled workers, is declining day by day. They may offer a course of vocational training. Knowledge and skills are required in the skilled workers in both the private and public sectors for industrial and agricultural development and productivity. The vocational education and training is our developmental need to produce skilled manpower. In India, vocational training is not increasing at alarming rates. At present there is a little data on the status of vocational education and training in the form of statistics. Vocational training comprises practical, on-the-job training with theoretical instruction at a part time vocational school. Thus, private and public sectors are jointly responsible to impart vocational education and training programmes to train the skilled workers.

Developmental tasks are important to the development of individual, family, society and nation. Vocational educational training may be the most important developmental task for the human resource development (HRD) of youth. A crucial task is to focus on youth's identity and survival. Also, acceptance of who they are and what they are doing is a task of HRD?

It is suggested that by imparting vocational education and training to the youth's we may help them to establish their roles and consequently to set their future developmental priority of the nation. In India more than two crore educated youth are unemployed. They may be more likely to be deprived in employment because of the lack of vocational training. Therefore, it is important to consider the vocational education and training as developmental tasks for HRD of youth.

Major transformations are associated with vocational education and training that in turn leads to HRD needs of the people. Increasing the skills and abilities of youth is key to "HRD need of the people with respect to health, education, safe water, food, environment and employment" (Rao, 1996, p.152). Vocational education can boost in living standards of households by expanding opportunities, raising productivity, attracting capital investment and increasing learning power. It may enable people to lead more fulfilling lives through "creations, mastery and utilization of modern science and technology to meet the basic HRD needs as well as to advance technologically" (Rao, 1996, p. 152). The importance of investing in technical and vocational education for economic development and development of new technologies have been recognized world wide. This realization has contributed to unprecedented global increase in technical and vocational schooling in recent decades.

Education is an essential aspect of HRD. General education gives people skills that they can later transfer from job to job and the basic intellectual tools are necessary for further learning. Vocational education augments the ability to perform skills or jobs, to adopt to new technologies and production practices. In India, areas where relatively few farmers had primary schooling at the onset of the green revolution experienced less growth than areas with the same technological opportunities but better educated farmers, vocational training exhibits a similar relationship with productivity. Thus agriculture sector becomes important.

Vocational training boosts one's learning power because market oriented economies reward the skilled worker who is able to deliver more output, or an output that is more highly valued in

Lack of information about what skills are required to be fostered, how marketing procedures are to be planned, what new technologies reemerging is a valid ground for the active involvement of organizations in vocational training programmes. These factors are particularly relevant with reference to the informal sector where paucity of information is likely to be more.

In India, government uses training to address such problems as low skill levels among the employed employees, job promotion, displacement of workers during economy — with transition and poor workers with petty jobs. State-sponsored training centres especially in vocational education, have proved expensive and often provided trainers with few marketable skills. We must reorient government or public training institutions to respond to consumer and market demands. In India, the provision of private training is emerging in various job-oriented courses just like computer skills, fashion designing and technology, food processing, hotel management, tourism, etc.

Need for Vocational Schools

Apart from learning on the job, the trainee has to attend a part time vocational school one or two days a week during the course of study. The schools teach general subjects and theory which trainees are better able to learn at school than at work. The curriculum has little relationship between economic activities and the resource base (e.g., agriculture-based activity, environment, animal resources like the sheep, human skills like weaving, leather work, dairying opportunities, etc.). Vocational schools should be obligatory for all under the age of 18 who attend no other type of schools. These students should be taught a pre-vocational training year in which they should be taught the theory which may facilitate their choice of training and HRD needs.

In addition to part-time vocational schools, there should be full time vocational schools offering one to three-year courses. The vocationally-oriented schools should admit students with a middle class or high school certificate. The duration of the course may be two years offering highly practice related study courses of a scientific nature. Courses should cover theory as well as workshop and on the job training.

Opportunity Beyond School

Vocational education and training centres should be established in rural areas to meet the HRD needs of the rural people for healthy and productive livings and it should extend to high technology required for technological progress. By expanding the scope beyond the schools, we may impart education and training to the primary school drop-outs, the literate youth who are in need of employment. At higher level it may also help additive value in terms of developing skills through short-term courses. The centers would have the overall responsibility of implementation, monitoring, development of career-oriented programmes, and managing good quality of education. The centers should take care in respect of the curriculum development, training and placement of the students and in interaction with the industry and trade.

National Institute of Information and Technology (NIIT) has taken a significant step towards providing computer training facilities among students throughout the country. The NIIT is not having affiliation to any university or institution. The computer professionals trained by the NIIT have been growing and they are in heavy demand. Accountancy, food processing, food technology, environmental technology, fashion designing technology, advertising, etc., are some of the new fields of job-oriented programmes required for youth to increase the employability.

Recommendations and Suggestions

(i) Surveys are needed to investigate the type of job-oriented courses and job opportunities available in different regions of the country.

(ii) Relationship between individual characteristics and effort of various types of information relevant to occupational choice, need to be explored.

(iii) Guidance needed in a school is mainly in vocational and professional fields. Private sectors should be involved in advising technical schools.

(iv) Efforts should be made to impart vocational education and training for the socially useful productive work. The curriculum should be linked with the market and economic resources.

(v) Production-cum-training centres should be established for boys and girls separately. These institutions must be recognized by National Open School (NOS).

(vi) The incident of drop-outs among various communities should be tackled by running affective monitoring education programmes.

(vii) Employers should be persuaded to find mechanisms to give employment to the students who attained degree/diploma certificates in vocational education. To achieve this objective one possibility may be to conduct national testing examination through specially designed aptitude test.

(viii) Atmosphere should be created to motivate students to study vocational courses. The vocational education of women belonging to various minority communities should be taken up on the priority basis.

(ix) There is a need for monitoring and evaluation of OJT programmes.

(x) Practical on the job training, usually called apprenticeship, should take one to three years, depending on the occupation. Training allowance should be paid during the apprentice period.

Conclusion

By introducing vocational education at the middle or secondary level, we can enhance the level of motivation and employability of our youth. However, the importance of general education cannot be undermined because it provides the foundation of chanelizing an individual's intellectual and scholastic resources in the direction of moulding the person as one capable of doing jobs available in the job market. The two streams of education have to merge at certain points so as to carry the person towards a happy and socially useful living.

REFERENCES

Bahl, S., 1995, Reaping rich dividends. *The Times of India* (Ascent), October 25, p. 23.

Rao, T.V., 1966, *Human Resources Development — Experiences, Interventions, Strategies*, New Delhi: Sage Publications.

SIXTEEN

Do Top Level Managers have Higher Quality of Work Life?

NAVAL KARRIR

The present cultural, social and technological period, the industrial era, which began in the eighteenth century, is slowly waning, impelled by changes in social values and development in technology. The relationship between work in its conventional form and economic performance is growing tenuous and, as a result, the meaning both of work and of man's relationship to society is called into question. The widely accepted belief that a dehumanized work life is the inevitable cost of acquiring material rewards above subsistence levels is also called into question. A growing number of people refuse to accept the inevitability of the kind of working life that is prevalent in most of the industrialized nations.

Trist (1975) made an eloquent plea for importance of Quality of Work Life (QWL) in a developing country like India. "In a developing country, the QWL can become both ends and means. It is an "end" in itself because it is a higher significant component in the quality of life — the goal of all development. It is a "means" because the experience of participation in decision-making at the work place and of progressive learning help workers to acquire the civic competencies and skills on which a country developing in social democratic mode must rely. It would be tragic if in industrializing, the less developed countries adopt the authoritarian management styles from which the advanced countries are beginning to break loose. It would retard development of their productivity, increase their comparative economic disadvantage, and all to rapidly create alienated workers, likely to cause severe political problems. The best strategy would be to "Century Skip" — to ignore the nineteenth century models of industrial organizations and the dehumanizing values embodied in them and experiment in ways suitable to the conditions of the third world, with new forms of organization that gives first importance to quality of life in work place.

In India, research on QWL has begun to take momentum. A number of studies have been conducted on various professional groups (teachers, industrial workers, bank workers, women workers, R&D personnel, etc.). But very few studies have been carried out on Managers (Singh and Maggu 1980; Gosh and Kalra 1982; George 1984; Kishore 1988).

For an organization to exist and survive, the key resource is the manager. In the present environment of tremendous technological and scientific advancement, it is the manager who plans and coordinates the workforce along with factors of production in a synergetic effort to achieve desired goals and objectives. Moreover, in an industrial set-up, the manager's role is very vital. He develops policies, plans, procedures and makes explicit the purpose of an organization. He is also a concrete bridge between the employers and employees. But for the managers, organizations would completely loose their structure and regress to the primitive state of more assemblage of individuals. It would be impossible for such assemblages to achieve the desired objectives. An organization and the manager cannot survive without each other. It becomes imperative for an organization to provide an atmosphere conducive for better quality of work life of its managers. It is, therefore, important for an organization to identify various factors which affect QWL of its managers.

The present study is based on theories of motivation, it is a modest attempt to compare QWL of managers in relation to job satisfaction, job involvement, work involvement alongwith management cadre), have been categorized as lower (first) level managers.

(ii) *Middle (second) level:* Managers supervising the lower level managers (not directly controlling the workforce, that is, forming a link between "Think Tank" and "Executioners" of the job), have been categorized as middle level managers.

(iii) *Top (third) level:* Managers supervising the middle level managers serving as "Think Tank" of organization have been categorized as top level managers.

Type of Organization

The total industry has been categorized into following sectors (based on Government of India norms):

(i) *Public Sector:* The organizations which are controlled by Bureau of Public Enterprises and in which Government of India has more than fifty per cent of share including in this sector. These exclude the state government owned industries and organizations in which state government has equity participation.

(ii) *Private Sector:* The organizations which are owned and controlled by proprietors, partnerships or board of directors nominated by shareholders come in this sector. This includes the private limited companies which have raised the equity through public distribution of shares.

(iii) *Cooperative Sector:* The organizations which came into existence during the cooperative movement launched by Government of India come in this sector. These organizations are directly under control of Government of India, run on the cooperative pattern (farmers or sections of farmers come together to form an enterprise).

These exclude cooperatives run by the state government equity participation.

Instruments used for Measurement of Variables

Personal Information Schedule (PIS)

The PIS was used to collect the background information such as age, educational qualification, experience, native or migrant status, number of dependents and income level of the respondent.

background variables in three sectors of Indian Industry (Public, Private and Cooperative), at all the three levels of managerial hierarchy.

Concept of QWL

From the review of literature, action studies and empirical researches conducted by various researchers and experts in the field of quality of work life, various viewpoints have been forwarded regarding what are to be the dimensions of QWL. However, neither consensus has been reached on what constitutes the dimensions of QWL nor a standard definition has been evolved. The dimensions for this multifaceted term 'QWL' entirely depends upon the researchers frame of reference. For the present study, QWL has been considered as an offshoot of quality of life concept and as a measure of individuals satisfaction or dissatisfaction at the workplace. This has been based on concepts forwarded by :

(a) Beinum (1974), who defined QWL as — the quality of relationship between men and his task.

(b) Seashore (1975), according to whom, "it is the individual's own personal satisfaction or dissatisfaction which defines the quality of his or her work life rather than any objective criterion".

Hypotheses

The present section of this study tests the three hypotheses with the rationale on which these hypotheses are based.

Hypothesis I

There will be significant differences in QWL of managers at different levels of managerial hierarchy, i.e., top, middle and lower levels of management in three different sectors of industry i.e., public, private and cooperative.

Rationale for the hypothesis: In nearly all the industrial organizations, professionals hold managerial positions and generally the entry level is at the lowest levels of management. A manager goes up in the hierarchy based upon his experience, seniority through age or acquired skills and educational qualifications. The decisions taken by managers also change with change in managerial levels and alongwith it there are changes in their needs. Porter (1961) found managerial level to be a significant variable in determining the extent to which the needs are satisfied. Slocum (1971) found that higher level managers showed greater degree of overall need satisfaction in their jobs than did lower level managers. Payne and Mansfield (1978) showed 'QWL' as a differentiating factor at various hierarchical levels. Jaine et al., (1982) found significant differences between managers with respect to their needs. These differences in the needs and satisfaction are likely to affect the QWL of managers. Sondhi and Bhardwaj (1986) found higher officials exhibiting better QWL than their counterparts at lower levels. Jain (1991) also found hierarchical differences with regard to QWL in a private organization. Hence it would be interesting to examine the differences in QWL of managers at top, middle and lower levels of management.

Hypothesis II

There will be significant differences in QWL of managers belonging to public, private and cooperative sector.

Rationale for the hypothesis: The three main sectors of industry: public, private and cooperative differ in their objectives, working style, organizational commitments, structure, rules, procedure, bylaws, etc., to name a few. These can have an effect on the QWL of managers. Very few comparative studies have been done in all the three sectors. With the change in industrial environment and globalization of markets, a comparative analysis would identify grey areas in each sector and good features from one sector can be adopted by other sectors.

Hypothesis III

There will be significant difference in QWL of managers with respect to levels of managerial hierarchy (top, middle and lower level) from three sectors of industry (public, private and cooperative).

Rationale for the hypothesis: This is micro analysis of the proposition made earlier in the hypothesis-I, with the superimposition of the

sectorial differences of public, private and cooperative sectors (from the hypothesis-II). Since the organizations differ in their objectives, working methodology, etc., in different sectors of industry QWL of managers may also differ.

Method

Survey method was adopted for the study. Questionnaire were used to collect data from randomly selected managers (N=491), in Indian industry. Data analysis was done by using various univariate, bivariate and multivariate statistical techniques.

Sample

Taking manager as the unit of analysis, simple random sampling method was adopted for the selection of managers. The sample consisted of 491 managers (public sector N=182; private sector N=143; co-operative sector N=166) at all the three levels of management, i.e., top, middle and lower levels.

Variables Included and Instruments used in the Study

Dependent Variable

The dependent variable is "Quality of worklife", further classified into two groups — conditions and feelings.

(a) *Conditions:* Conditions represent the perception of the respondent as regards to existing situation or conditions in work place. These can be considered as Objective Indicators of QWL (QWL-C).

(b) *Feelings:* Feelings are considered as psychological reactions to these various work situations or conditions and are thus categorized as Subjective Indicators of QWL (QWL-F).

Independent Variables

(a) *Managerial level:* Since disparity exists in the nomenclature of the designations of the managers, in the three sectors of the industry, the managers have been broadly classified according to the nature of supervision they exercise over their subordinates. These levels are categorized as:

(i) *Lower (first) level:* Managers directly in touch with the workers (supervising the workforce in non-

Sashkin and Lengermenn QWL Feelings/Condition (1984) (QWL F/C)

This instrument has two parts — Feelings and Conditions:

"Conditions" part consists of 25 items describing working conditions objectively on five dimensions: (a) Autonomy (b) Personal growth opportunity (c) Work speed and routine (d) Work complexity (e) Task related interfactional factors.

"Feeling" part consists of 10 strongly interrelated items measuring respondents subjective feelings about his personal relationship to work.

Statistical Techniques used in the Study

Various univariate, bivariate and multivariate statistical techniques have been used to analyse the data.

Pearson's product moment correlation has been used to study relationships between the dependent variable (QWL F/C) and independent variables. For the coded variables, wherever significant correlations are found, variables have been decoded, grouped and 't' test comparisons done taking two groups at a time.

Result and Discussion

Hypothesis I

To study the differences in QWL F/C of managers at different levels of management, comparison has been done by taking two levels at a time and computing their 't' value with respect to QWL-F and QWL-C. The results have been given in Table 1.

The results indicate a significant difference of QWL FC of managers from:

(a) Lower and top levels (refer Table 1, t=4.34 for QWL-F and t=2.57 for QWL-C, $p<0.001$).

(b) Middle and top levels (refer Table 1, t=2.75 for QWL-F and t=3.08 for QWL-C, $p<0.01$).

The analysis suggests (refer Table 1) that top level managers have higher QWL than middle and lower level managers. This clearly shows that top level managers are able to satisfy all their needs through resources available at top levels of management, middle and lower levels managers may be having less satisfied needs at their levels of managerial hierarchy. Results on similar

TABLE 1

't'—TEST (COMPARISON) OF QWL F/C OF MANAGERS FROM TOP, MIDDLE AND LOWER LEVELS OF MANAGEMENT (N=491)

Sr. No.	Managerial level	N	Mean		S.D.		Comparison of levels	Degree of freedom	't' value	
			QWL-F*	QWL-C	QWL-F	QWL-C			QWL-F	QWL-C
1.	Top Level	95	41.49	69.0	4.75	5.75	Top level v/s Middle level	266	2.75**	3.08**
2.	Middle Level	173	39.7	66.6	5.27	6.13	Middle level v/s Lower level	394	1.47	0.96
3.	Lower Level	223	38.9	67.2	4.77	5.64	Lower level v/s Top level	316	4.34***	2.57***

*QWL-F = Feeling; QWL-C = Conditions ** $p < 0.01$ *** $p < 0.001$.

TABLE 2

't'—TEST (COMPARISON) OF QWL F/C OF MANAGERS BELONGING TO THREE DIFFERENT SECTORS, VIZ. PUBLIC, PRIVATE AND COOPERATIVE (N=491)

Sr. No.	*Sector*	*N*	*Mean*		*S.D.*		*Sector comparison*	*Degree of freedom*	*'t' value*	
			QWL-F	*QWL-C*	*QWL-F*	*QWL-C*			*QWL-F*	*QWL-C*
1.	Public Sector	182	40.01	68.21	5.09	5.98	Public v/s Private	323	0.69	2.46*
2.	Private Sector	143	39.62	66.61	5.00	5.59	Private v/s Cooperative	307	0.28	0.72
3.	Coope-rative Sector	166	39.66	67.09	4.99	5.95	Cooperative v/s Public	346	1.01	1.75

* $p<0.05$

TABLE 3

't'—TEST (COMPARISONS) OF QWL F/C OF MANAGERS IN THREE SECTORS OF INDUSTRY WITH RESPECT TO MANAGERIAL LEVEL. (N=491)

Sr. No.	*Sector*	*Mean*		*S.D.*		*Sector comparison*	*Level of manager*	*N*	*Degree of freedom*	*'t' value*	
		QWL-F	*QWL-C*	*QWL-F*	*QWL-C*					*QWL-F*	*QWL-C*
1.	Public	41.77	71.35	4.28	5.28	Public	Top	31	63	0.74	3.75***
	Sector	40.92	68.25	5.47	5.85	v/s	Middle	55	103	1.64	2.82**
		38.91	67.17	4.89	5.96	Private	Lower	96	153	0.76	0.71
2.	Private	40.94	66.91	4.79	4.24	Private	Top	34	62	0.71	1.46
	Sector	39.26	64.96	4.87	6.10	v/s	Middle	50	116	0.23	1.44
		39.16	67.84	5.18	5.56	Cooperative	Lower	59	125	0.39	1.14
3.	Coope-rative **	41.83	68.96	5.25	6.84	Cooperative	Top	30	59	0.05	1.53
	Sector	39.04	66.60	5.30	6.12	v/s	Middle	68	121	1.93**	1.52
		38.83	67.17	4.27	5.27	Public	Lower	68	162	0.11	0.47

** $p<0.01$ *** $p<0.001$

lines have been reported by others (Porter, 1961; Slocum, 1971; Jaine, et al., 1982). The differences in QWL of managers with respect to their managerial hierarchy have been found in other studies (Payne and Mansfield, 1978; Sondhi and Bhardwaj, 1986; Jain, 1991).

To sum up, results have been showing significant difference in QWL F/C of managers among :

(a) Lower and top levels
(b) Top and middle levels

Hypothesis II

To study the difference in QWL of managers belonging to three sectors, namely, public, private and cooperative, comparisons have been made by taking two sectors at a time and computing their 't' value with respect to QWL-F and QWL-C. The results have been tabulated in Table 2.

The comparisons of quality of work life of managers belonging to three different sectors of industry reveal significant differences in public and private sectors (refer Table 2, 't' value = 2.46, $p < 0.05$) in QWL-C. This indicates differences in subjective evaluation of the quality of work life by managers. Differences in their means, further reveal, that managers in public sectors have better quality of work life than managers in the private sectors. Similar findings have been reported by Ghosh and Kalra (1982) and Kishore (1980) in their studies on managers of public and private sectors. This may be due to the fact that governmental policies of pay, compensation, etc., are such that the manager feels high job security and is able to satisfy all his needs at the workplace. An important fact that cannot be overlooked is, that the cooperative sector has fallen in between the public and private sectors, in comparison to the quality of worklife of their managers. Further analysis has been carried out to bring out the differences in quality of work life of managers with respect to managerial hierarchy in public, private and cooperative sectors.

Hypothesis III

The 't' test comparisons of QWL-F/C of managers at three levels of managerial hierarchy, taking two sectors at a time have been given in Table 3.

The superimposition of sectorial differences on the differences in QWL F/C of managers at top, middle and lower levels of managerial hierarchy reveals, that there are differences at:

(a) top level managers in public and private sectors (refer Table 3, t= 3.75, p<0.001 for QWL-C) in their objective evaluation of the quality of work life.

(b) middle level in (i) public and private sectors (refer Table 3, t= 2.82 at p<0.01 for QWL-C) in objective evaluation of quality of work life by managers. (ii) public and cooperative sectors (refer Table 3, t= 4.93 at p<0.01 for QWL-F managers about their feelings towards quality of work life. Also the top level managers in public sector have better QWL than private sector managers (differences in means, refer Table 3). The possible reason could be that managers at top level in public sector are able to satisfy all their needs through resources available at that level (due to governmental policies and laws) and feel more job satisfied, work involved than their counterparts in private sector. Similar is the case of managers at the middle level in public sector, who have better quality of work life than their counterparts in private and cooperative sectors. An interesting observation is that there is no significant difference among managers in their QWL at the lower level of managerial hierarchy in all the three sectors. The possible reason could be, that in all the three sectors, at entry level, managers (lower level) are able to satisfy their basic needs or may be getting a job itself is a satisfying experience in itself (considering unemployment in India).

Conclusion

After testing the hypotheses, the question addressed to in this chapter "Do Top Level Managers have Higher Quality of Work life?" can be answered with confidence that Yes! the top level managers have highest quality of work life amongst the three levels of managers. Moreover the managers in public sector exhibit higher quality of work life than their counterparts in private and cooperative sectors.

Recommendations for Future Research

1. In the present study only three sectors have been covered, attempts should be made to extend the study to other sectors, joint ventures, services sector, etc.
2. More variables need to be included as pay and compensation, benefits and environmental factors given due considerations.
3. The study of blue collar workers on the same lines would help in comparisons to be drawn between white and blue collar workers.
4. Attempts need to be made to devise instruments for measurement of QWL in Indian conditions after a 'Delphi' is done so as to reach at a consensus for broad definition and dimensions of QWL.

REFERENCES

Beinum, V., 1974, On the strategic importance of the quality of working life, a paper presented at the 5th International Personnel Conference, Montreal Canada, November.

George, S., 1984, Perception of Quality of working life, an exploratory study in two public sector undertakings, An Unpublished M. Tech. Dissertation, I.I.T. Delhi.

Ghosh, S. and Kalra, S.K., 1982, Perceptual differences in quality of worklife factors, *Indian Journal of Training and Development*, 12 (3 and 4): 10-12.

Jain, S., 1991, *Quality of worklife*, Deep & Deep Publications.

Jaine, C. Jaramitlo, M.P., Torres, M.C. and Urdaneta, O., Motivational Differences According to Hierarchical Levels in Finance Services Organizations.

Katz, B., and R. L. Kahn, 1966, *The Social Psychology of an Organization*, New York: John Wiley.

Kishore, M., *Factors Related to Need Satisfaction, Focus on Managers of Public and Private Sectors*, Unpublished PhD dissertation, IIT, Delhi, 1988.

Oldham, G.R. and Rotchford, N.L., 1983, Relationships between Office Characteristics and Employee Reactions, A study of the Physical Environment, *Administrative Science Quarterly*, 28: 542-56.

Payne and Mansfield, R., 1978, Correlates of Individual Perception of Organizational Climate, *Journal of Occupational Psychology*, 51.

Porter, L.W., 1961, A study of perceived Need Satisfaction in bottom and middle management jobs, *Journal of Applied Psychology*, 45: 1-10.

Sashkin, M., and Lengermann J.J., 1984, *QWL Conditions/Feelings* (Eds.) Pfeiffer, J.M., and Gold Steins, L.D. Developing Human Resources 13th Annual University Associates, California, 131-44.

Sashkin, M., and Morris, W.C., 1984, *Organizational Behaviour and Management: Concepts and Experiences*, Reston, VA: Reston Publishing.

Seashore, S.E., 1975, "Defining and Measuring the QWL" in Davis, L.E., and Chern, A.E. *The Quality of Working Life*. (1): New York: Free Press.

Singh, P. and Maggu, A., 1980, Quality of working life in Indian Organizations, *Management and Labour Studies*.

Slocum, J.W., 1971, Motivation in Managerial levels. The Effect of Need Satisfaction on ones' Job Performance, *Journal of Applied Psychology*, 55: 312-15.

Sondhi, N. and Bhardwaj, G., Quality of working life in the Indian Industrial Scene: A myth or reality? *Indian Psychological Review*, 1986, 31 (special issue).

Trist, E., 1975, Planning the first step towards quality of work life in a developing country. In Davis S, L.E. and Cherns A.B. (eds.), *Quality of working life*, Vol. One. New York: The Free Press.

SEVENTEEN

Cooperation and Competition among Industrial Employees

CHITTRANJAN N. DAFTUAR *and* ANJULI SRIVASTAVA

History of small group research is virtually identical with the history of social psychology and certain areas of sociology. In the early1920s, the social psychologists and research workers of small groups did not so much involve themselves in philosophical issues as with its methodology. They began to concentrate on studying limited specified aspects of man's social behaviour. In 1930s, the small group researchers widened their field of study to include mass movements, lynchings, prejudices, rumours, etc. In 1940s, methodological developments and empirical knowledge both acquired significance and gave thought to the study of leadership. In 1950s and 1960s, particularly in the USA, much more interest developed in this area. Four decades back, three eminent American social psychologists (Kelly, 1953; Fetinger, 1954; and Thibant, 1956) focused their attentions on the research of small groups. Identifying the set of roles and a network of interpersonal attraction that distinguish small groups from other groups. They gave many guidelines for the future research. Daftuar (1967) was the first Indian scholar who nicely worked in the field. But it is a matter of great surprise and sorrow that his initiative was not followed by other research scholars in spite of the fact that the techniques of dealing with groups might prove rewarding in terms of influencing behaviour, attitudes, and possibilities of the participants in these groups.

Scientific Approach to the Study of Group Dynamics

A basic premise of group dynamics is that method of science can be employed in the study of groups. Social science, of which group dynamics is a part, has during the last quarter of the nineteenth and in the present century, increasingly adopted experimental procedures. In the first three decades, significant advance was made in the measurement of attitudes. The "Social distance" scales developed by Bogardus (1925), Thruston (1928) and Likert (1932) were important landmarks. Apart from this, there was development in statistical methods which helped in efficient experimental design and quantitative findings. The following three scientific methodologies are worth noting.

Experiments on Individual Behaviour in Groups

Experimental technique for conducting experiment on the conditions affecting human behaviour was a valuable gain for group dynamics. One problem experimentally investigated was to see the change in an individual's solitary performance occurring when other people are present. The laboratory answer to this question came from Triplett (1897) when he compared the performance of children in winding fishing reels when working alone and working together with the other children. Triplett's conclusion was that the group situation tended to generate an increase in output of energy and achievement. A similar line in research attempted to compare the performance of the group and the performance of the individual. Gardon (1924), Watson (1928) and Shaw (1932) experimented on tasks which could be performed either by individuals or by groups.

Controlled Observation of Social Interaction

This method has been used extensively in field of group dynamics where observational technique is combined with experimental procedure. The principal researches responsible for these important advances were those of Thomas (1918), Parten (1932), Jack (1934) and Olson (1934).

Methods were also developed for sampling the interaction of large group of people over a long time to ensure efficient estimates.

Sociometry

Moreno (1934) was responsible for initiating this technique in the USA. A questionnaire was prepared and each person was required to indicate those other people with whom he would prefer to share some specified activities. This procedure led to finding of valuable information about interpersonal attraction and repulsion among the members of the group. The data concerning "who chooses whom" helped in preparing a SOCIOGRAM which revealed the picture of cohesiveness with the help of sociometric techniques in the field of group dynamics. It was easy to find, for example, features of groups patterns of friendship and sub-group formation, etc., by this method.

Group atmosphere has assumed considerable importance in the present social setting. A very important discussion among social theorists is popular which has divided them into two groups. Some scholars say that effective cooperation inside the group among the group members can yield better results. i.e. the performance of team work gives perfection in work because no body is absolutely perfect, so without the cooperation of other members an individual cannot effectively do any work. Opinion of the second group is absolutely different from the first group. They prefer individuality not group atmosphere.

Works of Lewin (1939), Lippitt (1940), White (1940) and Bavelas (1942) have made excellent contributions in this field. We may note certain basic aspects of the dynamics of the group in regard to cooperative v/s competitive social situations. In a study made by Martin M. Grassack (1954), following points were noted:

1. A cooperative situation is one of "task directions" within the group which is not readily available in a group working under a competitive situation. A situation of "task direction" is one in which an individual's goal is reached by the achievement of a group task.
2. According to Deutch (1949), the basic difference between cooperation and competition is in the way an individual achieves his goal in both situations. Cooperation was defined

by him as a situation in which no individual reaches his goal unless all other individuals also enter their goal region.

3. Cooperation may be viewed as an example of cohesiveness due to task direction. Back (1948) demonstrated that the relatively high amount of cohesiveness existed in situations where the group mediated individual goal.
4. Conditions of task direction are likely to produce instrumental communications, while the competitive situations will tend not to have such an effect.

Cooperation and Competition

In groups which are motivated to cooperate, all the members work towards a group goal which depends on interdependence of activities performed by the members. In competition, individual's reward depends upon his own achievements which can usually be maximized only at the expense of other group members (May and Doob, 1937).

Competition requires at least a degree of prior cooperation that is necessary for the setting of rules and imposing of sanctions without which competition would dissolve into open war. Conversely, it is doubtful that cooperation would be the major force in the absence of pressure of competition that spur some to cooperate with others as a means of enhancing their own effectiveness in the struggle for existence. In any event, a purely cooperative or competitive relationship is normally not found.

Biesanz and Biesanz have said that competition is the striving of two or more persons for the same goal, which is limited so that all cannot share it. According to Southerland, Woodworth and Maxwell (1952), competition is an impersonal, unconscious, continuous struggle between individuals or groups for satisfaction which because of their limited supply, all may not have at the same time. Hence, it can be said that competition is a struggle in which minimum two competitors are involved and they try to achieve the same goal(s). In the views of Fairchild (1944), competition is the struggle for the use or possession of limited goods or resources. According to Bogardus (1925), competition is a contest to obtain something which does not exist in a quantity sufficient to meet the demand.

The concept of cooperation and interrelated concept of competition are rarely missing in discussions of interpersonal and intergroup relations. Both play important roles in the writings of many social theorists. Yet, despite the obvious significance of these concepts for the understanding and control of social process, there has been little in the way of explicit theorizing and virtually no experimental work with respect to the effects of cooperation and competition upon social process. The work in this area has largely been concerned with the effects of the individual's motivation to achieve under the two different conditions. None of the experimental studies have investigated the interactions between individuals and the group process that emerges as a consequence of the cooperative and competitive social situations.

Cooperative and Competitive Situations

According to Cartwright and Zander (1953), in a cooperative social situation, the goals for the individuals or subunits in the situation are defined so that a goal region can be entered by any given individual or subunit only. All the members of the group are interdependent on each other and they have their common goals which are interrelated.

In competitive social situations, the goals for individuals or subunits in the situation under consideration have the following characteristics: If a goal region is entered by an individual or a subunit, the other individuals or subunits will, to some degree, be unable to reach their respective goals in the social situation under consideration. However, it is important to note that in real life, "pure cooperative" or "pure competitive" situation does not exist. Therefore it is possible for individuals to be promotively interdependent with respect to one goal and contritely interdependent with respect to another goal. On an analysis of cooperative situations, it is revealed that if one individual makes a move in a direction, the other also moves in the same direction. On analysing the competitive situation, it is often seen that the movement of an individual towards a goal has no necessary effect on the movement of others. When pairs or larger groups are compared in the solution of the same types of problems, the groups are found to be more efficient when a division of labour is possible.

Among the 8 Cooperative groups, the members chosen for 4 groups were friendly or most friendly with each other while the members of other 4 groups were less friendly or indifferent to each other. In the same way, competitive groups were also formed.

In Cooperative groups, the subjects were told to work together in cooperation by helping each other. In competitive groups, the subjects were told to work individually, they could not help each other. In this way, each subject was given an experience of working in cooperative or competitive conditions for four hours, spread over four. days. The detailed instructions given to each type of groups are described in the 'data collection' section.

Tasks

The following four tasks were given to the subjects :

1. Reproduction of Geometrical Designs
2. Solving different kinds of Puzzles
3. Solving Arithmetic Sums
4. Greeting Card Making

Geometrical Designs

The subjects were shown twenty geometrical designs for about 5 minutes. Subject had to recall and draw those designs with the help of scale and pencil. After half-an-hour, another set of twenty geometrical designs were shown to employees for 5 minutes only. Again they had to recall and draw those designs. The instructions given to the cooperative groups was that the group which would draw maximum number of correct designs would get the prize. In competitive groups, the prize was to be awarded to the individual drawing maximum number of correct designs.

Solving Puzzles

Cross-word Puzzles: Some Cross-word Puzzles were given and the employees had to solve with the help of the clues given.

Jigsaw Puzzles: Three Jigsaw Puzzles were given to the subjects for solving. In these puzzles, two different types of pictures were shown to the employees. They had been given two hundred multicoloured pieces of the pictures. With the help of multicoloured pieces, subjects had to prepare the picture. Each picture was to be prepared with 100 multicoloured pieces.

The instruction given to cooperative group was that the group which would solve the puzzle first would get the prize, provided all the answers were correct. In the competitive group the prize was to be awarded to the individuals solving the puzzle first with correct answers.

Arithmetic Sums

The third task involved adding three given sets of numbers. The subjects were required to multiply each digit beginning from left. After this, subjects were given few sums wherein they were required to find out the missing numbers. The subjects were told that they would be eligible for the prize only when all the answers were correct.

The cooperative groups consisting of 3 members each were to complete the task in one hour. The competitive groups were required to do as much as each member could do in one hour. The condition for the prize was that each sum should be correct. (The winners were given a flower pot and key ring as reward.)

Greeting Card Making

Subjects were given some material. With the help of these material they had to make greeting cards. In cooperative group, the subjects were given instructions that the group which would prepare more greeting cards in one hour would be awarded a prize. Each worker should make at least 2 greeting cards. Thus, there should be at least 10 greeting cards in each group. Reward will be given upon neatness and uniqueness of the card. In the competitive group, the workers were told that the individual preparing maximum number of neat and beautiful greeting cards would get the prize.

Other Tests

One sociometric test was prepared to know the extent of friendliness amongst the employees which helped in forming the groups. On the left side of the page, names of the 48 employees (subjects) were written and against each name five response categories were indicated, i.e., most friendly, friendly, just friendly, less friendly and indifferent. Each employee was required to rate every other employee under these categories.

For measuring interpersonal relationships, a small 7-point Semantic Differential scale was used. Only three item - scale was used, i.e.,

Good	Bad
Intelligent	Foolish
Active	Dull

Collection of Data

For data collection, at first, the sociometric test was administered to 48 subjects. These 48 employees were divided into 16 groups on the basis of their sociometric scores, i.e., in each group, there were 3 employees, 8 groups were for cooperative work and the remaining 8 for competitive works. First, one cooperative group was called and following instruction was given.

"The group which would make the maximum designs would get the prize. So, you should work cooperatively. You can help each other. You will be shown 20 geometrical designs for 5 minutes and will be required to reproduce those designs within 30 minutes. After you complete the work, another set of 20 designs would be shown tomorrow and the same procedure would be followed".

However, they preferred to work together. As soon as they started drawing designs, the watch was set. While subjects were performing, some observations were being noted such as how they were talking with each other, how they were responding to each other, whether they were friendly with each other or not and so on. When the test time was over, they were asked to stop their work. The number of designs made by the group was also noted.

While administering this scale and the questionnaire, they were seated at some distance and were asked not to consult each other. In this way the first work session of one group was concluded. Next day, the same group was again called. They were given the second task which was Puzzles Solving Task. They were given all the material required for solving puzzles with proper instructions.

After the task was over, similar data, as in the first session, were collected from the subjects. The same procedure was repeated for next two days with the remaining tasks.

In the competitive groups the instructions were different. At first one competitive group was called and the following instruction was given:

"Now I am going to give you some interesting problems to solve. All of you have to solve each problem individually and as quickly as possible. The time limit is one hour. Within these 60 minutes, you will have to solve as many problems as you can. The one who will solve the largest number of problems will be awarded a prize".

Excepting change in instructions, the same procedure was followed with competitive groups as which was followed with the cooperative groups.

According to the group productivity, the members of the cooperative groups were given prizes and according to the individual productivity the members of the competitive groups were awarded the prizes (Flower Pots and Key Rings).

Observations

During the data collection, some personal observations were also made. Each member of the group whether cooperative group or competitive, was kept under close observation while performing their assigned task. Their behaviour towards each other, their attitude and conversation was also taken note of.

Observation for Cooperative Groups

On the first day, the subjects were filled with curiosity as to what they would be required to do. When they were told the nature of the task to be done, they were also posed this question — "would you like to work together on this task individually?" All the 3 members of a group sat very close to each other, discussing their plan of action. Suggestions were made to each other and help offered. All of them had a keen desire to commence their operation.

In the greeting-card making task, the members of the groups had divided the work among themselves. Some folded the papers, some did the cutting and some did the painting work. Each prodded the other to be quick. They were all keenly interested in the assignment and were full of enthusiasm. While working, they talked to each other continuously.

In the task-solving arithmetical sums, each of the 3 members of the group divided the sums amongst themselves and started doing them. As they worked on sums, they asked each other to get the sums right and not to commit a mistake. If a particular group completed the task earlier than the assigned 60 minutes, the members constituting the group checked the correctness of each other.

Thus, it was seen that the members of the cooperative group displayed a sense of unity. In order to gain the prize for the group, each member wanted to contribute to the maximum. They took interest in the work and were eager to know the score of the other groups. Their keenness was sustained and interest unflagging. They appeared to be determined to do better in succeeding in the test in order to improve their overall score.

Out of 8 cooperative groups, 4 had such members as were friendly to one another and 4 were such whose members were indifferent to one another (as shown on sociometric scale). The members belonging to the second type of groups rarely talked to each other on the first day but from the second day onwards got friendly with each other and indulged in mutual help.

Competitive Groups

The interpersonal relationship of the competitive group in the performance of different tasks were also observed. The members (3 in each group) did not talk to each other. Almost unconsciously they sat apart at some distance from each other and as soon as the task was allotted they started doing their work. It was seen that when a particular member failed to make a Geometrical design or to solve puzzle test, he made a sly attempt to note the design of the neighbour. When one succeeded in completing a design quickly, the other felt jealous of this and also felt a sense of humiliation. It was seen that one subject who succeeded in making a geometrical design early enough, shielded it with the notebook, lest others should copy his design.

Results and Discussions

As has been stated earlier, the semantic differential test with only 3 scales was used to measure the dependent variable, i.e., interpersonal relationship.

On the basis of individual ratings each individual had been given scores on a 7-point rating scale. These scores were added and averaged individually as well as group-wise. Lastly, the average for all cooperative groups and for competitive groups was calculated. To test the hypothesis, the average of all 3 scales was calculated separately. The t-test was applied to know the significance of difference between means of the two groups.

The average scores of each cooperative and competitive group have been shown in Table 1. The table also gives means of all cooperative groups and competitive groups for each of the semantic scales.

TABLE 1
THE MEAN SCORES OF INTERPERSONAL RELATIONSHIP OF COOPERATIVE AND COMPETITIVE GROUPS

Groups	*Cooperative Group*			*Competitive Group*		
	Intelligent/ Foolish	*Good/ Bad*	*Active/ Dull*	*Intelligent/ Foolish*	*Good/ Bad*	*Active/ Dull*
	1	*2*	*3*	*1*	*2*	*3*
1	6.8	6.9	6.8	5.0	4.9	4.9
2	6.6	6.5	6.3	4.1	4.7	3.9
3	6.5	6.6	6.4	4.8	3.9	3.9
4	6.8	6.9	6.9	4.6	4.4	3.8
5	6.7	6.9	6.9	3.8	4.1	3.7
6	6.7	6.6	6.6	4.6	4.6	4.3
7	6.8	6.8	6.9	4.8	4.6	4.5
8	6.8	6.9	5.8	4.0	4.1	4.8
Average of Means	6.7	6.7	6.6	4.4	4.4	4.2

On comparison of overall means of the cooperative and competitive groups for the three semantic scales, Intelligent/ Foolish, Good/Bad, and Active/Passive it was found that the three sets of means differed significantly. The t-values for the three comparisons were 13.3, 89.05, and 10.43, respectively.

On examining the above data, it is clear that in cooperative group there was very good interpersonal relationship. The highest rating of the scale is 7 and here the average of the interpersonal relationship for cooperative group is 6.7 which is very close to the maximum possible score. While in competitive groups, the mean score for interpersonal relationship is only 4.4 which leaves a relatively big gap of 2.30.

In the three scales of interpersonal relationships in the cooperative group, the average for "intelligence" (Intelligent or Foolish) is 6.7, average for "Activity" (Active or Dull) is 6.6 and for "Goodness" (Good or Bad) the average is 6.7. It indicates that the members of cooperative group perceive each other favourably. In competitive group the average rating for "Intelligence" is 4.4, average for "Goodness" (Good or Bad) is 4.4 and the average "Activity" (Active or Dull) is 4.2. It can be easily said that there is a better interpersonal relationship among the members of the cooperative group than in competitive group.

Making observation of behaviours during the period when the subjects were busy in performing their tasks it was found that the members of the cooperative groups displayed a sense of unity. In order to gain the prize for the entire group, each member wanted to contribute to the maximum. All the 3 members of a group tried to move and sit very close to each other and discussed the possible mode of their attack, gave suggestions to each other and offered mutual help. Whereas in competitive groups, the group members unconsciously sat apart, at some distance from each other. There was, of course, no question of giving suggestions or offering help to each other at all. It was also seen that when one subject succeeded in completing the geometrical design task earlier than others, he often tried to shield it with his notebook or by some other material lest others should copy his design.

One more thing was also marked that in the condition of cooperation, in which the members who were indifferent to each other, they did not rate other group members very high on the first day, but from second day onwards when they got acquainted with each other and grew friendly they started rating each other, more favourably. Exactly opposite was found to happen in the competitive groups. On the first day, the subjects rated their other group members for interpersonal relationship at quite a high point, but on the third and the fourth day, they did not rate them as

Deutsch, M., 1949, 'The effects of Cooperation and Competition on group process', *Human Relations II* abridged in Cart Wright and Zander, *op. cit.*

Duke, S., 1977, *Theory and Practice in Interpersonal Attraction*, London, New York: Academic Press.

Dowell, L.J., 1975, The effect of a Competitive and Cooperative environment on the Comprehension of a Cognitive task, *Journal of Educational Research*, 68 (1): 274-76.

Foulkes, S.H., and Anthony E.J., 1957, *Group Psychotherapy*, London: Penguin.

Festinger, L., Schachter, S., and Reck, K., 1950, *Social Pressures in informal groups*, New York: Harper.

Festinger, L. and H.A. Hutte, 1954, An experimental investigation of the effect of unstable interpersonal relations in a group, *Journal of Abnormal Social Psychology*, 49: 513-22.

Faroqui, M.A., 1973, Motivation and Morale in a Cooperative Group. *Research in Personality and Social Problems*, Madras, India XVI, 324.

Gordon, K., 1924, Group Judgements in the field of lifted weights, *Journal of Experimental Psychology*, 7: 398-400.

Ghiselli, Edwin, E. and Clarenes W. Brown, *Personnel and Industrial Psychology*, Toronto, London: McGraw Hill Book Company Inc.

Gross, N., Martin W.E. and Darley, J.G., 1953, Studies of group behaviour, *Journal of Abnormal and Social Psychology*, XI. VIII.

Gross, N., and Martin, W., 1952, On Group Cohesiveness, *American Journal of Sociology*, 533-46.

Guigan, MC, F.G., 1990, *Experimental Psychology, Methods of Research*, New Delhi: Prentice - Hall of India Pvt. Limited.

Gleb, Richard and Jacobson, Joseph L., 1988, Popular and Unpopular children's interactions during Cooperative and Competitive peer group activities, *Journal of Abnormal Child Psychology*, 16 (3): 247-61.

Horney, Karen, 1945, *Our Inner Conflicts*, New York: Norton.

Husband, R.W., 1940, Cooperative versus solitary problem solution, *Journal of Social Psychology*, 11, 405-409, P.A. 14: 4936.

Homans, G.G., 1959, *The Human Group*, New York: Har Court Brace.

Heider, F., 1958, *The Psychology of Interpersonal Relationship*, New York: Wiley.

Hagstrom, W.O., 1965, The Dimensions of Cohesiveness in small groups, *Sociometry*, 28, 30-43.

Hare, A.P., 1968, *Handbook of small group research*, New York: The Free Press.

Hurwitz, J.I., et al., 1956, '*Some Effects of Power on Relations among Group Members*, in Cart Wright and Zander, op. cit., Ch. 30.

Hemphill, J.K., 1950, Relation between size to group and the behaviour of superior leaders, *J. Social Psych.*, XXXII.

Horwitz, M., 1953. The recall of interrupted group tasks: an experimental study of individual motivation in relation of group goals, *Human Relations VI* and abridged in Cart Wright and Zander, op. cit.

Hersey Paul and Kenneth M. Blanchard, 1972, *Management of organisation behaviour: utilising human resources*, New Delhi: Prentice - Hall of India.

Josephine, Klein, 1963, *Working with Groups*, London: Hutchinson & Co. (Publishers) Ltd.

Judd, Charles, M. and Pak, Bernadetta, 1988, Out group homogeneity: Judgements of variability at the individual and group levels, *Journal of Personality and Social Psychology*, 54 (5).

Klein, D.J., 1968, *Working with Groups*, pp. 178-202, London: Hutchinson and Co., (Publsiher) Ltd.

Kirscht, L.P., Lodahi, T.M. and Haire, M., 1959, 'Some factors in the selection of leaders by members of small groups, *Journal of Abnormal and Social Psychology*, LVIII.

Kantowitz, H.B., 1984, *Experimental Psychology, Understanding: Psychological Research*, H.L. Roediger, 2nd Edition, New York, Los Angeles: West Publishing Company.

Leonard, R. Sayles, 1958, *Behaviour of Industrial Work Groups*, New York:: Chapman & Hall Ltd.

Larry, B. Christenson, Allyn and Bacon Inc., 1989, *Experimental Methodology*, International Student Edition, London.

Lewin, K., Lippitt, R., 1939, Patterns of Aggressive behaviour in experimentally created "Social climates", *Journal of Social Psychology*, 10: 271-99.

Lippitt, R., 1940, *An Experimental study of Authoritarian and democratic group atmospheres*, University of Iowa, studies in child welfare, 16 (3): 43-195.

Likert, R.A., 1932, *Technique for the measurement of attitudes*, Archives of Psychology, No. 140.

Maller, J.B., 1929, *Cooperation and Competition, an experimental study of Motivation*, in Crafts, Schneirls, Robinson and Gilbert, op. cit.

Moreno, J.L., 1937, Interpersonal the rapy and the Psychopathology of interpersonal relations, *Sociometry*.

———, 1953, '*Who shall survive?*" (Revised) Beacon, N.Y.: Beacon Howe.

———, 1960, *The Sociometry Reader*, The Free Press of Glencoe, Printed in USA.

Moore, H.T., 1921, The Comparative Influence of Majority and Expert Opinion, *American Journal of Psychology*, 32, 16-20.

Redle, F. Wineman, D., 1951, *Children who hate*, Glencoe, III: Free Press.

Scheidlinger, S., 1952, *Psychoanalysis and Group Behaviour*. New York: Norton.

Slavson, S.R., 1950, *Analytic Group Psychotherapy*. New York: Columbia University Press.

Sigmund, Freud, 1965, *Group Psychology and the analysis of the Ego*, Liveright Publishing Corp.

Smith, Henry Clay, 1955, *Psychology of Industrial Behaviour*, New York, London: McGraw Hill Book Company Inc.

Shaw, M.E., 1932, A Comparison of Individuals and Small Groups in the Rational Solution of Complex Problems, *American Journal of Psychology*,. 44: 491-504.

———, 1971, *The Psychology of small group behaviour*, McGraw Hill Boom Company.

Srivastava, Ashok, K., 1986, Structural factors in cooperative and competitive game behaviour, *Psychological Studies*, 3 (2).

Thurstone, L.L., 1928, Attitudes can be measured, *American Journal of Sociology*, 33: 529-54.

Triplett, N., 1897, The Dynamogenic Factors in Pace Making and Competition, *American Journal of Psychology*, 9: 507-33.

Watson, G.B., 1928, Do Groups Think More Effectively than Individuals?, *Journal of Abnormal and Social Psychology*, 23: 828-326.

Zandu, A. and Havelin, 1960, A Social Comparison and Interpersonal Attraction, *Human Relations*, 13: 21-32.

EIGHTEEN

Educating Socially Disadvantaged Children

SHAMSHAD HUSSAIN

Children are a supremely important asset of a nation and the future of any country lies in the hands of her children. Equal opportunities for the development of all children during the period of growth should be the aim of any society. For the purpose of achieving this aim the inequality must be reduced and social justice must be ensured.

As a state we are also party to the U.N. declaration of human rights of the child (defined as 'every human being under 18 years of age unless, under the law applicable to the child majority is attained earlier) which emphasies on the following rights which entered into force in 1990.

- The right to life and to protection from capital punishment.
- The right to acquire a nationality.
- The right to leave any country and enter his or her own country.
- Protection from separation from parents.
- The right to enter or leave another state party for the purpose of family reunification.
- Protection from being illicitly taken abroad and prevented from returning to his or her own country.

- Protection of the child's interests in cases of adoption.
- Freedom of thought, conscience and religion.
- The right of health-care services.
- The right of social security.
- The right to education, with states making primary education compulsory and free.
- Protection from economic exploitation.
- Protection from involvement in the illicit production, trafficking and use of narcotic drugs and psychotropic substance.
- Protection from sexual exploitation.

The government of India has also launched various programmes for the upliftment of children coming from different sections of society. Special attention is needed to promote education to socially disadvantaged group of people, as they feel themselves alienated from the mainstream of society.

It is generally observed that the so-called socially disadvantaged children develop such behavioural manifestations which reflect the attitude of the people towards their bringing up. They mostly grow in a social environment which does not provide healthy and enriched foundations. The atmosphere is charged with criticism, hostility, ridicule, shame, disapproval, non-acceptance and hate. These living conditions generate learning of unhealthy reactions which interfere in developing an organized self concept and ego strength which ultimately interfere with their adjustment in different walks of life and the educational environment is one of them. It has been rightly remarked that if a child lives with criticism he learns to condemn, if he lives with hostility he learns to fight, if he lives with ridicule he learns to be shy and if he lives with shame, he feels guilty. Such unhealthy reactions are learned under an environment which treats the socially disadvantaged children as alienated from the mainstream of socio-cultural and economic background, while dealing with the problems relating to the education of socially disadvantaged children and their upliftment, the behavioural manifestations and attitude resulting from unpoverished environments and ill-treatment of such children are to be considered otherwise they would not be benefitted by the programme for providing education to such children. An atmosphere is to be created in which they receive praise, security, fairness, approval and acceptance which may help them in attaining confidence, appreciation, faith and finally learning to find love in the world.

The term 'socially disadvantaged' commonly covers a large number of factors which handicap children in school and keep them away from using their potential capacities. Keach et al., (1967) defined the socially disadvantaged child as one who is handicapped in the task of growing-up and living a competent and satisfying life. On the whole, it can be said that a child who is culturally deprived or socially disadvantaged is deprived of some favourable aspects of social life in comparison to other children. The educational deprivation lies at the core of this problem.

The term 'social disadvantage' has such a wider connotation that it is difficult to restrict its scope. Broadly, this category includes socially disadvantaged, culturally disadvantaged and economically disadvantaged people.

The problem of socially disadvantaged children has attracted sociologists, psychologists, educationists and the administrators. However, this is to be noted that mostly the problems of socially disadvantaged group have been raised in context of education. Their poor achievements and faulty social interactions have been taken for investigation, though other aspects of their personality and environment should also be considered for having a comprehensive picture of socially disadvantaged children. Factors like perceptual discrimination, self-esteem, level of aspiration, time perspective, emotional feeling, insecurity, inferiority, anxiety and other personality dispositions like approval seeking, dependence proneness, adjustment, etc., should also be focussed upon as the educational failure may be the result of some personal factors and not only that of environmental facilities. These factors are interlinked.

The author himself (1989) has made empirical studies on the personality patterns of socially disadvantaged children and has found some pointers to their personality. Her conducted an empirical study on social deprivation as it leads to maladjustment in different areas as well as on the whole, by administering social deprivation scale (De & Sinha) and Mohsin Shamshad adaptation of Bell's adjustment Inventory (Student form), on a sample of 600 male and female undergraduate college students of Bihar. The adjustment was taken in the form of a process which helps in achieving a balance between an individual's needs and those of environment. (Coleman, 1960; Schenider, 1965; Madigan, 1962;; Kaplan, 1965; Lazarus, 1961; Hussain, 1985).

These findings were supported by early studies of Nijhawan, 1968; Patel, 1961; Gunthy & Sinha, 1983; Sagar, 1971; Kumar, 1975. The findings in general showed that the greater the social deprivation the greater the home, health, social, emotional and overall maladjustment. Thus, on the basis of this finding it can be assessed to what extent socially deprived people cannot take advantage of education because of their maladjustive patterns. However, the author restricts the area of his discussion to the education of socially disadvantaged children, which is of much importance. Special care is to be taken of them as they feel to be cut-off from the mainstream of culture and pass their life amidst frustrations, apathy, insecurity, low level of aspiration, lack of self-confidence and other pathological behaviour patterns. They feel themselves to be handicapped in the task of growing up to lead a competent and satisfying life. Some of them have been found of having poor health conditions due to poor nutrition and medical facilities. They may be victims of unhealthy child-rearing practices.

Frustration and Apathy

The low level of motivation and lack of stimulation affect their performance in school or college. That is why, it has been remarked that children who have severe school learning problems by reasons of their isolation from the mainstream of middle class culture are culturally deprived or socially disadvantaged. The key to advancement in a society is education for which willing participation and responses to teacher's demands are needed which do lack in disadvantaged children. Growing up poor, many of them seem unable to learn the proper skills ana aptitude. They find themselves doomed to life of frustration and apathy which interfere with the learning of curricular activities. They have to develop proper attitude of curricular activities. They have to develop proper attitude and learn skills to pass a healthy life, failing which they find themselves to an increasing degree alienated from the rest of the society. They do not have long-range personal planning, commitment and dedication. Consequently they have their own simplified version that success is a matter of luck and chance and there is no place for dedication and commitment; they are unlucky and, hence, they cannot achieve educational attainment.

The legislature and public feel that because the attitude and expectations of these children and the school are so apart that the education system does not work effectively for majority of the children. The school is meaningless, incongruous and wrong for lower class people. Their presence may be irritant to school authority. They display scorn, resentment, rejection and hostility. Such children attempt at creating fear in their teachers. Sometimes there may be physical assault on the teachers. The teachers remain in perpetual state of fear nowadays because of their crowding in the class.

Ground Rules

Such children show defiance of discipline and destructiveness. The study of Samao conducted on the children of slum areas has indicated the difficulties encountered by the teachers and the patterns of behaviour of such children. These children are unaware of the ground rules for success in school setting and behave in a disturbing manner. They are less able to learn as compared to middle class children; for example, when a teacher showed a picture of a policeman crossing the road with a child, to give training in traffic rules, they insisted that the policeman was taking the child to a jail, which was a reflection of their living conditions, attitude towards life and society at large.

Further, the children are unable to make simple symbolic interpretation, and have a short attention span and difficulty in following directions. They could not benefit from the work of other children and wanted teacher's direction at every step. They were unable to use language in a flexible way. After learning about animals, when a picture of a cat was presented, the child simply said that it was not an animal but a cat, as he had little concept of relative size.

Socially disadvantaged children, thus, are less likely to perceive adults as people to whom they can turn for help. They have low level of curiosity in general and have poor cognitive life. Such children do not have faith in values advocated by middle class children. They in their home are less likely to be regarded as persons having different personalities. They are not sent to school as the parents can't consider it to be important. They think that there is only playing and recreation in the school and, hence, they can better play at home.

Social Reinforcement

As far as social reinforcement is concerned, it is to be remembered that operant conditioning is important. Various types of rewards have been given to such children in order to examine their relative effectiveness. The rewards may be ego-reward or social approval or some concrete reward for correct responses. The ego-reward and social approval are attractive in nature, whereas third type is concrete and real. Middle class people have been found to respond positively to symbolic socialized rewards than to tangible ones in schooling, whereas disadvantaged children believe more in tangible rewards. Indirect method is not effective. Olsen in his study found that children from socially disadvantaged conditions are likely to be unmoved by grades nor are other kinds of positive or negative reinforces effective. Such children rarely respond to moral preachings as they evoke feelings of guilt and shame. The disadvantaged children believe in the reinforcement which is applied promptly and don't have faith in future rewards. The immediate and concrete reward is effective because of prolonged deprivation and feeling of negligence on the part of the learners. Promise means nothing to them and what is given is to be given immediately. School marks are of little importance to them. Need for affiliation in such children is greater as compared to middle class children. They are always suspicious of motives of others. Need for achievement is not so strong in them. If achieving means success in academic competition, such students prefer not to achieve.

Early environment is more important for the development and growth of socially disadvantaged children. Social and intellectual stimulation can help such children in developing correct attitude towards achieving success. The personal relationship with teacher is also counted. They work hard for such teachers who are supportive and show their interest in them, whereas they seem to be apathetic or hostile towards those who are highly discipline-oriented and solely interested in cognitive aspect of learning.

Proper Planning

In the light of this discussion the educationists and the teachers can chalk out plans and find ways which can cater to the needs of socially-disadvantaged children. Their expectations and frustrations, their future goal, level of aspiration, parental encouragement and involvement, prolonged deprivation, cognitive style, intellectual attainment, impoverished social environment, their inferiority or hatred towards middle and upper class people, attitude towards education and schooling, mode of thinking, study habit, lack of stimulation, lower need for achievement, emotional and social apathy, social defiance and many other such factors are to be considered while planning any correctional and educational programme for them. For a proper planning, to educate such people there must be proper task for remedial programme. There should be preparation for free choice. We should not be solely concerned with trying to mould such children in order to fit them into a predetermined role in rigid and unyielding situations. There must be freedom for considerable degree of choice and self-determination. Various arrays of experiences are to be provided to them. Ego strength must be built upon so that children may feel self-confident and consequently can realize that they can also earn experiences from schooling at par with middle and upper class people.

The feeling of inferiority and alienation must be removed or at least be minimized. They should develop proper attitude towards teachers and school authorities. A remedial programme must be properly staffed by people having warm understanding and acceptance of such children and not by people who are disgusted or afraid of lower class people and of their behaviour. Remedial programme should concentrate on children's attitude, values, interest as well as skills that are more obviously identified with school success. Deprived children must be given individual attention for the purpose of generating interest, enthusiasm and motivation in them. The ego-strength should be developed to make them able to face the frustrating situation. Rewarding task should be introduced to encourage such children.

Wrong Presumption

All these need a careful planning and sincere effort. It takes more than enthusiasm and hard work to produce a successful enrichment programme for deprived children. Only such learning programmes will succeed, which have considerations for environmental influences, child rearing practices and motivational patterns, the children have already with them. To achieve this aim a carefully structured syllabi and trained and skilled personnel are needed. Hence, the problems of learning of socially disadvantaged children are manifold and must be solved by planning a realistic syllabi and adopting methodology which considers the personality of the low achievers, as well as their exposure to unhealthy environment. However, it will be a wrong presumption that every socially disadvantaged child is dull, defiant and a problem creator. Carl Rogers, a famous psychologist, has rightly said that every child is creative and possesses creative potentials within him. It is the society and schooling which hinders with his upbringing and growth. Studies on personality and ability of socially disadvantaged children are also not highly conclusive. Hence, let the educationists and administrators start their planning and work with an optimistic outlook by accepting socially disadvantaged children as useful members of the society and who can learn and achieve success in life. With this conviction and determination, the educationists and the administrators should assume the responsibility for imparting education to such children.

REFERENCES

Coleman, J. C., 1960, *Personality dynamics and effective behaviours*, Chicago: Scott, Foresman and Comp.

Gunthy, R. K. and Sinha, P., 1983, SES as determinant of anxiety adjustment and affiliation in teen ages, *Indian Psychological Review*, 24, 40: 1-4.

Hussain, S., 1985, *Adjustment and its measurement*, New delhi: S. Chand and Company Ltd.

Kaplan, Louis, 1965, *Foundation of human behaviour*, New York : Harper and Row.

Keach, E.T., Fulton, R. and Gardner, W.E., 1967, *Education and Social Crisis*, N.Y. John Willey and Sons.

Kumar, A., 1975, *Survey of Research in Psychology*, Part-I, A project sponsored by the ICSSR, New Delhi.

Lazarus, R.S., 1961, *Adjustment and Personality*, New York.

Madigan, M.E., 1962, *Psychological Principles and Application*, St. Louis : The C.V. Mosby Comp.

Nijhawan, 1968, and Patel, 1961, A Survey of Research in Psychology, A project sponsored by the ICSSR, New Delhi.

Sagar, 1980, A Survey of Research in Psychology, Part-I. A project sponsored by the ICSSR, New Delhi.

NINETEEN

Memory Strategies and Learning Disability

NEETI RANA *and* S.P. SINHA

It is common experience that children in classrooms have different levels of abilities to learn and perform. Some children learn pretty fast and learn with ease. There are also children who require relatively more time and effort to learn. Generally teachers complain there are number of children in their classrooms who have learning problems and require special efforts from them to learn and perform even though their intelligence quotient (IQ) is comparatively no less than their 'normal' classmates (Scott et al., 1993; Mehta, 1995).

The inability of these children to perform adequately in the areas of academic achievement despite sufficient intellectual skills and educational opportunity is referred as learning disability.

The learning problems of children generally arise out of the interplay of three sets of factors (Ahuja et al., 1999);

(i) Problems with psychological processes like perception, attention, memory and problems of visual-motor coordination resulting in specific learning difficulties in reading, writing, spelling and arithmetic;

(ii) lack of opportunity for interaction and learning and inappropriate child-rearing practices; and

(iii) absence of quality teaching matched to individual special needs.

Before turning to empirical or experience-based knowledge, we first consider the general issue of how we improve our memories or how we learn. Memory strategies are deliberate, purposeful activities that we use to improve our memories. There are four kinds of memory strategies: Rehearsal, Organization, Retrieval and Imagery (See Matlin, 1994). These show clear changes as children's memory have included that older children remember more information than younger children. This is not because of an inferior capacity of children but due to frequent use of memory strategies by older children.

Researchers believe that many learning disabled children are passive rather than active learners. Many of their problems can be attributed to the fact that they often lack the ability to use appropriate strategies (Torgesen & Kail, 1980).

A fundamental problem with the earlier studies and with status studies generally, that may account for inconsistency in findings is heterogeneity in the samples of learning disabled (LD) children. There is little disagreement among professionals concerning the presence of academic deficits in LD children. Indeed, such deficits are the hallmark of learning disabilities. Some children have deficits in all scholastic areas while others have problems in only one or two academic subjects. We decided to focus on those children, showing marked discrepancy between IQ and achievement and having specific learning problems in reading, writing and spelling. The tests administered were developed by Ahuja et al., (1990) reading and writing tasks, questionnaire for teachers and background information proforma, standardized on Indian school going children.

Organization

A central problem in memory research is to discover just how memory is organized so as to provide relevant knowledge when it is needed. Regarding this, normal and LD children were tested under two recall conditions. A set of 24 cards with a picture of a words belonging to six categories was shown for a brief period. Whether children organized the words or not we took under consideration the types of words recalled. If the child continuously recalled at least three words of the same category, it was referred to as organization.

In immediate recall, just after presentation of all the cards, subjects were instructed to recall the previously learned material in free-recall test. For delayed recall condition, subjects were asked to perform the picture drawing task for 15 minutes and then recall the previously learned material. The order of presentation was randomized across subjects.

It was noted that the two groups did not vary vastly in the performance when tested immediately. However, delayed recall condition influenced the performance of LD children. These children suffered from a performance collapse by the duration of this interval, although normals remained least affected. LDs have proven to be slow to capture the flexible use of knowledge that characterizes normals cognition. This failure, however, should be viewed with the understanding that the general problem of relevant access is overwhelmingly complex. It is important to understand can LDs organize and enhance their performances.

From this, it can be stated that information does not get processed at least not in the same way that normals do. Normals learned by organizing the material, they were able to retain it for a longer duration; highlighting self-regulation in learning (Butler, 1995; Prasad, 1995).

Imagery

Often we are presented with some information, we not only encode its meaning, but we elaborate or explain it. These elaborations provide a means of integrating and retaining information to the extent that they help relate the current information to our knowledge.

The foregoing experiment specifically compares, recalls concrete and abstract words under different recall conditions (Immediate and Delayed, procedure similar to our previous experiment). Subjects were exposed to ten items out of which five were concrete words (e.g. peach, board) and the remaining were abstract words (broad, below). Almost without fail, the conclusion of this effort was that children with learning disabilities were deficient in use of imagery strategy. Post-experimental inquiry found that LDs were rather passive in processing the words by developing some associations that would have enhanced their performances like normals.

At this point, we should note once again that there is no variation in the performance between the two groups for immediate recall condition but, a marked deterioration during delayed condition. These data also reveal an important relationship as items become less abstract. They are recalled more readily in the similar fashion by LDs.

Memory is best when an item represents itself, when it is the actual object (concrete word), with more abstract representations, recall is poorer. The word 'tent' for instance, has a strong visual image, while an abstract word e.g. 'irony' does not. Some items can thus be stored in analog code (Kosslyn & Koeing, 1992). Naturally these items will be better remembered since they have a greater chance to closely resemble the original stimulus.

Recall was best for the concrete words and worst for the abstract words for the LDs. Normals are assumed to store information in a prepositional code, an abstract language representation that describes relationship between items. Normals deliberately process and produce appropriate learning strategy spontaneously. Lack of this manifests deficits in executive processing (Watson & Willows, 1995).

Controlled Processing Deficits

Sethia et al. (1993) provide further experimental evidence of controlled processing deficits among LDs. They found that an LD child lacks strategic control to adjust with varied task demands i.e., cognitive loads. For example, LD and Control group cancelled letter under low cognitive load (i.e., cancellation of letter P), moderate cognitive load (i.e., cancellation of letter B proceeded or succeeded by letter R) and high cognitive load (i.e., cancellation of letter N which is succeeded by letter O but not preceded by letter M) from random arrangement of English alphabet. As anticipated, the LD group took significant higher time for cancellation in comparison to control group. Both groups were quite accurate and efficient in task performance when cognitive load is moderate or low but when high, a step increase in the errors of LDs is obtained which indicated that due to controlled processing deficit, they are not able to adjust energy allocation according to task demands.

Mode of Instructions

At this juncture, it is sufficient to point out inadequate utilization of learning strategies by LDs. Still another factor of considerable importance is the similarity of performance during immediate recall condition, recall of concrete words and as reported by Sethia et al. (1993) during moderate and low cognitive load condition.

Most often, scant attention is paid to the children's capacity to adapt to instructional sets and learning situations. Bauman & Burgeron (1993), report that some form of instruction improves child's comprehension and recall of stories. The nature of prior knowledge activated can result in different information process and try to account for the facilitation effects in recall patterns (Machiels - Bangaerts, et al. 1995).

To accomplish this purpose, we conducted an experiment (Rana & Sinha, 1996) to explore the nature of performance during different mode of instructions and recall conditions. Like, in the previous experiment (Organization), subjects were not instructed any particular method of learning. Now, subjects were tested both under Implicit and Explicit mode of instructions. In the explicit mode (unlike implicit mode), subjects were informed that they can learn the given material by organizing or grouping into categories. The categories of objects were also mentioned beforehand, viz., transportation, human beings, sports materials, dresses and furniture.

Analysis of the number of items recalled by counting the categories formed by the object showed 65 per cent of grouping by normals during implicit mode of instructions and only 30 per cent for LDs. It is interesting to observe the facilitatory impact of explicit mode of instructions. LDs organized 60.2 per cent of words as compared to 65.6 per cent of Normals group. During delayed recall condition implicit mode of instructions produced low free recall scores as compared to immediate recall condition, whereas, performance of LDs was stable along recall conditions when explicit mode of instructions were given.

Walkinson et al. (1995) reported individual differences in story comprehension and recall of poor readers. Poor readers tend to recall less of the stories overall, recall less information from story-grammar categories to varying extents and show patterns of category recall different from normal readers.

There is a dearth of good evidence for the view that supports the training of LDs in the use of executive strategy (Metacognition). The executive actions are concerned with planning of action, allocation of attention, selection and monitoring activity. These actions have a management or regulatory function across all cognitive domains (Clunnappan & Lawson, 1996).

The stability in performance of the normals during mode of instructions under immediate and delayed recall condition supports the notion that unlike LDs, normals can transfer strategies accordingly and deal non-instructed tasks strategically. The inferior performance of LDs during implicit mode of instructions suggests low utilization of metacognitive skills (executive processing) within on line processing (Swanson et al., 1993).

Conclusion

More generally, our findings suggest that LDs have an inadequate grasp of what methods and strategies are available for learning. Having an average range of intelligence with adequate memory capacity these children have a limitation in deciding when and how the strategies should be applied.

Experiments (Organization & Imagery) are based on the work done in the Deptt. of Psychology, Dayalbagh Educational Institute, Agra on "Memory Strategies Among Learning Disabled Children". — Unpublished dissertation of Pratibha Gulati (1995). Supervisor Dr. S.P. Sinha and co-supervisor Neeti Rana.

REFERENCES

Ahuja, A., Jangira, N.K., Kaur, C. and Sibia, A., 1990, *Fundamental Assessment Guide: A Handbook of Primary Teachers*, NCERT.

Bauman, J.F., and Bergeron, B.S., 1993, Story map instructions using children's literature: Effects on first grader's comprehension of central narrative elements, *Journal of Reading Behaviour*, 25: 407-437.

Butler, D.L., 1995, Promoting strategic learning by post secondary students with learning disabilities, *Journal of Learning Disabilities*, 28(3): 170-90.

Chinnappan, M., and Lawson Michael, J., 1996, The effects of training in the use of executive strategies in geometry problem solving, *Learning and Instruction*, 6(1): 1-17.

Kosslyn, S.M. and Koenig, O., 1992, Wetmind: The new cognition neurosciences, New York: The Free Press.

Machiels-Bongaerts, M., Schmidth, Henk G., Boshuizen, Henny P.A., 1995, The effect of prior knowledge activation on text recall: An investigation of two conflicting hypotheses, *British Journal of Educational Psychology*, 65: 409-23.

Matlin, Margaret W., 1994, Cognition Holt, Rinehart & Winston, Inc., p. 173.

Mehta, N.P., 1995, Slow learners: Handle with care, *The Hindustan Times*, p. 16, September 26.

Prasad, Sheetla, 1994, Hypoxican characteristics in learning-disabled and non-learning disabled children, *Journal of the Indian Academy of Applied Psychology*, 20(1): 69-74.

Rana, N and Sinha, S.P., 1996, Impact of recall conditions and mode of instructions on memory performance of learning disabled children, *Journal of Psychological Researches*, 40(1-2): 35-43.

Scott, M.S., Perou, R, Grenfield, D.B. and Swanson, L., 1993, Rhyming Skills; Differentiating among mildly mentally retarded, learning disabled and normal achieving students, *Learning Disabilities Research & Practice*, Vol. 8: 215-22.

Sethia, P., Saxena, S. and Sinha, S.P., 1993, Control processing among learning disabled children, Paper presented in the International Symposium on Cognition, 14-17 December, BHU, Varanasi, India.

Swanson, H.L., Christe, L. and Ruleadeau, R.J., 1993, The relationship between metacognition and analogical reasoning in mentally retarded, learning disabled, average and gifted children, American Educational Research Association Meeting, *Learning Disabilities Research & Practice*, Vol. 8(2): 76-81.

Torgesen, J.K. and Kail, R.V., 1980, Memory processes in exceptional children, In B.K. Keogn (ed.), *Advances in special education Vol. 1: Basic constructs and theoretical orientations*. Greenwich, Conn: J.A.I. Press.

Watson, C. & Willows, Dale, M., 1955, Information-processing patterns in specific reading disability, *Journal of Learning Disability*, Vol. 28, 216.

Wilkinson, Ian A.G., Elkins, J. and Bain, John D., 1995, Individual differences in story comprehension and recall of poor readers, *British Journal of Educational Psychology*, 65: [illegible]3-407.

TWENTY

Role of Implicit Memory in the Development of Prejudice

SAEEDUZZAFAR *and* RAMA SHARMA

The social perceiver is continuously confronted with a formidable array of environmental information to interpret. According to Bruner (1957, 1958), this information is manageable only by selectively attending to certain features of the stimulus field and by further reducing this limited range of information through assigning it to cognitive categories — abstract representations of conceptually related information. Hence, perception is considered as an interaction between the cognitive structure of the perceiver and the environmental context (Cantor, 1981; Mischel, 1979; Neisser, 1979; Norman and Bobrow, 1976). The relative accessibilities of these categories partly determine the selection and interpretation of social information (Bruner, 1957; Higgins and King, 1981; Wyer and Srull, 1981). As a matter of fact the more accessible category, the more likely it is to be used to process relevant information. Thus, category accessibility is critical to the outcome of social perception. In a study Higgins, Rholes and Jones (1977) asked their subjects to perform first a colour naming task in which they were presented with a word to hold in memory until the colour had been named. These memory words included four personality trait terms, either positive or negative and either relevant or irrelevant to the stimulus material of the next task. In the second task, unrelated to the first, all subjects read the same behavioural description of a stimulus person. Subjects exposed to the relevant trait terms evaluated the stimulus person in line with the denotative character of those traits, i.e., either positively or negatively, whereas the positive and negative irrelevant trait terms had no effect on the subjects evaluation. Higgins et al. (1977) concluded that earlier exposure to the trait terms had activated trait categories that influenced subsequent processing of trait relevant but not trait irrelevant information. Srull and Wyer (1979, 1980) not only reported more or less similar findings but also contended that the effect of this processing can influence judgments along other trait dimensions as well.

It has been reported that a given category can also differ across individuals in its long-term or chronic accessibility. In general the more frequently a category is activated, the more accessible it becomes, requiring decreasing amount of energy to detect congruent information (Higgins and King, 1981; Shiffrin and Schneider, 1977). Individuals vary in the frequency with which different categories become active, due to variation in their past experience and their repertories of chronically accessible categories will vary accordingly (Higgins, King and Mavin, 1982).

Higgins and King (1981), Bargh (1982) and Bargh and Pietromonaco (1982) have argued that category priming effects can be passive, that is, these may not require a conscious expectancy or set on the part of the subject. In an investigation, Bargh and Pietromonaco (1982) studied the influence of trait information presented outside of conscious awareness on impression formation. In their experiment, they examined the possibility that information relevant to a trait category (e.g. hostility) presented outside conscious awareness can temporarily increase that category accessibility. Subjects initially performed a vigilance task in which they were exposed unknowingly to single word. Either 0 per cent, 20 per cent or 80 per cent of these words were semantically related to hostility. In another, unrelated task, subjects read a behavioural description of a stimulus person that was ambiguous regarding hostility and then rated the stimulus person on several trait dimensions. The results strongly suggested that the impression, subjects formed of the stimulus person was directly related to the amount of hostile information to which they had been exposed (of which they had not been aware). The more hostile information to which subjects were exposed, the more negatively they perceived the stimulus person on both hostility related or unrelated traits. Thus, Barg and Pietromonaco (1982) concluded that social stimulus of which people are not consciously aware can influence conscious judgment. In the light of these findings, it is reasonable as well as logical to assume that social stimuli such as words which express communal prejudice, if exposed outside conscious awareness may contribute in rating or judging the stimulus persons as prejudice and hence may help in the development of communal prejudice. The present study is designed to examine this possibility. More specifically, the present investigation is carried out to explore the possibility that information relevant to a trait category (Prejudice) presented outside conscious awareness may temporarily increase that category's accessibility which in turn may influence conscious judgments about the individuals belonging to same community in general and other community in particular.

Methodology

Subjects were assigned to either the rate or test conditions. Those assigned to the rate condition were exposed to either 0 per cent, 20 per cent or 80 per cent prejudiced words (the remainder being neutral control words) while performing the vigilance task. This vigilance task required subjects to react as quickly as they could to flashes (actually words but subjects were told nothing about the nature of flashes) on a screen. After completing 100 traits of the vigilance task, rate condition subjects read a brief description of a stimulus person and rated him on 12 trait dimensions half of which were related to prejudice and half unrelated. Subjects assigned to the test condition were exposed to either 20 per cent or 80 per cent prejudiced words in the vigilance task and then were given a recognition memory test on the prejudiced and control words to which they had been exposed.

Apparatus and Stimulus Material

Automatic Slide Projector was used to present each stimulus word for a period of 100 msee at one of the four locations of the screen. The location order was randomized and was the same for all subjects.

Techno Digital Display Response apparatus was used to record the reaction time of the subject.

Three lists of 20 words were prepared containing either 0 per cent, 20 per cent or 80 per cent prejudice words with remainder being neutral or control words.

The 20 prejudice words were selected from a large pool of prejudice words by conducting a pilot study. A list of 100 prejudice words was presented to 100 subjects and the subjects were instructed to rate each word on a 5-point scale ranging from least expressive of prejudice attitude to most expressive of prejudice attitude with the middle point as moderate expressive of prejudice attitude. Only those 20 words were selected for the study for which there was complete agreement among the subjects with regard to expressiveness of strongest prejudice attitudes. These words were:

> Dishonest, Traitor, Disloyal, Unfaithful, Cruel, Narrow minded, Violent, Uncultured, Unreliable, Backward, Unkind, Unfriendly, Anti-nation, Biased, Selfish, Anti-religion, Self-centered, Unfair, and Cheater.

The twenty control words were selected from 200 most frequently appearing words in English language (Carroll et al., 1971); the selection criteria was that these words should be approximately of the same length as prejudice words. The control words were:

> Water, Long, Number, Something, Little, Between, Another, Many, Always, Inkpot, Every, Climate, Various, Though, Event, People, What, Together, Different and Said.

High frequency words were used as control words in order to rule out an alternative explanation for a finding of relatively greater stimulus words processing by the 20 per cent and 80 per cent prejudice word group in terms of the subject's greater familiarity with prejudice words. Ten additional low frequency words were used during the initial practice task.

The brief duration of each word, its immediate asking, its unpredictable location and time of occurrance and its placement outside the foveal area were all intended to prevent subjects from becoming conscious of the word contents. As a manipulation check the following recognition test was administered to subjects in the test condition.

Recognition Memory Test

The 60 items of this test were composed of equal number of prejudged targets (actually presented words), prejudiced distractors (not presented), control targets (actually presented) and control distractors (not presented). The prejudice distractors were taken from the prejudice word rated by the subjects in the pilot study mentioned above but that were not presented in the vigilance task. Like the control targets, the control distractors were taken from among the 200 most frequent words in the English language (e.g. down, house, about). The presentation order of the items was randomized.

Behavioural Description

Subjects in the rate condition did not take the recognition memory test but were given a 12-sentence paragraph to read. The paragraph described a stimulus person engaging in somewhat prejudiced behaviour.

Trait Rating Form

Immediately after reading the behavioural description, subjects in the rate condition were given a form consisting of 12 items on which to rate the stimulus person. Subjects indicated their rating by circling a number from 1 (not at all) to 5 (extremely) for each trait. Six of the trait scales were descriptively similar to prejudice; three were negative in evaluative tone (hostile, unfriendly, dislikable) and there were positive (kind, considerate, thoughtful). The remaining six-trait scales were evaluatively denotative but not related to prejudice, three were negative (boring, dry, crude) and three were positive (interesting, intelligent, humorous), the presentation order of the 12 scales was randomized.

Procedure

Subjects were told that the experiment would consist of two separate parts, and that instruction of second part would be given following completion of the first part. Subjects were next informed as to the nature of vigilance task. They were instructed to sit comfortably and to maintain their gaze on the fixation point on the screen in front of them throughout the task. They were also instructed to press the button corresponding to the side of the fixation point on which the flash has occurred as quickly as possible after seeing a flash. Accuracy and speed were stressed. Subjects first performed 10 flash practice trails. Each subject responded to the 100 trails of the vigilance task. In the rate condition 60 subjects were exposed to the 0 per cent, 20 per cent and 80 per cent prejudice word lists and half of the 40 subjects in the test conditions were presented with 20 per cent prejudice word list and half with the 80 per cent prejudice word list.

In the rate condition, the subjects were informed that the second part of the experiment would concern how people form impressions of other people. The subjects were given the behavioural description to read. As soon as a subject finished reading the paragraph, he was given trait rating form to complete.

In the test condition, after the completion of vigilance task, the subjects were told that the flashes on the screen were actually words. Then recognition memory test was distributed and the subjects were instructed to check/make a tick mark against those items they thought had been presented. They were informed that some of the items on the test had been flashed during the vigilance task and others had not been.

Result

Recognition Test

The proportion for correct and incorrect recognitions of prejudice and control words for 20 per cent and 80 per cent lists were separately calculated. In Table I, mean correct and incorrect recognition for 20 per cent and 80 per cent prejudice list and their respective proportions, and t-values are given:

TABLE I
SHOWING PROPORTIONS AND T-VALUES OF CORRECT AND INCORRECT RECOGNITIONS FOR 20 PER CENT AND 80 PER CENT LISTS

Recognitions		*Percentage* 20%	*t-value*	*Percentage* 80%	*t-value*
Prejudice	Correct	.50	.10	.50	.10
words	Incorrect	.50		.50	
Control	Correct	.56	1.30	.25	5.00
words	Incorrect	.43		.75	

TABLE II
SHOWING PROPORTIONS AND T-VALUES OF CORRECT RECOGNITIONS FOR 20 PER CENT AND 80 PER CENT LISTS

Recognitions		*Percentage* 20%	*t-value*	*Percentage* 80%	*t-value*
Prejudice words	Correct	.50	.50	.50	1.20
Control words		.56		.25	

The correct and incorrect recognitions for both the prejudice and control items were computed and a series of t-tests were performed, comparing correct and incorrect recognition within prejudice and control items as well as between prejudice control items for each proportion (20 per cent and 80 per cent). In case of 20 per cent proportion group, incorrect and correct recognitions of prejudice words were not different rather these were identical as shown in Table I. The incorrect and correct recognition of control words were also not different. The t-value was highly insignificant (i.e. 1.30). When correct recognition of prejudice and control words were compared, subjects did not differ significantly (t= .50). In case of 80 per cent proportion, correct and incorrect recognition of prejudice words were also found identical whereas incorrect recognitions of control words were significantly higher than correct recognitions (t = 5.00). When correct recognition of prejudice and control words were compared no significant difference was found (t = 1.20). Thus subjects could not detect prejudice targets at better than chance level. The results of the recognition test did not demonstrate any memory for the terms actually presented.

Reaction Time

An analysis of variance of average reaction time with proportion and trait block as factors revealed a reliable effect of trait block. More specifically response lantencies increased over time most likely due to fatigue. There was no reliable effect of the proportion factor. It appears that differential processing of the prejudice information had its effect on response accuracy rather than on speed. In short, accuracy reliably decreased as amount of prejudice information presented increased.

Impression of Stimulus Person

An overall prejudice rating was computed for each subject by taking the mean of the ratings on the six prejudice traits, after reversing the scales for the three positive traits. Similarly, an overall prejudice unrelated trait rating was computed for each subject by taking the means of the ratings on the six prejudice-unrelated traits after scale reversal on the three positive traits. These average ratings were then subjected to a repeated measure of analysis of variance, with proportion as between subjects factor and relatedness as the within subjects factor.

In general, as shown in Table III, the higher—the proportion of prejudice words to which a subject was exposed, the more negative his impression of the stimulus person. Subjects also rated the stimulus person in a more extremely negative direction on those traits related to prejudice than on the prejudice unrelated traits. The F values for proportion and relatedness were found highly significant.

An examination of the simple main effect of proportion on prejudice related traits showed that 80 per cent prejudice word group have rated the stimulus person significantly more negatively than the other two groups, $F(1, 128) = 12.15, p<.01$. For prejudice unrelated traits, however, both the 80 per cent and 20 per cent groups rated the stimulus person reliably more negatively than the 0 per cent group, $F(1, 128) = 9.69, p<.01$. For both prejudice related and unrelated traits, therefore, those subjects exposed to more prejudice words during the vigilance task rated the stimulus person reliably more negatively.

Discussion

The pattern of results strongly suggest that the formation of the impression about a stimulus person by the subjects is directly related to the amount of prejudice information to which they had been exposed (of which they had not been consciously aware). The more prejudice information to which rate-condition subjects were exposed, the more negatively they perceived the stimulus person on both prejudice related and prejudice unrelated traits. These findings are in consonance with the findings obtained by Higgins et al. (1977), Srull and Wyer (1979) and Bargh and Pietromonaco (1982) showing that social categories can be primed passively by presenting the priming information outside of the subjects awareness. The prejudice stimuli produced a negative halo effect that may be responsible for an overall negative reaction to the stimulus person. Different explanations may be extended to account for this phenomenon. First, prejudice stimuli could have activated the prejudice traits category and this activation might have spread to other trait categories. The traits that are associated with prejudice in ones implicit memory are likely to be negatively toned as well, and so their activation would result in negative halo effect. Alternatively, perhaps a more general social category such as 'undesirable ' or 'unpleasant' was directly primed by the prejudice stimulus. The activation of this more global concept would then affect all trait ratings in a negative direction, regardless of their relatedness to prejudice.

Still another possible explanation for the phenomena may be that subjects might have extracted the emotional tone of the information, and this affective processing might have produced both the vigilance task performance decrements and the differential trait ratings. This interpretation gains a strength from findings obtained by Nielsen and Sarason (1981), and Bargh (1982).

It may be argued that automatic category activation by congruent information increases the category's acute accessibility and thus it influences the interpretation of subsequent information.

One does not have to be aware of a source of environmental information for it to affect conscious judgments such as impressions of other individuals. The present research makes it crystal clear that not only do people lack awareness of the ways in which they process information, they can also be unaware of the presence of influential information.

It is interesting to note that importance of information outside the consciousness as a determiner of behaviour was recognized as early as in 1704 by Gottfried Wilhem Leibniz. He emphasized the importance of 'insensible' or 'unconscious' perceptions, ideas of which we are not consciously aware, but which do influence behaviour (Leibniz, 1916). More or less similar viewpoints were expressed by Johann Friedrich Herbart in 1816, who introduced the notion that suppressed ideas "which are unable to exceed the threshold of conscious awareness, can nevertheless influence conscious thinking (Herbert 1896). Later on, Hearing (1920) also agreed that it is necessary to consider unconscious memory, which is involved in involuntary recall, the development of automatic and unconscious actions.

The findings of the present study provide impressive evidence to the effect that unconscious perceptions — ideas of which we are not consciously aware, have tremendous impact on our behaviour. These findings imply that an abusive or pleasant childhood experience may remain imprinted on the childs brain till the end of his life without any memory remaining of it afterwards (Haldane and Ross, 1967). These childhood experiences may influence his behaviour when he becomes an adult. Accordingly, impression formation is also likely to be affected by the childhood experience or by the information provided at the outside of the consciousness. What type of impressions, whether positive or negative, will be formed depends on the type of childhood experiences or the type of information presented at the outside of consciousness. In other words it may be argued that what is now known as implicit memory (Graf and Schacter, 1985, 1987; Schacter and Graf, 1986 a, 1986 b) may have a profound impact on the impression formation about other people. The findings of the present study have clearly demonstrated that information presented outside the consciousness significantly contributed in the development of prejudice, i.e., the more prejudice information to which subjects were exposed, the more prejudiced they perceived the stimulus person. In the light of the above findings, it may be argued that child rearing practices, during which parents impart information about other persons or community, may be a critical determinant of his/her future behaviour towards other individuals. Thus, the findings suggest that implicit memory like other personality and social variables, may contribute in the development of prejudice attitude. If it is so then the parents should be educated that they should be very careful about content and nature of the information given to the child during the childhood period. If aversive information about other individuals or community is not given to the child during childhood period then as an adult person he is unlikely to develop prejudice attitudes towards other individuals or community and hence the development of prejudice may be checked. If prejudice, a social evil, is controlled it would be a great contribution to the advancement of a nation and to the strengthening of national integration.

REFERENCES

Bargh, J.A., 1982, Attention and automaticity in the processing of self-relevant information, *Journal of Personality and Social Psychology*, 43: 425-36.

Bargh, J.A. and Pietromonaco, P., 1982, Automatic Information processing and social perception: The influence of trait information presented outside of conscious awareness in impression formation, *Journal of Personality and Social Psychology*, 43: 437-49.

Bruner, J.S., 1957, On perceptual readiness. *Psychological Review*, 64: 123-52.

———, 1958, Social Psychology and perceptions. In E.E. Maccoby, T.M. New Comb and E.L. Hartley (eds.), *Readings in Social Psychology*, (3rd ed) New York: Holt, Rienhart and Winston.

Cantor, N., 1981, A cognitive social approach to personality, In N. Cantor and J.F. Kihlstrom (Eds), *Personality, Cognition and Social Interaction*, Hillsdale, N.J. Erlbaum.

Carroll, J.E., Davies, P. and Richman, B., 1971, *The American Heritage word frequency book*. New York: Houghten Mifflin.

Graf, P., and Schacter, D.L., 1985, Implicit and explicit memory for new associations in normal and amnesic subjects, *Journal of Experimental Psychology: Learning, Memory and Cognition*, 11: 501-18.

———, (1987), Selective effects of interference on implicit and explicit memory for new association. *Journal of Experimental Psychology: Learning, Memory and Cognition*, 13: 45-53.

Haldane, E.S. and Ross, G.R.T., (eds.), 1967, The Philosophical works of Descartes, Cambridge: Cambridge University Press.

Herbart, J.F., 1896, A textbook in Psychology, New York: D. Appleton.

Hering, E., 1920, Memory as a Universal function of organized matter, In S. Butler (ed.), *Unconscious memory*, pp. 63-86. London: Jonathan Cape.

Higgins, E.T. and King, G.A., 1981, Accessibility of social constructs: Information processing consequences of individual and contextual variability. In N. Cantor and J.F. Kihlstrom (eds.), *Personality, Cognition and Social Intervention*. Hillsdale, N.J: Erlbaum.

Higgins, E.T., King, G.A. and Mavin, G.H., 1982, Individual construct accessibility and subjective impressions and recall, *Journal of Personality and Social Psychology*, 43: 35-47.

Higgins, E.T., Rholes, W.S., and Jones, C.R., 1977, Category accessibility and impression formation, *Journal of Experimental Social Psychology*, 13: 141-54.

Leibniz, G.W., 1916, *New essays concerning human understanding*, Chicago: Open Court.

Mischel, W., 1979, On the interface of cognition and personality: Beyond the person-situation debate, *American Psychologist*, 34: 740-54.

Neisser, U., 1976, *Cognition and reality*, San Francisco: Freeman.

Nielsen, S.L. and Sarason, I.G., 1981, Emotion, personality and selective attention, *Journal of Personality and Social Psychology*, 41: 945-60.

Norman, D.A., and Bobrow, D.G., 1976, On the role of active memory process in perception and cognition. In C.N. Cofer (ed.), *The structure of human memory*. San Francisco: Freeman.

Schacter, D.L., and Graf, P., 1986a, Effects of elaborative processing on implicit and explicit memory for new associations, *Journal of Experimental Psychology: Learning, Memory and Cognition*, 12: 432-44.

———, 1986b, Preserved learning in amnesic patients: Perspective from research on direct priming, *Journal of Clinical and Experimental neuropsychology*, 8: 727-43.

Shiffrim, R.M. and Schneider, W., 1977, Controlled and automatic human information processing: II Perceptual learning, automatic attending, and a general theory, *Psychological Review*, 84: 127-90.

Srull, T.K., and Wyer, R.S. Jr., 1979, The role of category accessibility in the interpretation of information about persons: Some determinants and implications, *Journal of Personality and Social Psychology*, 37: 1660-72.

———, 1980, Category accessibility and social perception: Some implications for the study of person memory and interpersonal judgements, *Journal of Personality and Social Psychology*, 38: 841-56.

———, 1981, Category accessibility: Some theoretical and empirical issue concerning the processing of social stimulus information. In E.T. Higgins, C.P. Herman, and M.P. Zanna (eds.), *Social cognition: The Ontarios Symposium* (Vol. I) Hillsdale, N.J. Erlbaum.

Index